Where is Belgrade?

First published in 2011 by
What's Your Story

British Library Cataloguing in Publication Data
A catalogue record for this book is available
from the British Library

ISBN   978 1 903623 51 0

Scripture quotations from various
translations of the Bible

Typesetting and print management
by What's Your Story, Luton, UK
www.goodnewsbooks.net

Where is Belgrade?

Paulette Coldham

To Peter, Gerard, Christopher,
Clare, Paul, and Alan
for all the love and help
I have received from them.

Contents

Biography

Paulette Coldham was baptised into the (Roman) Catholic Church when she was three days old and remembers her childhood and teenage as a happy if well-disciplined time. She counts herself as blessed to have been sought out by Peter, her husband-to-be. Together they have encountered and eventually been able to overcome the problems which face all married couples, not least the call to deepen their spiritual lives without compromising their commitment to the practicalities of raising their four children Gerard, Christopher, Clare, and Paul (together with a foster son, Alan). Peter spent his working life mainly in the Central Office of information and for a short spell in the diplomatic service overseas; Paulette as a home economics teacher in a local Church of England school.

A short time before the Second Vatican Council was called they both discovered they were encountering some serious misgivings about their spiritual growth, and especially questioning whether there should not be more to life than going to church, obeying its rules and practices, and working hard in between. So they began a fundamental search which led in 1977 to an experience which was the beginning of a thrilling immersion into a quite new way of life.

Together in that same year, with not a little misgiving coupled with a powerful sense of anticipation, they determined to start a local prayer group which, after 33 years of ups and downs, is still active and vigorous even if a bit lacking in numerical strength. And during all those years Paulette and Peter have managed to organise many Life in the Spirit seminars in the Southwark Archdiocese and more recently in their own parish Alpha and CaFE courses.

Paulette since her childhood has kept records and written about events in her life. She conceived the idea some years ago, with the encouragement of her family, of preparing a book about her spiritual development with the intention of encouraging other Christians as well as those of no faith to take hope from her witness. For that reason she has chosen to disclose many of her private thoughts challenges hopes, and disappointments but - more than that - her conviction that nothing can stand between us and the love of God.

Chapter One

Pilgrims in a Foreign Land

P ETER AND I had been married about 18 months, when the phone rang whilst I was having lunch with my parents. The year was 1955. Our first child Gerard John was then about nine months old, (he was named after the Jesuit John Gerard who lived through the persecutions in the reign of Elizabeth 1).

"Do you know where Belgrade is?" I heard Peter saying. I vaguely knew that it was over there beyond Austria and Switzerland in the mêlée of Bulgaria, Romania and Yugoslavia, but not quite as far as Russia! Peter was also a little uncertain of the geography but assured me that it was the capital of Yugoslavia. I was intrigued to know what all this was leading up to when he told me that he had been asked to take up a diplomatic post at the British Embassy in Belgrade. The idea was not so foreign to us as Peter's father and mother had been involved in the diplomatic service for many years, and had lived abroad most of their married life. They had served in Rome, Poland, Mexico and Venezuela as well as in London. For the moment I was stunned as we had bought a house and spent many months decorating and furnishing it. I was very happily settled and had not really considered a diplomatic career for Peter, as this move would involve him being seconded to the Foreign

Office from the COI (Central Office of Information) where he worked. We knew that there was a strict communist regime in Yugoslavia under the leadership of Marshal Josip Broz Tito. We also knew a little of what had gone on during the 1939-45 war there, and that Britain had backed Tito after some hesitation, that must surely be good. I was to find out later so much more, which was horrifying. We knew no-one in England who had ever been to Yugoslavia, and the invitation to go there carried with it an air of mystery and intrigue. Against all the warnings we received from well meaning friends our sense of adventure won. We found ourselves in a buzz of activity once our decision was made, buying and planning, letting the house and making arrangements. By this time I was pregnant with our second child. My mother was extremely worried as I had to make arrangements for the birth to take place abroad, and was strongly advised not to stay in Belgrade as the only hospital was very primitive. My doctor in England investigated several possible options, including Rome, but finally I seemed to have very little choice since I would not be allowed to fly after the 5th month of pregnancy.

The other thing we had to study was protocol. I had not realised how important this was, and indeed never quite completely got the hang of it. However, amongst my wardrobe apart from maternity dresses etc. were six little hats to be worn at cocktail parties. This was absolutely compulsory. I remember when we first arrived feeling very confused having been invited to dinner at another address straight after a cocktail party, and some kind soul making a pssst... pssst in the cloakroom, telling me to remove my hat, such as it was, a fluff of tulle and a couple of feathers. Hats were compulsory at cocktails, no hats at dinner of course.

Peter's mother who was an expert traveller and organiser for diplomatic purposes showed us how to run up a large account with Saccone and Speed for drinks and cocktail fancies, for which, in the end, I was grateful, as entertaining was high on the diplomatic agenda. Amazingly I was not a bit daunted by these arrangements, and remember comforting my mother when she expressed her fears about my ante-natal care. She was quite right of course as I only saw a doctor twice in the whole of my pregnancy, and then it was from my own choice. At that time in Belgrade, life was fairly cheap. No-one had a car except diplomats and high ranking communists, certainly not doctors who were fairly near the bottom of the list. If you needed a doctor you either went on public transport or if you were more fortunate like ourselves you collected the doctor in your own car, otherwise you either got better or died. It was as simple as that. It was very rare to see a car on the roads, which were filled mainly with carts pulled by oxen. I remember Wolf Mankovitz's article written about that time focussing on the one set of traffic lights in the whole of the city.

Our household goods were packed and shipped by container, which were to arrive six weeks after us. The remainder of goods that we would need meanwhile was packed into our Morris Minor, including disposable nappies for the journey, which were then very costly and used by very few people, leaving room for the Karricot on the back seat, where Gerard lived for most of the journey, strapped in with side clips and reins!!! We built up a shelf by the back seat so that the Karricot could not fall forward and we had storage space under it. We decided to take our time across Europe and enjoy the journey to the full, which we did, taking in many places of interest on the way. By the time we left England, seemingly for ever, Gerard was just one year old. Air travel at that time was very expensive and was therefore limited. We had a grand family farewell party, and then made our round of friends to say goodbye, or they came to us at my parents' house where we were now staying. On the actual day after our tearful farewells we made our way to Lydd Airport. There was a very nice baby room which I made full use of but our flight was called early and urgently, so I had to run with Gerard only half dressed. There were very few people on board the tiny car transporter plane, and Peter and I were both quite nervous as the plane had no inner lining and you could see all the nuts and bolts holding the sections together, and the sections moved and groaned just like Meccano.

We had our lunch in Le Havre, Gerard sitting in his newly acquired baby seat which fixed on the back of a dining chair, with a little tray in front of it. He loved it and this proved to be one of our most useful and helpful items. We could eat in any hotel or restaurant and know that we could manage. Then the provision of high chairs in a restaurant was unknown even in England. I guess people did not travel too much with young children. I remember Gerard's cries of glee at the steamed fish and mashed potato which were produced with such aplomb and dignity by the waiter, as if Gerard was their best customer, followed by the cries of mo-mo (which we liked to think meant more... more) when it had all gone. We made our way across France, Germany and Austria, then over the Dolomites to Venice, staying in small hotels. It worked out very well. I gave Gerard cooled boiled milk, often prepared in an espresso coffee machine; our reasons seemed to mystify everyone, but he kept very well. This was my first visit to Venice and I can remember being appalled at the colour of the water, the stench of the canals and the general odour of decay. I have since adjusted my dream of perfection and have come to love it very much, and see it with different eyes. We later returned year after year to holiday in Venice after a month on the Yugoslav coast at Novi Vinodolski as Peter had to attend the Venice Biennale as part of his job, but that is another story.

Our excitement mounted as we drove over the north of the Istrian peninsula to cross the Yugoslav border at Rijeka, which was previously Italian and called Fiume, both words meaning river. My first impression was of the smell of the motor fuel; it was very distinctive and different from anything we had experienced before. We lunched in a rather darkened restaurant, with beaded curtains, suitable for any spy film. The smell which pervaded everywhere was garlic and coffee which was actually made from acorns. The mashed potato was superb and Gerard charmed everyone with his obvious appreciation of the meal. He was our passport through every difficult situation. Everyone there seemed to love a baby and found it amazing that we had travelled with him from London in the car; now, it would be commonplace.

The feeling of anticipation in both Peter and myself was tremendous as we drove towards Ljubljana and Zagreb. Few English people had ventured before us so far by road and we had very little idea of what to expect. When we arrived in Zagreb we stayed at one of the International Hotels on the main square. We were given a suite of rooms with a large lounge, a bedroom and a bathroom plus an entrance hall. Gerard was tired and we decided not to take him to the dining room for dinner. We gave him something to eat that we had with us and tucked him up to sleep, safely strapped into his harness which he had become very used to by now, and he was able to get very comfortable. He was a good and reliable sleeper at this stage, so we decided to take it in turns every quarter of an hour to check that he was okay. With the changed climate of safety one would not now leave a child like this, but we were very trusting and seemingly had no fear. Everything was fine, but when we returned together at the end of the meal, we discovered that someone had been through our apartment and fixed two flags to our very large balcony, overlooking the main square. When we complained of the intrusion we were told that this was quite in order because an important head of state was arriving in Zagreb the next day. Gerard had slept peacefully through it all.

At this stage language was not a problem. Peter's fluent Italian was understood in some places and in the hotels someone usually could understand a little French or possibly a little English. Everyone tried to speak to us in German when they knew we were English, but neither of us spoke German. We were not really prepared for the shock that was to come later. It was Saturday when we started the last stage of the journey, the 200 kilometre 'Autoput', the only paved road, even to this day, between Zagreb and Belgrade. This road was a narrow ribbon of rough white single lane concrete, with no other traffic. For the most part the scenery on either side was flat, dull and uninteresting. Sometimes groups of peasants could be seen, often women, dressed in black, with black head scarves working in groups or rows, with primitive implements. I wondered how far they had to walk to their fields as there was rarely a house or any habitation to be seen. There were two main dangers on this long boring stretch of road. The first was peasants with ox or donkey carts crossing from one side to the other at a very slow pace, none of whom seemed to have any sense of the speed of an oncoming car, or the realisation that their right of way was a hazard to themselves and others. The second danger, more personal, but equally uncontrollable, was the intense desire to fall asleep. The straight white road with its mirages dancing in front of you had an hypnotic effect, and many a driver ended up in a field, some in the hospital, if they were lucky enough to be spotted by someone passing.

In recent years as the motor car became more universal, the autoput became a solid traffic jam in both directions with traffic travelling at the speed of the slowest vehicle. It was the main through route to Turkey, and farms and restaurants sprang up on each side of the narrow highway which became worn and dirty with rubbish strewn on either side. The journey down the autoput took approximately five hours, the only resting places were a few identical 'Ristoran' built at intervals. They were simply designed and spartanly furnished with bare wooden tables and chairs. It was at one of these that we stopped to eat. There was no choice of menu, and as there were so few travellers this was understandable. What was served was extremely acceptable. Beef, which in Yugoslavia was always very young and tender, cooked in a pan in a little fat on a low heat with a very little liquid added, served with 'pire krompir' which was mashed potato, almost certainly from a packet, because of its unnaturally smooth texture, but nevertheless made tasty by the meat juices which were poured over it, quite delicious. Even Gerard could eat this as the meat was so tender, and his "mo mo" echoed through the emptiness. Just one swarthy unshaven man with an apron round his waist controlled the entire place, cooking, serving, and taking the money; such a small amount for the meal we could hardly believe it. There was not another building in sight, and no sign of his transport. Did he live on the premises? It all remained a mystery as we could find no common language other than signs. The need to stop again arose and we trundled down a lane through the fields suddenly coming upon a small group of shacks and outbuildings, our wheels suddenly heavy in the mud, chickens fluttering, clucking and squawking all around us. We were alarmed at first in case our intrusion would not be welcome, but children and black-scarved old ladies alike came out and stared without a word, as we refreshed ourselves with a drink. There were apparently no young men or women. Perhaps they all moved into the towns to find better work? No-one spoke, no-one objected and no-one came to help as we turned with difficulty and waved our farewell. It was as if we had landed from outer space.

It was late afternoon when we eventually arrived in Belgrade. We had received clear instructions, in theory anyway, to find the flat which was to be our temporary home, and the directions for collecting the key. The culture shock which we experienced is difficult to describe. We had even dipped into the Serbo-Croat dictionary which we had with us, which presented us with no difficulty at all beyond knowing that we would have to make some effort to master this up to now, unheard language. Crossing Slovenia and Croatia we had only experienced Croatian which is 'latinica' a language written and spoken phonetically. One could either read words and find them in the dictionary, or someone would find them for you. Here in Serbia the language is written in 'Cyrillic' which is an alphabet rather like Greek or Russian, completely unintelligible to the stranger. We could neither read nor write nor understand. The street signs were in Cyrillic and we had our address written in latinica. It was only the fact that our flat adjoined the British Reading Room that gave someone a clue to help us find No.1 Nikola Spasiča which was to be our home for the next eight months.

As we were not sure which day we would be arriving it was impossible for anyone to meet us, and of course on Saturday night the British Reading Room was closed. We found our way into a courtyard through a large double door with the help of several conflicting and gesticulating women in head scarves, who inhabited rooms around the courtyard, telling us where to put the car, and where to go, wanting to unpack the car there and then, giving us some difficulty in holding them off. We climbed the staircase which led to what seemed to be the back door into a very small primitive kitchen, and then into a very large square room with parquet flooring and large windows down one side, at each end of which were spectacular double doors, one set leading into the only bedroom, again extremely large, with windows on one side, and the other into a small hall, which led in turn to the Reading Room office. A small primitive bathroom led from the kitchen. These four rooms were our new home. Fortunately we had food with us, as we had already been picnicking on the journey. We unpacked what we needed. I had brought blankets and bed-linen with us, sufficient for the first six weeks. We discovered that there was no cooking stove in the kitchen but fortunately we had a small spirit stove, which was sufficient for our needs that night. We slept well, and in the morning we had a call from Ratko Kalafatovič who was the factotum of the Reading Room and completely managed it. He spoke excellent English, and could answer many of our questions. He showed great interest in Gerard even though he was a confirmed bachelor. Ratko was a great organiser, and not a truly typical Serb. He had someone lined up for us to cook and housekeep, who he thoroughly recommended. Her name was Louisa and he said she was honest, which was a rare quality. Louisa turned out to be a gem. She was due to present herself for scrutiny on Monday morning at 8.00am.

As it was Sunday, we decided to find a church. We had been warned and fully understood that being a Roman Catholic in a Communist country could be difficult. We were therefore surprised when Ratko found no problem in recommending two or three Catholic churches in the surrounding neighbourhood. We set off with light hearts, only to find that these were all Serbian Orthodox churches. We witnessed a wedding in the first, the second was empty, and in the third a service was going on that was completely alien to anything we had previously known. Even to this day we have not fully understood what was happening. We decided to make a more concerted attempt to find a Roman Catholic Church, if indeed there was one. I felt terribly homesick and longed for the familiarity of our own congregation and friends. At this stage in my life God was important but I had not then begun to realise how much He knew about me, and what more he wanted to do for me, this was to take many more years. Although I had been brought up in a Catholic family, and had been educated for the most part in a convent, I had not then grasped the true meaning of being a Christian. I held the view that if I tried to lead a fairly good life, went to church and kept away from sin, which was then always spelled out very clearly, I would be alright. Everything was cut and dried, as my mother used to say. My father was my headmaster until I was eleven and he was always very strict about things to do with religion. It seemed mostly a matter of being on time for church and paying attention. There were times in my life when I had been touched in a special way, for instance when I was in the upper fifth at school, sitting in my classroom overlooking Greenwich Park and the Thames, the loop of which is now well known from the 'soap' East Enders, I became conscious of Mother Agnes speaking about perfect love, the love that God has for us, but through His grace the love that we also can have. This is the love that wants nothing in return, agape love. I wanted to have that kind of love but it seemed an impossibility. I can remember as a young child having quite revolutionary ideas which on the whole I kept to myself as I quickly came to learn that adults didn't think much of them. I had read children's books about Jesus, so I used to think, when I came to a problem or obstacle, 'What would Jesus have done?' and would take this as my guideline, but it often got me into trouble. My church, the Catholic Church, was for me like a hospital, where people could go if they weren't alright, but most people's idea of church was that you got alright first, or you weren't acceptable. I could never understand this, if I tried to express this at home or at school I was suppressed. The friends that I brought home from school were often in need like Emily White who lived with her grandmother and seemed to have no parents. She was always a bit dirty and their house was smelly. Then there was Iris Denton who cried a lot and was very thin. They didn't go to church although they were at my school and I was always discouraged from bringing them home. Then there was John Murray who nearly drowned on a scout camping holiday in Folkestone and was rescued by a boy named Colin who dived into the harbour and disentangled him from some ropes. John used to call for me to go out to play, but he again didn't go to church and was a bit scruffy. The answer was always 'No'.

However, finding a Catholic church this day proved impossible as we could not read anything, or indeed ask, owing to the language difficulty. Louisa arrived as arranged on Monday morning, and proved to be everything that we had heard about her. She could prepare food amazingly well, and was not at all put off by the absence of any evident means of cooking. She had learnt a kind of pidgin English very badly from previous Embassy appointments. With Ratko interpreting both her Serbian and her efforts at English, we covered a lot of ground. She was willing to do everything, cook, clean, shop in the market, (which she did at 4.30am), the washing and ironing...... " Louisi do all," and all was what she did. I was her "mali reine" her little queen. She used whatever language she had heard, and I did not disillusion her. She would not let me work, she protected me with her life. She made up a bed on the floor behind a screen in what seemed to be the little entrance hall, with blankets she brought from her own little flat. This was all folded and had disappeared by the time we were up in the morning. She hired us a two ring electric stove from a friend, on which she could cook an amazing three course meal, even for visitors. She cleaned and washed, boiled the terry towelling nappies, and was always ready to do anything that was needed. As well as all this, she started to teach me Serbo-Croat. We both realised that running a flat without being able to communicate properly was too difficult. We could always call in someone from the Reading Room to interpret, as they were only separated from us by the locked double door after all, and they were always very willing to practise their

English. Two ladies on the staff were on call at a moment's notice and their English was excellent, but for Louisa and me, being able to speak directly to one another was very exciting. We started with numbers, one to ten, jedan, dva, tri, četiri, pet, čest, sedam, ossam, devet and deset. As soon as Peter returned from the Embassy, which was about 15 minutes' journey by car, I would teach him what I had learnt. We counted up to a hundred, then practised the days of the week, everything Louisa touched in the kitchen she named and would make me repeat it. It worked wonderfully well, but nevertheless Peter was particularly pleased when the day came for Mr Angelkovič to start official lessons for him which I was allowed to attend. Peter had found kitchen language rather limiting on the diplomatic front.

We were very soon to realise that acquiring Serbo-Croatian was not as easy as we had at first thought. Learning words and speaking a 'pidgin' language was far removed from an acceptable way of speaking. The nouns declined rather like Latin and so did all the pronouns. It entailed learning and understanding many endings for the same word, according to the action, declining in ablatives and genitives and so on. I knew from the beginning I would never master this but learnt what I could and tried to imitate Louisa. I stopped worrying about correct grammar and was pleased when people could understand me. Mr Angelkovič came weekly and proved to be a very good friend. Whenever he wanted to talk to us about his life and his family, and what had been going on in the country, he would get up and look behind the sofa and chairs, peer into the bedroom and kitchen with an "Excuse me, please?" and then even though we were on the first floor he would open the window and look out. Having satisfied himself all was clear, he would draw close and speak in a whisper. UDBA, the secret police were everywhere. Strangely they were often recognisable in a city of rather run-down buildings and people. They often wore regulation light-coloured raincoats and trilby hats. We came to see quickly that they were taken very seriously. As a citizen of Belgrade as long as you kept within the rules and did what you were told, usually everything was alright. As diplomats we of course were privileged, although undoubtedly we were watched and sometimes bugged.

As we listened to the stories of the people that we came to know well and who trusted us, we realised just how much everyone had suffered. Houses had been commandeered and whole families moved into two rooms. Family treasures, silver, and anything of value had been confiscated. We saw situations in which many people, who had previously lived quite comfortably, were sharing kitchens, toilets and washing facilities with many other families; sometimes a person living alone would have just one room with no toilet or bathroom. They would sometimes be forced to use an outside toilet several blocks away with no washing facilities. It was a familiar sight to see people carrying water from a communal tap. Those who had no work would often spend all day in bed, either to keep warm or to be comfortable. Some families had managed to move to a smaller self-contained flat. The Angelkovič's considered themselves very fortunate to be together as a family. One of their daughters was a dancer in the Belgrade Ballet Company, and this was deemed by the government to be of national value so they had been slightly privileged. We went several times to share a meal or a party with them, but the air of cautiousness was always present amid the fun.

When I communicated to Louisa with signs and actions that we wanted to find a Roman Catholic Church, not a Serbian Orthodox one, she knew exactly where to take us, telling us not to worry. We made an expedition the following Saturday in order to be able to find our way on the Sunday morning whilst Louisa cooked the lunch. She indicated that being half Bosnian and half German, (I think she had a German great-grandfather), she was actually a Roman Catholic, but she didn't always go to church, in fact I don't think she ever did, as events showed. She took us miles right across the town and through the outskirts on the other side. "Još, Još... (Keep going)" she commanded, holding up her right arm and pointing her hand forward. She certainly knew her way to St Anthony's. A very large church faced us, beautiful inside and out. An air of wealth and care pervaded every corner. An army of black head-scarved women were cleaning and polishing and others brightly clothed with carefully groomed hair were arranging flowers. We were amazed at the beautiful marble pillars and the exotic lace altar cloths. All we had heard about the persecuted church in Yugoslavia could not have been true. We looked up the times of Masses for Sunday and knelt and said a prayer of thanksgiving. Perhaps things were not so bad after all. Sunday came and we arrived in plenty of time for Mass. We were welcomed by an extremely pleasant priest, who spoke both French and Italian, who invited us to visit him in his house after Mass and take some refreshment with him. The Mass as far as we could tell was the same as we knew, but we still had difficulty in lining up our experience with all that we had heard about the disappearance of priests and the anti-religious regime. The congregation was made up mainly of women, but there were certainly some men. We had been told that men were kept busy with compulsory parades on Sunday so that they could not attend church. In the priest's house we were offered slivovič which is plum brandy fire water, the national drink, or cherry brandy. Two nuns were present and they also had a drink. Peter made a rather generous donation to the priest and we arranged, in view of the apparent lack of anywhere else, to make St Anthony's our parish church. We continued to make this journey on Sundays for another five weeks, becoming more and more amazed at St Anthony's wealth in contrast with the hardship we saw all around us elsewhere. We did speak to the priest about this but he shrugged his shoulders and said people supported their church, of course, it was very important to them.

It was only when we made friends with Ied and Hein Schaapveldt from the Royal Netherlands Embassy, who were also Catholics, that we came to understand the situation better. St Anthony's was one of the few Catholic churches which had pledged loyalty to the Communist Government, and had severed all ties with Rome and the Pope. We were horrified and not a little upset. Ied and Hein introduced us to our proper parish church, one of five surviving in the whole of the capital, a poverty stricken darkened building with a Hungarian parish priest. He told us that he never left the building. He lived in a room above the sacristy which was reached by a spiral staircase. Evidently the UDBA watched the church from a window on the first floor opposite and left him alone if he obeyed their instructions. His fellow priest, a younger Yugoslav, had been removed and disappeared in the spring, just before our arrival in Belgrade.

Chapter Two

La Vie Diplomatique

For a while, life was full of new things to learn, new experiences and new people. The container with our household goods and clothes arrived from England and we were able to start to organise the flat and try to make it comfortable. Louisa scrubbed and polished, she could not do enough to help. She could be found in the early morning with steel wool strapped to her slip-in mules, in which she always shuffled about, smoothing the parquet blocks so that she could polish them perfectly, nothing was too much trouble for her. Louisa's day started at 4.30am with a visit to the market. An early start meant fresh meat and the pick of the vegetables. There was no refrigeration in the market, and it was most probably better not to see where our meat came from. The butcher's shop, and there was only one, was refrigerated but the meat was much more expensive. The meat everywhere was of excellent quality usually with a choice. Serbians ate a great deal of meat, when they could afford it, at least. It was usually prepared from young animals and was of good quality. Restaurant meals often consisted of grilled meat served with chopped raw onions chilli peppers and lots of bread. There were various national meat dishes, čevapčiči, small tube-shaped rissoles made from minced lamb, beef and pork, cooked over charcoal, razniči, pieces of succulent pork on a wooden skewer, again cooked over charcoal.

The Serbians are also very fond of suckling pig cooked on a spit, very often over an open fire. In a restaurant we once had a lamb, roasted to perfection and served in its entirety in the centre of the table, each person pulling or cutting a piece as they fancied. Another popular meat dish was duveč, a kind of stew made with beef, vegetables and paprika; čorba is the basic peasant soup made from marrow bones and vegetables, it is delicious.

Vegetables were scarce. The peasants would bring their goods in from the countryside to the market, very often tied in cloths, and lay them out on a table. Potatoes, peppers, cabbages and onions were usually available, but it was the early bird who found the spinach, parsley and other green vegetables, carrots were small and inferior. There were fresh fruits in season but only for the first arrivals, and again the quality was poor unless you had the first pickings. It was impossible to make a firm decision in advance about vegetables and fruit for the day. It was a matter of what was available. Nothing imported like oranges or bananas were ever seen. Bread was bought by the kilo, brown in colour, delicious when hot, but stale within the hour. Louisa made white bread every other day, and it was also delicious. She would sometimes keep a little of the dough back and fry it, sprinkling it with sugar as a treat with my mid-morning drink.

When we were entertaining she really excelled herself. She was full of ideas and had a very high standard, even when it was just for Peter and myself, although you would not always guess this from looking at her. She liked to wear the universal head scarf at all times except when she was serving at table, when she made herself look very smart.

One evening not long after we arrived in Belgrade, Louisa was baby sitting for us. We came in as usual through the kitchen door and switched on the light. It was as if a black carpet moved across the floor and disappeared in a matter of seconds. We recognised it as a plague of cockroaches. We had already found one or two lurking in corners, but this was terrible. They had retreated into the cracks between the floor and the walls. Ugh! The kitchen had already been thoroughly cleaned by Louisa. We realised that cleaning alone did not solve the problem. Louisa took the matter in hand and heard, on what only can be called the grape vine, that a substance, if you could get it, called Rapin, was the only thing that was known to kill cockroaches. It smelt rather like low grade petrol. We set about trying to procure some Rapin, and were eventually successful. We borrowed a spray gun. At this time the shops, such as there were in Belgrade, were almost completely empty and it was impossible to buy anything like this. People were used to lending and borrowing, and were most obliging.

Peter and I started a campaign. Before we went to bed we sprayed round the bottom of the walls in the kitchen where the wooden skirting board joined the stone floor. What a sight greeted Louisa the next morning. She left it for us to see, there were dozens of dead cockroaches waiting to be swept up. The next night we sprayed not only the kitchen but all round the flat where the wooden skirting board met the parquet, but omitted the bedroom because we were afraid of the fumes hurting Gerard. We continued this for three days, sweeping up hundreds of dead cockroaches, but they still seemed to keep coming.

We decided to spread our campaign into the Reading Room Office which adjoined Louisa's sleeping area through the large locked double door. We went in at night and sprayed round all the edges when everyone had gone home. As well as other duties in the Embassy, Peter was in charge of this office, so we were quite in order. We perhaps overstepped the mark when we discovered that some of the drawers were littered with old sandwiches, cakes, biscuits and apples. We got rid of them all. Our harvest of insects which we swept up early the next morning was tremendous. Peter put out a friendly edict to the nineteen people working there, that storage of food was forbidden unless it was in a sealed container. Our campaign worked like a miracle and within a week there was not one cockroach to be found. Most of the Reading Room staff could not understand what all the fuss was about saying that cockroaches never hurt anyone!

Living in two rooms was not easy even though they were very large. We had been promised a villa when we arrived, but weeks went by and nothing materialised. We were doing the rounds of cocktail parties and dinner parties, but entertaining for me was difficult because of our limited accommodation. We were committed to giving small dinner parties as our table only sat six. We had experienced having dinner with our Ambassador and his wife, Sir Frank and Stella Roberts. There were eighteen of us at the table, and dinner had been delayed because of a power cut, which was not an uncommon experience. Lady Roberts was in many ways very natural and unassuming, but she managed an excellent staff, and always presented a very good table. On this occasion each one of us had our own miniature cruet in front of us, and the main course was served to the ladies first from the left by a team of skilled waitresses and waiters. A silver sauce boat was also set on the table, one between two people. I was seated beside one of the First Secretaries from our own Embassy, whose reputation for absent-mindedness had gone before him. He was a bachelor, very much liked by everyone. As the waiter and his junior assistant put my warm dinner plate in front of me and served my food, my dinner companion offered me the sauce. On taking it back not realising that he had not yet been given a plate, he poured it carefully all round his beautiful lace mat. He did not immediately notice his faux pas, as he was busy relating a story to me. A waiter appeared from nowhere with a silver tray and a cloth, removed all the mess, to a horrified "O my God!" and reset the place with hardly a soul noticing.

I was by now feeling my pregnancy. The summer brought with it very hot humid weather. The climate in Belgrade is continental, that is, very hot in summer and extremely cold in winter. There was hardly any spring or autumn. One day snow would be thick on the ground, the next day bright sunshine and the leaves starting to come forth on the trees. I was invited to spend as many days as I liked at the house of the Naval Attaché on the outskirts of town. He and his family had gone to spend the summer at Bled in Slovenia where the climate was more gentle. The whole Embassy moved there for major business with the Ambassador, the Naval Attaché and his wife had lent their house in Belgrade to the First Secretary who lived with his Italian wife and children in the centre of town. There was a lovely garden with pleasant shade, and even a small pool with this out of town house. We were already close friends with the First Secretary Keith and his wife Marisa, and this gave a wonderful chance for Gerard to have a free run in the beautiful garden. He was now walking of course and my daily exercise with him previously had always been in Kalemegdan, a large park at the confluence of the Danube and Sava Rivers, just five minutes walk along the 'Corso' from our flat in Nikola Spasiča. Most hot countries are known for their Corso and Belgrade was no exception. From about six o'clock in the evening for at least two hours it seemed as if the whole of Belgrade, with their children dressed in their best, walked up and down the Corso. In our flat you could hear the loud noise of tramping feet and a thousand conversations. The whole building trembled with the vibrations. This was mixed with the typically Serbian music which was churned out constantly through public loudspeakers. Although at this time Kalemegdan was very beautiful I used to tire of it. Marisa also had a baby boy, named Patrick, not quite as old as Gerard, so she was very simpatico company. She also lent me some very cool fashionable maternity wear. These were pleasant days.

The diplomatic bag left the Embassy for London every Monday morning. This meant that any letters had to be ready for delivery by Sunday night. Sending them any other way was very unreliable. I usually started a letter home during the week but we never seemed to get everything completed. There was often a mad rush, especially if we had been particularly busy with engagements, or if we had been on a group picnic to the banks of the Sava on Sunday, where there was a safe and very pleasant place for swimming. I was by then too far in my pregnancy to be seen in a swimming costume even if it had fitted. Gerard always enjoyed the water, and although he could not paddle as the water was deep, he went in with Peter. Down by the river the main difficulty was to find protection from the mosquitoes.

As my pregnancy moved into the sixth month I became a little concerned that I had not seen a doctor, and my mother was constantly exhorting me to seek medical attention in her letters. There was no organised maternity care as far as we could understand, so I went privately to see a Dr Fotič. Without my knowing it at the time of making the appointment, he was the person who lived in the flat across the road, which overlooked our bedroom. He caused us a great deal of distress with his night time cough. In the great heat everyone slept with their windows wide open. He had been recommended to us but I only saw him twice. He spoke no English and only a little French. He took my blood pressure but otherwise showed very little interest. His surgery was a rather dirty room in his flat, and I saw little purpose in going for a third time. Although I had already given birth to one child, I was rather vague about the importance of ante-natal care. Because I felt well, I presumed everything was okay. Later when I realised the tremendous care that is always taken of mothers in England, I was truly thankful that nothing had gone wrong.

It was at this time that something very distressing happened. Louisa's daughter Branka was engaged to a young Serbian man named Miloš. Branka loved Miloš very much. We had met him as Branka sometimes came to our flat when she had finished her work, to both help Louisa and keep her company. Miloš would occasionally come to meet her. Branka was a beautiful girl, with dark curly hair, just twenty years old; she lived with Louisa in their small flat. One day Louisa was summoned home, I think by the police. A neighbour who had a key to Louisa's flat had noticed that Branka had not followed her normal routine and, thinking she might be ill, had gone in to see if she could help. She found Branka unconscious, slumped across her bed, with an empty bottle of tablets beside her. The poor girl was taken to hospital where she was treated immediately. She did not die as she had wanted but lay for several days without regaining consciousness, and then only gradually did her senses return. Evidently she had become suspicious that Miloš was dating another girl and had then seen him with his arm round her. She had tackled him about it to find that he had been trying to pluck up courage to break off their engagement. Branka saw no point in living any more. We were to find out later that suicide was very common in Belgrade. Life was hard for everyone. It was several weeks before Branka was well enough to return home and even then she dragged her paralysed leg behind her which never recovered. Louisa continued working for us during Branka's stay in hospital, giving us plenty of notice that we would need to find a temporary replacement. Branka was going to need constant care for a while as she was emotionally disturbed as well as physically disabled.

It was Ratko who found Maria for us, again someone who he could wholeheartedly recommend. Maria started work just at the time when I was making arrangements for the birth of our baby. Before we left England my doctor had been very helpful in finding out where the birth might take place. The only hospital in Belgrade had been completely ruled out except as a last resort. It was known to be ill equipped and run down. I was there on several occasions, helping people through their labour, as there was very little professional help or guidance. There were rats freely scavenging at night and no running hot water at all on the third floor where the maternity department was situated. This hospital has since been rebuilt.

When the final choice of hospital for me was made it was under-stood definitely that flying was not allowed after five months of pregnancy, so it was decided that I went by train to Vienna direct from Belgrade. The journey would take eighteen hours. A place was reserved for me from November 16th at the Rudolfinerhaus in the Billrothstrasse. This was an exclusive private hospital and the maternity department had an extremely high reputation. As a diplomat's wife it was expected that I would be well looked after, no equality laws then. Our baby was due on the 23rd November so I had a week's leeway. Word had gone round the diplomatic grape-vine, and I was invited to stay with the officer in charge of Embassy security in Vienna, who lived with his wife in a flat in the centre of town. I was to be under the care of Primarius Skamnakis, the top gynaecologist in Vienna.

Maria, like Louisa, came from a very good background. Whereas Louisa was of German origin, and spoke German, Maria was from an area which was previously Italian, and although she was partially Serbian and had lived in Serbia for many years, she spoke fluent Italian. We explained to her that when I went to Vienna I would have to leave Gerard. We asked her if she would be willing to look after him for two weeks or so. She was delighted. It was no problem for her as she also had a daughter who was willing to help. Louisa had also said she would sometimes come in to give a hand. I was very concerned about leaving my beloved little nineteen month old son with a comparative stranger, but by now I had several good friends who would keep an eye on things. None of them, though, was willing to take charge of Gerard completely because all had either English nannies or Yugoslav girls to look after their own children. The diplomatic life did not lend itself to carrying out maternal duties. This aspect of diplomatic life was to cause me much distress in the months to come. Until a week before my departure for Vienna we were not sure whether Peter would be able come with me. There was important work to be done in the Embassy and it would be difficult for him to be spared. However at the last moment he was free to accompany me, and providing that I had the baby on time, he would be able to stay in Vienna until my return. I was very unsure whether I preferred him to remain at the flat in Belgrade with Gerard and Maria, or support me in Vienna. I thought I would not be able to bear the pain when I said goodbye to Gerard. However he took to Maria straight away and she to him. He seemed quite happy and of course was too young to understand what was to happen, although I had talked to him about the new baby. By this time winter had set in and snow was falling heavily and settling.

On our arrival at the main railway station in Vienna, we were met and warmly greeted by our new friends, Mr and Mrs Lamb, after the long uncomfortable and fairly hazardous journey when we were nearly roasted because we had a sleeping compartment with heating that we could not control ourselves. If we opened the window to get some fresh air, we not only froze in the icy wind, but were bombarded with pieces of red hot coals, coming from the funnel of the engine as it got up steam. It was an exciting journey, crossing the frontier into Austria, where we had listed the hospitals in case of an early labour, starting with Maribor and Klagenfurt, which was then a military hospital. They had all been alerted.

Everything went according to plan and we soon settled down with the Lambs. They were a very kind old-fashioned couple, with quite definite ideas. Peter stayed in a local hotel and I was put in their only spare room which was single. Peter and I spent our time shopping and sight-seeing in the icy cold snowy weather. We were well wrapped up and I was really pleased to see some of the beautiful sights in Vienna, as well as sampling the world famous coffee and cream cakes. In so few months we had forgotten about well stocked shops and luxury tea rooms, at which the Viennese excel. We bought many things, including table ware, to augment our own china, which matched very well, glasses, dress material and baby-ware. We had it packed and delivered to our friends' flat, ready for the journey home to Belgrade. I remember the exhilaration of quite ordinary things; for instance, drinking real milk on breakfast cereal, instead of diluted 'Carnation' which we fortunately could buy in the wonderful Embassy NAAFI in Belgrade. Fresh milk in Belgrade was sold from the churn in unhygienic conditions and because of the fear of tuberculosis which is spread through infected cows, absolutely everyone boiled milk for twenty minutes. This was very difficult to do as it constantly boiled over, was reduced to half its quantity and on top of that, had a terrible taste. The man who delivered the milk in our district was swathed in furs in the winter and his fur-clad arm and dirty hand would disappear into the churn with the measure; the milk was then tipped into whatever receptacle was provided, and the same hand took the money.

I loved the excitement of Vienna even though I was rather uncomfortable and I guessed our baby would be quite large. We were watching outdoor skating in one of the parks on Sunday afternoon, just four days after our arrival, when I felt the first signs of the arrival of our new baby. We returned to our friends' flat and ate supper, which was always egg and bacon. They planned this for easy management, as neither liked housekeeping or cooking. The dirty washing up was left for the maid, who came in by train each morning from the south of Vienna and worked until three o'clock. She cooked a very good lunch at midday. On this night we played cards until bedtime at eleven o'clock when I announced to Mr and Mrs Lamb that I would have to call the ambulance and go to the hospital. Pains had been getting stronger all the evening but only Peter knew. Even the ambulance men were surprised when I told them I wanted to walk down the two flights of stairs to the ground floor. They would not hear of it and insisted that I went on the stretcher-chair.

My entrance to the hospital was an anticlimax. Primarius Skamnakis was already waiting for me. He greeted us, examined me briefly, gave me an injection, sent Peter back to his hotel for a good night's sleep, and left me to sleep soundly until morning. After another injection at daybreak, with no consultation, the labour continued normally. I was taken into the delivery room and as I went into the second stage of labour, I was expecting to have 'gas and air,' however, I was in for a big surprise. My hands were fixed to the edge of the bed with handcuffs. I could not move and remonstrated with the nurses as best I could as none of them spoke English. At last they sent for Dr Skamnakis, who explained that it was the custom to tie Austrian women down as they often screamed and hit out at the doctors and nurses. I was astonished and promised I would not do this. Reluctantly the handcuffs were removed. Then instead of 'gas and air' a pad of cotton wool, soaked in chloroform was pressed onto my face. The next thing I remember was Dr Skamnakis saying in his broken English, "Mrs Coldham, if you don't wake up and do something you will never have this baby." I had vaguely thought in my dreamy state that it was all over.

Christopher was duly born at half past two. It was November 21st 1955. He weighed ten and a half pounds. We thought this was possibly due to my large meat consumption during the pregnancy, and certainly a large proportion of my diet had been protein. The young nurse, whose job it was to whisk the baby away and clean him up before allowing the mother to see him, quickly brought him close to my face and allowed me to kiss him. She would have put him in my arms but a harsh voice obviously scolding her caused her to slide quickly away with our baby, without a word. I then underwent another dose of chloroform while I had twenty two stitches, sewn by Dr Skamnakis. All was as well as could be expected in the circumstances. Sadly then, both in Vienna and in England, husbands were deprived of the privilege of witnessing the birth of their baby. Afterwards I actually felt well and was very hungry, only to find that my special delivery room lunch, a kind of vegetable puree, served on the usual silver dishes, had been eaten by Peter, the nurse having persuaded him that I would not want it. Even though it was such a first class establishment, there was absolutely no provision of food of any kind until the next meal time. We were not yet in the age of 'take away', so I just had to stay hungry until the evening.

After the birth, when our baby had been washed and dressed, both Peter and I had almost as long as we wanted to hold Christopher and admire him. Peter was allowed in my room to stay with me all day with no restrictions, but Christopher was taken away and tucked up in a cot in the nursery with seventeen other babies. I did not once set eyes on any of the mothers as I was encouraged to stay in bed and rest. Primarius Skamnakis came in every day to see me. He often stayed to chat with us, and told us many horrific stories of the Russian occupation of that section of Vienna. It had been a very traumatic time for them, and they hated the Russians more than they hated the Germans. The soldiers drank a lot and were often out of control, abusing the citizens verbally and physically and even raping.

The day to day routine in the hospital was very strict and very Teutonic. The baby was weighed before and after feeds to make sure that he was having sufficient milk. We were allowed a little cuddle with him after feeds and that was that. The other rule which I found impossible to obey was no bath for me for fourteen days after the birth. I never quite got to the bottom of the reasons for this because in England the first thing that happened after a birth was a 'nice hot bath'. The time finally came to choose a name as it was necessary for Peter to register the birth. We were undecided whether it would be Christopher Paul or Paul Christopher. We wanted both Paul and Christopher for the first name. In the end I sent Peter off and asked him to make the decision. When he had finally decided we were both very happy with the name for our little (or rather very long) Christopher.

One day when I had just finished feeding Christopher, I reached up to the strap handles over my bed to pull myself up, so that I could get more comfortable. There was a tremendous cracking noise and the whole iron structure snapped and fell on me, badly bruising my shoulder. Once again Dr Skamnakis was sent for. He was not in the hospital but arrived very quickly. I believe they were all really afraid that Peter would sue the hospital. They could not do enough to help us, and I was even allowed to have a bath so long as I remained kneeling! This was a great concession. During my stay in the Rudolfinerhaus Peter did not need to go out to get a lunch. I was always served far more than I could possibly eat, beautifully presented on silver salvers and quality china with plenty of cutlery so that I could share it with Peter. One morning as he came into my room I knew at once that all was not well. His manner was different although he tried to disguise it. He obviously had some news to tell me but did not want to upset me. He had had a letter from my mother and father to say that Cyril, my eldest sister's husband, had been taken very ill with poliomyelitis. He was in an iron lung and the prognosis was not very good. Josie, my sister, had moved back home with my mother and father and was learning to drive so that she could visit Cyril more easily each day in the hospital, leaving her two very young girls with them. It took her one hour each way to get to the hospital as it was near their own home in London, and of course he was too ill to be moved. It was a very worrying time. Cyril was in hospital for over a year. When eventually he was well enough to return home he was unable to walk as both legs were paralysed.

During this time in the Rudolfinerhaus in Vienna there was quite a lot of trauma. The way the midwives managed feeding was unknown to me in England. Apart from weighing the baby before and after meals they preferred to have mother's milk to feed the eighteen babies in the night. The mother was never woken up to feed except in the day. As I seemed to have a lot of milk, they brought me a pump and showed me how to take off any extra milk.

Innocently I did this as I thought it was good for my welfare and that of Christopher. I came to see that I always had far too much milk and it was obviously because I was stimulating my supply each feeding time. Because there was no one at all who spoke any English except Dr Skamnakis it was difficult for me to stand against the rather strict authoritarian regime and refuse to do this. They all said I would be worse, when I had my message translated through Dr Skamnakis, who although an excellent gynaecologist knew little about day to day breast feeding. My breasts became enormous, I was in agony and sore and I stood out in front like a large table. Finally I found the courage to refuse the pump but in actual fact because my milk was flowing so freely nothing improved. We found out that they were feeding the eighteen babies in the night entirely with my milk.

Our friends, particularly Mrs Lamb, had been visiting me each day, flooding me with flowers, fruit and every kindness; she was very concerned about my welfare, but although they had been living in Vienna for quite a long time, she hardly spoke German, only just enough to manage her maid. She was very motherly and understood that what was happening to me was not correct procedure, as far as English standards were concerned, anyway. After nine days and much consultation, permission was grudgingly given me by the Matron to return to Belgrade. I was not really quite well enough but Peter was needed in Belgrade and neither of us wanted to travel separately. As another great kindness, the Matron gave Peter permission to take me out to lunch on the last day. This proved to be a disaster as the local restaurant that was recommended had typically Austrian carved hard wooden chairs, and I was barely able to sit down as I had been sitting on a rubber ring whilst I was in bed. I was still very weak and very sore and in great pain from my twenty two stitches. My breasts were enormous and tender. I was concerned because there was very little skilled medical help in Belgrade and we had an eighteen hour journey on the train before that to face. I begged Dr Skamnakis to give me an injection to reduce my milk. He was loath to do this. He said as I became more active and was managing without so much rest my milk would naturally reduce; however he said he would give me a minute dose by injection. I should have listened to him.

The Lambs were very kind to us, they had helped Peter organise all my luggage in the flat, and arranged for a car to take us to the railway station in time for the night train to Belgrade which left at 9.00 o'clock. Goodbyes were said, and with Christopher tucked into his Karricot, a Harrington square completely covering his face to filter out the bitterly cold snow laden wind, we said farewell to Vienna, carrying with us the impressive looking documents registering Christopher Paul as Austrian and English. It was quite sad saying goodbye to the Lambs who even brought beautiful roses to the train for me. I felt I would most probably never see them again as Mr Lamb was near retiring.

By the time we arrived in Belgrade my milk flow was already greatly reduced. I felt very tired on the journey through the night and because of the heat and the movement, Christopher slept. I fed him much less than in the hospital partly because I felt unwell and very hot. When we opened the carriage window to let in cold air, it not only became too cold very quickly, but as before lumps of burning coal flew in the window and I was very worried something would happen to Christopher. When we eventually reached our flat in Nikola Spasiča by taxi it was 5.00pm and I was exhausted. We had been travelling from 8.00pm the night before and Peter and I were looking after Christopher entirely on our own whereas I had only previously touched him to feed him. I went to bed and when I came to feed Christopher the second time after arriving I had no milk. Peter immediately phoned a doctor explaining the situation; this time it happened to be a lady doctor, she was with us almost immediately as Peter had to go and collect her and she was ready. No doctor had a car in Belgrade at that time, only party members and a few clever elite ran a car. I can't remember the doctor's name, but she understood my predicament and gave me yet another injection to bring back the milk. She said I was to rest quietly in bed until it flowed again.

Christopher was crying and I was desperate. We could not give him diluted cow's milk. This was too dangerous as no westerners ever drank local milk in Belgrade, certainly not children or babies. Louisa or Maria used to buy enough just for themselves. When Christopher was a few months old Danny Kaye came to visit with UNICEF primarily to promote pasteurised milk and the new pasteurisation factory which he opened. It so happened that we looked after him. It was much later when they managed to rid cattle of tuberculosis and have some sort of control on this, as pasteurisation does not reach a high enough temperature to kill the tubercular cocci. All we had to give Christopher at this time was Carnation milk. I got up intending to give him a bottle of diluted Carnation to tide him over. When Peter saw what I was doing he snatched it all away from me and made me go back to bed. It was one of the occasions that he really asserted himself and I did exactly what he said immediately; I was already in tears with great distress.

I suppose I knew he was right. He picked Christopher up and nursed him for several hours. At last I could feel the tingling and surge of the milk returning, and what joy when I could feed him again. At first it was only a little and we gave him water as well. I did feel unwell for quite a while, I guess the stress of the journey and the fuss over the milk and also having been waited on in Vienna and not encouraged to look after my own baby was to do with this. I hadn't even bathed him or changed a nappy until I left the Rudolfinerhaus. They had their own baby clothes, pure white beautiful little cotton things, which I think they could wash at a high temperature. I had a case of my own baby clothes but they were not touched until we came home. One had the feeling that everything was so well looked after and neat and tidy that they did not want anyone disturbing their apparently perfect management. I was also upset because we had been away from our home for nearly two weeks and I wanted to be with Gerard who was only 19 months old. I was even now not allowed to have him with me as I had to rest quietly. It was a very difficult time for all of us.

Chapter Three

Things to be Learned

Immediately we returned to Belgrade we had news that one of the Embassy villas was to become vacant, and we would be able to move in January. This was a difficult time as it took me a while to regain my energy. Gerard not only had to get used to a mother and father again, but also a little brother; he had been rather spoiled by Maria who had looked after him very well, however, he was overjoyed to see us.

It was customary then to have a baby baptised before it was a month old, and as Christmas was already so near we decided to make arrangements immediately. Our friends from Holland had agreed to be godparents. There were many people to be invited as it was never possible to do something like that very quietly, all our friends wanted to join in the celebration. Louisa was ready to return to work with us as Branka was very much better although she could still only walk with one leg dragging behind her. Louisa was openly very jealous of Maria's success with Gerard although they appeared to get on well, and she was anxious to establish herself as one of the family again. Maria was happy to come and help if she was needed, which was a very good situation for me. Maria was not entirely dependent on the money from her work as she had some sort of pension.

Louisa prepared the food for the christening party with some help from me; it was an afternoon event but, in a two roomed flat, even though they were very large pleasant rooms, entertaining in the day with two young children, was not easy. Visitors needed access to the bedroom as it was the only place to put their coats when we returned from the church, so that had to be left tidy. Keeping in order seemed to be a big job when we had to have lunch, feed Christopher, get ourselves ready and have everything prepared for the party. Maria came to help serve, but it was only afterwards I learnt about hiring extra staff. We were in a new world and felt completely incongruous with poor, oppressed people all around us, yet we were living in a way that was far above our normal standard; it seemed very hypocritical but there was no escape. It was brought home to me very strongly by our Hungarian priest, after he had baptised Christopher in the darkened church, with so many people dressed in their smart clothes. We asked him if he would return with us to bless the flat and celebrate with us. He then told us that he never ventured out because of the danger of arrest. He asked us to kneel before him in the sacristy so that he could give us the blessing for our home. We were caught in a trap. The lesson I learned at that time was not about the oppressed or the persecuted but about the importance of employing more staff for important diplomatic occasions! Several older diplomatic friends gave me advice, and it was obvious that I had to take notice.

How long does it take to learn the important things? I buried the unpleasant thoughts in the recesses of my mind and tried hard to be a good wife and mother as well as a good diplomatic hostess. It was a difficult job. I felt I was not only stifling my strong spiritual and political leanings, as I always had to support the government line, but that I was living a totally hypocritical life. I remember a discussion one day when Peter and I had lunch at the Ambassador's residence. I stood out against everyone when it was suggested that a wife's first duty was to stay beside her husband at all times. I believed that I should stay and look after my children when Peter was going on tour to Southern Yugoslavia known for its very primitive state. It would be impossible to take the children and I would not leave them. I felt I received a black mark, or possibly Peter did. Fortunately Peter understood and agreed with me.

The Christmas season in the Embassy had started, and there were no excuses allowed for anyone who thought they might escape the Embassy celebrations. The cerise velvet I had purchased in Vienna was made up into a beautiful evening dress. Louisa had a friend who worked exquisitely, as long as you followed her ideas. Her name was Ivanka. She lived in two small rooms with a little kitchen, and you visited her by appointment when she would then provide you with refreshments and keep you for several hours. The Embassy Ball took place just before Christmas; I remember struggling into my cerise dress having spent two hours with Kosta my hairdresser. I found a visit to Kosta really enjoyable. He spoke very little English so I found it a good place to practise my Serbian as he liked to know what was going on. There was sometimes a big discrepancy between the news heard on the Belgrade radio and the BBC news. Every day Peter's office put out a bulletin based on the early morning BBC news, but this had to be collected from the Reading Room. Kosta knew that I had up-to-date information, and he was very pro English.

I had to take my own towel and shampoo, and for this I was grateful, as nothing was very clean. I had previously tried the hairdresser in the so-called international Majestic Hotel where we sometimes ate. I soon tired of this as Maritsa spoke English and all the diplomatic wives who did not want to mix too much with the locals went there. It was particularly popular with the older American ladies who would discuss their latest beauty treatments. It was possibly a little more hygienic but on balance Kosta won.

My size seemed to vary every day but I was determined to feed Christopher myself. Diplomatically the Embassy Ball was a great success. I spent the whole evening dancing with people other than Peter, this is how protocol worked. The men entertained all the other wives in turn except their own until the rounds were completed. I did not see Peter until it was time for me to slip home, hopefully unnoticed, to feed my new baby, but of course we had to return to the ball afterwards, no-one was allowed to leave until the end. We did, however, have quite a lot of fun, very often at other people's expense, some of which I really came to regret as I got older and wiser.

About this time a young man named John had joined the Embassy staff. He was the product of a well known Catholic public school, and had spent a few years at the Foreign Office in London. He was fairly pompous and apparently knew everything. He took a fancy to me and liked to spend his time talking to me and sometimes trying to dance. Peter's immediate boss Dugald Stuart a senior member of the Embassy staff with whom we were friends, and who was completely unimpressed with the strict compliance to protocol, decided to teach him some lessons. Dugald knew Yugoslavia well having been deeply involved there with his wife during the war, and he loved the people. He explained to John that it was not only protocol but Embassy tradition that the newest member of the Embassy staff was privileged to have the first two dances of the evening with the Lady Ambassadress. Of course it was really the most senior man, the Counsellor, who danced the first dance with her. Our friend Dugald, with great seriousness, rehearsed with John what he should say exactly, and those of us who knew what was happening watched carefully. Lady Roberts was too polite to refuse and we watched them struggling together as John was an appalling dancer and she an extremely good one. At the end of the dance he held on to her and did not let her go. When the music started again whatever she said no-one will ever know, but she escaped.

At a party in another Embassy, Dugald explained to John that it was the custom when greeting the Lady Ambassadress to bend over and kiss her hand and that this was how she really liked the British men to say hello. In actual fact she disliked this form of greeting intensely, and foreigners used to this style quickly learnt to change their ways. Dugald showed astonishment that John had not already gone straight to Lady Roberts to say good evening and started rehearsing him in the correct methods of hand kissing. We again watched the comedy show with glee as John even clicked his heels. It was some time before John realised that everyone was 'taking the Mickey.' Even then he could not see how objectionable his behaviour was. Now I am sad to think how mean we were to him.

Christmas came amidst many preparations and parties, which I found quite difficult whilst feeding Christopher. I seemed either to be hurrying to go out, or hurrying home. I always left my phone number with Louisa when I was out, but fortunately, Christopher was a good baby. A friend, Sheila from the Indian Embassy was surprised to see me going home to feed the baby at night. She told me that I should 'take measures', but I did not understand what she meant. She had a baby slightly older than ours. When she was pregnant she had very little idea of what preparations to make, she told me the grandmother in India always took charge of the mother and prepared everything for the baby. She was extremely ignorant about her own body as well and I had been able to help her quite a lot. My mother had sent woollen garments and wool for knitting. When her baby was six months old, however, he was eating 'black curry' and sleeping on a double bed under an eiderdown. When we went to dinner with her, she took me into her small son's room, opened a tiny silver box, licked her finger and dipped it in the powder, brushing it then on the child's lips. "Poppy seed," she said "you must try it; he will sleep soundly until the morning now." Of course, I never did.

We went to midnight Mass, which was a wonderful celebration, but I was already missing the familiarity of our Christmas preparations at home. My mother and father had sent some presents for Gerard, and we had brought a few things from Vienna, although he was still too young to understand. We had decorated a lovely Christmas tree but nothing seemed to help me. We had received several invitations to Christmas lunch as well as dinner in the evening, but all from people who had no children. This meant leaving our two at home. I refused to do this. Louisa cooked a lovely traditional English Christmas dinner under my tuition, although I was rather nervous as I had always celebrated

Christmas at home, and my mother, of course, had been in charge of the kitchen. I was desperately homesick. I tried hard to overcome my feelings but could not hold back my floods of tears. No one from our families had seen my lovely baby, and to go through Christmas without them all was almost too difficult. Louisa and Peter did all they could to comfort me, but it was no good. I think Peter felt it too. We had an open house invitation from Betsy and Derek Ferguson (the Naval Attaché, whose house and garden I had enjoyed in the summer), which included all children from 2.30- 5.00pm. By the time we had finished lunch and I had cried and cried, the afternoon went on, and amidst my tears I had to feed Christopher again. I felt in no state to go out. Peter however made me wash my face and helped me get the children ready; we arrived at the Ferguson's just as the last guests were leaving, and there was a mad flurry of maids putting the furniture in place. I shall never forget the kindness of the whole family. Instead of saying that they were sorry but we were too late, they treated us like royalty. Their two lovely daughters, who were in their late teens, looked after the children. I guess that they could see I was finding my first Christmas abroad very sad. There was no mention of the fact that they were dining with the Ambassador that evening and needed a rest. I learnt something very important that afternoon, which was Christianity in practice, although they would not have put it in those terms. I was surprised how much better I felt when we returned to our flat. I was ready to start again. I have never forgotten their kindness.

It was just at this time that we moved from Nikola Spasiča to the other side of Belgrade. Our villa, Suvoborska 27 was on the outskirts of the town in a rather pleasant residential district. It was in a road which led into the main street going up to the 'White House' where President Tito lived. Ours was an impressive looking detached house, standing in a garden, with a semi-circle of steps to the large oak front door. It was heated entirely by tiled stoves. I was expecting it to be well appointed inside, as it had been occupied by a senior member of the Embassy and his attractive wife. We found it needed a good clean, particularly the kitchen and the bedrooms. All the curtains were dirty and the linings of all of them were in ribbons. The furniture on the whole was acceptable. I refused to move until we had some assurance of help, both financial and physical. There was no carpet on the very wide rather beautiful sweeping staircase, which went up from the large hall. This concerned me as it seemed slippery. The prospect of carrying a new baby up and down was alarming. There were glass folding doors, allowing the reception rooms to be opened out, which made a very attractive space but several of the small panes of glass were either cracked or broken.

Officials at the Embassy were surprised that I was dissatisfied because of the previous occupants, and they agreed for an inspection to take place. We were rather afraid that the villa would be given to someone else if we made too much fuss, but I knew I was not prepared to live in it as it was. The Embassy agreed that we needed help. We were given an allowance for cleaning, and the glass panes were repaired. Louisa set to work with assistance from some friends and spring cleaned everywhere. The biggest job of the day was to light the fires in the tiled stoves and it was obvious that I was going to need more help in the house on a regular basis. While the spring cleaning was going on we advertised through the various Embassy outlets for a maid. Girls from Slovenia gathered every Sunday night at a special site on the Corso, arrayed in their beautiful national costumes, but being inexperienced I really was not sure how to tackle this. You had to make up your mind there and then. It seemed risky.

Meanwhile we started preparing our flat for the move and our time was spent between the two buildings. I was refused money for new curtains with the promise that I would be first on the list. We decided to remove the rotten linings in the curtains downstairs and risk washing them. Louisa actually trampled them in the bath with bare feet as some of them were very large. She seemed to be able to cope with anything. The curtains were old and rather ugly but at least they made a covering for the windows for the winter. They would never stand another washing that was sure. On the day of our move it was snowing hard, Louisa who was now sleeping in the villa on some blankets, without a proper bed, had the stoves alight downstairs. We decided to light them upstairs in the late afternoon. The house looked lovely, clean and polished. The Rapin treatment had been given with great success, and the old wood stove in the kitchen had been pulled out and cleaned. I saw the inches of grease that had lain hidden behind it for years. Louisa was delighted with this stove; it cooked her bread to perfection but to me it was anathema. I was glad of the simple electric cooker and oven for the few occasions when I would be working in the kitchen, although there were to be many times during electricity cuts when the wood stove proved its worth.

We had a list of names and addresses of women of various ages seeking work in Embassy houses, which had been gathered for us from various neighbouring Embassies. It all seemed simple, just call at the address, interview them, look at references, and make a decision but Peter and I were in for a shock. Although we knew what had been happening in Yugoslavia, it was difficult to understand the people's fear, until it was encountered first hand. No one gave their own address; it was always that of someone they knew who would vet a caller for them. Sometimes we had to go to two or three addresses, most of them in obscure back streets, before we could even begin to make contact. Then it was left to the person when they eventually received our address if ever they did, to make contact with us. It was a lengthy and frustrating mission. People were terrified of being picked up by the UDBA.

During the state visits of foreign officials, hundreds of people would be arrested, if they could be found, there only needed to be a slight suspicion of their having anti-government views. As we were not familiar with the names of the streets which were all in Cyrillic, and we were always visiting in the dark it felt a hopeless task. Most of the houses we visited were occupied by many people living perhaps with one room each, and they were almost all in semi-darkness. We were often taken in to talk with someone who would be in bed or stretched out on a sofa. It gave us an insight into the many difficulties that were experienced, not only oppression and fear, but lack of money and lack of anything that one might call beautiful. It should have prepared me for what was to come, but it didn't.

These methods, time consuming and difficult as they were, eventually produced no one that I felt I could trust with my children. Everyone who eventually appeared at the house was so willing to do anything from the smallest to the most difficult job, and assured us of their ability and efficiency, that we had to be suspicious. References, if they existed at all, were scrappy. We were to learn that this was very typical of the Serb, always saying what the listener wanted to hear whether it was true or not. A friend in another Embassy knew of a Hungarian girl, only fifteen years old, who was looking for a job. Her name was Veronica. She was living in Belgrade with her family but conditions were not good for them. Veronica was the eldest of a large family who needed the money. She was a hard working charming girl, wonderful with both the children. I always doubted in my mind that she was only fifteen; she looked mature and was full of wisdom. She had a strong faith and had been brought up as a Catholic, but did not go to church. She prayed every night before she went to bed, wearing a beautiful long white smocked cotton nightdress and a white bonnet, which she said was traditional where she came from.

Louisa and Veronica got on very well. Veronica was strong and carried the coal up from the cellar each day for all the stoves, cleared away the ashes, prepared them with wood and lit them at the planned times. She cleaned the house, looked after the children's rooms and their clothes and took care of the children while I was out. Neither she nor Louisa wanted a whole day off each week; they were both happy to have just a short time away from the house when it was convenient for me. Louisa enjoyed two hours sleep in the afternoon, only if it was possible. She cooked and cleaned and washed and ironed. I was not allowed to do anything. Louisa taught Veronica how to serve at table and insisted that they had matching dresses and head pieces made so that they could present a really high class service for Peter and myself. These were made by another friend of Louisa's who sat at her own sewing machine in a corner of Louisa's room which was really only a large cupboard by the kitchen, frugally furnished, but it was all she wanted. This lady had previously made some maternity dresses for me when I was in the flat, again crouched in a corner out of sight. The material was purchased by my mother and sent with speed in the diplomatic bag. My mother was an expert at procuring the many things which we needed and which were unobtainable locally. Life was good, and entertaining went well, the children were well cared for. Veronica had good moral values and was prepared to say no to Gerard quite firmly if he was being naughty, and he loved and respected her. Friends were amazed that I had kept my household staff so long and that I was happy with them. I felt really safe.

Winter came to an end as suddenly as it had started; the sun came out and the snow melted. There was the usual flooding across the Voyvodina, the enormous plain which stretched out behind the villa, and eventually became Hungary. Leaves in profusion sprang out on the trees and flowers started to bloom. Winter and spring had passed and summer was here. Exactly what the reason was we never quite understood, but possibly to do with the political events, Veronica gave us two weeks notice that she would be leaving. It was to do with her family and work permits, a complicated story difficult to understand anyway, I am sure, but with both of us only speaking broken Serbo-Croat the details were impossible to understand. (Veronica had tried to teach me Hungarian, but with little success). All I know is that it was a sad time for all of us, especially for the children. The difficulties of finding another girl were again with us. Ratko had exhausted his knowledge. It was possible to manage in the house with just Louisa but it was quite difficult and it meant that she had the burden of everything. In the summer, at least, there were no stoves to be lit, but the weather was extremely hot and everyone had less energy. We decided to try yet another method of finding help. We advertised for young ladies with experience of diplomatic household work and good references to come to the villa at 9.00 am on a certain date. Peter took the morning off to help me make a decision, if in fact anyone came. At 8.00am on that day Louisa came rushing in to say a queue was forming, I could hardly believe it. By 9.00 am there were ninety three people forming a queue along Suvoborska. We had to sit down and think how we would deal with this extraordinary situation. We decided to send Louisa along the queue saying that it was pointless for anyone without written references to wait. I went with her and asked to see the references to ascertain they existed. This was Louisa's suggestion because of course she knew the Serbs well. This got rid of more than half of the queue with much murmuring and annoyance. It was easy for me to see at a glance who else I would not want just from their appearance although I was to learn that this was not necessarily a good way of judging.

Peter and I set ourselves up with chairs and table in the large hall at the bottom of the stairs which still remained uncarpeted, and Louisa acted as doorman, whilst keeping an eye on the children. It took us all the morning to find Jovanka, a trim nicely spoken presentable girl of twenty one, with excellent references from someone in the French Embassy. She had looked after children, served at table etc.etc. and she was available to start work the following day. The seamstress was called back to alter Veronica's serving dress, Louisa showed Jovanka the household jobs that were to be done and everything on the surface seemed to be fine. I was always very wary of leaving a new person alone with the children until I had become confident that they were trustworthy. Jovanka seemed to understand both the children and was very fussy about cleanliness. She asked if she could have one day and one night out each week. We had a rule in the house that if we were in we would answer the telephone otherwise a message could be taken for us. I began to be aware that Jovanka was using the phone each morning before we were up for which she should have asked permission. She denied this absolutely. However, we then started having mysterious phone calls sometimes even waking us up. If I answered immediately the person would ring off, then sometimes Jovanka would answer first and then tell me it was a wrong number. She was unable to tell me the truth that she had a man friend. I actually spoke to him one day when he phoned and asked him not to phone so early because it woke us up. This was the first sign of Jovanka's lies, but I still wanted to trust her.

I had cause to go into her room one day when she was out, to look for some clothes belonging to the children which I usually left to Louisa. I was astonished to see a photograph of Jovanka wearing one of my best outfits. I found out later of course that this was common practice with Serbian maids. I went through my wardrobe and found that several things had been worn. I spoke to Louisa about it to find out if she knew. She told me that Jovanka had experienced a very hard time and that she had an illegitimate baby, whose father was not the current boyfriend, that she had been beaten by the father of the child and had no means of support. The child was evidently in a home. I was filled with compassion and decided to give Jovanka another chance. When I spoke to her and told her that I knew she had taken my clothes and that she had a baby, she was in tears. I told her that she could stay as long as she was honest with me. I started to give her some extra money towards the care of her baby which she accepted.

It was decided that at the end of July Louisa would accompany us by car to Split where we would meet up with Peter's mother and father, who were going to travel through Italy and cross the Adriatic to Split by boat. Peter and I had booked a villa by the sea. We were to leave Jovanka in the house, which I was not very happy about, but she had nowhere else to go. I tried to persuade her to take a paid holiday but she said she would be on the streets. I left her money for her keep and asked her to write an account of her shopping. I had a lock fitted to my bedroom door. I didn't have anything of great value but felt it was wise. I had already given her some dresses of mine and things that I thought would help her. She promised she would look after the house and keep it clean.

Our holiday in Split was a great success. The journey took two days and we stayed the night in Banja Luka in the International Hotel. Again, we had a large suite, with lounge, bedroom, bathroom and hall. Louisa slept on the sofa and assured us it was all she wanted. She refused to have a meal sent up to the room when we went to dinner and said she would go to the kitchens and get something. You could not argue with her, she was adamant. She looked after the children who had eaten earlier, while we went to the dining room. I wanted her to have the same as we had but she could not accept it. I had many times tried to tell her that in England I did not have anyone to look after me, but she did not want to know this. She still liked to call me her 'mali reine,' and she practically worshipped the ground Peter walked on. Gospodin could do no wrong. Louisa was loyalty personified. I found it very difficult at first, but it is amazing how quickly one is caught up in this artificial lifestyle. The next day was a Sunday, we were on a very dusty unmade road between Banja Luka and Split. There had been no petrol available in Banja Luka. Although we always carried an extra can of petrol as there were very few petrol stations, we had used all of it and could not go on any further without re-fuelling. We came to an obscure village with a petrol station which was closed. We begged someone who was there on the premises to give us some petrol but they refused saying the owner was out hunting and kept the keys with him and that it was no use our waiting, he would not be back until nightfall. We were desperate as we were expected in Split that night and were meeting Peter's parents the following day. It was very hot and the outlook was grim. Louisa got out of the car and said, "Louisi ide, može može," meaning "Louisa will go." Može is an all purpose word used all the time in Serbia, meaning "Of course it's possible," or "You can manage," or "It will be okay," or "They will do it." And sure enough they did. Someone ran down the road and after five minutes returned with an older man with a key, he unlocked the pump, filled the tank and with much bowing and scraping and apologies, tried to insist that we did not pay. However Peter made him take the required amount of dinars, still not understanding the mystery. When we were on the road again we asked Louisa to tell us what she had she said to the man. "I told them you were friends of Moše Pijada, (then Tito's deputy), and that you were from the British Embassy, and that there would be a great fuss if it became known we had been refused petrol when we were travelling." We had once told Louisa that we had met Moše Pijada at a cocktail party, which was true. Although we strongly disapproved of this method of intimidation, it certainly worked on that occasion with no one being hurt. I forbade her to do anything like that again! She said it was the only way things worked.

Our villa in Split was superb. We met Peter's mother and father as arranged, and we were delighted to see each other; Louisa insisted on looking after us all on her own. We ate out on the terrace each day, and spent most of our time on the beautiful beach. Louisa did all the shopping and cooking. Her only request was to have a dip in the sea every afternoon to ease her rheumatism. She washed and ironed and wanted no help. When we returned to Belgrade Jovanka seemed to have looked after the house. The kitchen had not been used at all, and she produced receipts for meals in a local Serbian café, which were comparatively cheap, she explained that she had not wanted to dirty the kitchen. I was lulled into a sense of trust for several weeks. However as the season changed again and it was time to get out winter things I soon found many things missing from my clothes and from my jewellery and from Peter's and the children's clothes. I realised then that the stealing had perhaps been going on for some time. When I went through the things in my room in more detail, much that I had not noticed before had been stolen, obviously just before I had the lock put on the door, and even since we returned from our holiday. Peter phoned the Frenchman who had given Jovanka such a good reference, telling him what we suspected. He then confided in Peter that she had stolen from them and worn his wife's clothes and finally she had stolen two very valuable watches from them, one of which she was still wearing when she was with us, the other she had sold. His excuse for writing the reference was that she had threatened him.

We decided that it was no good challenging her, there was little one could do. On the whole the police were not interested in petty crime. We decided to ask her to leave and pay her the two weeks wages in lieu of notice. I was sad because she seemed to be very good with the children. We were already expecting our third child and although I had a genuine desire to help her I did not want any fuss. We told Louisa before breakfast what our plan was so that she would not be surprised. Louisa then said she did not like Jovanka and had been concerned about her behaviour; she had also heard that the story about her baby was not true. After breakfast I called Jovanka into the dining room and we asked her to leave, saying that we were no longer satisfied with how things were and that we had reason to believe she had been stealing from us. She was very abusive and shouted, particularly at me. I asked her to pack up her belongings, take the money, a fairly generous amount, and go immediately. She took the money and went out of the room without a word. Peter and I sat and talked for a while, wondering what we should do to find someone new to replace Jovanka, as we had many diplomatic duties and now could not run the house without help. We were just saying how we dreaded the very thought of going through this procedure again, when suddenly Louisa came into the dining room in great alarm, breathlessly calling "Izvinite Gospodja, izvinite Gospodin," (Excuse me Madame, excuse me Sir,) Jovanka was nowhere to be found, and the downstairs cloakroom door, which was beside the front door, also a large oak structure, was locked; there was no reply when we knocked and called. We had no means of seeing into the cloakroom apart from the round window which, although quite high from inside, was even higher from outside because of the steps beside it, leading to the front door. We did not possess a step ladder to look in the window, so the three of us carried through the garden the large wooden kitchen table so that we could stand on it and look in.

A horrible sight met our eyes. Jovanka was lying on the floor with blood everywhere. I sent Louisa to look after the children and phoned the police, while Peter started to break into the cloakroom. When I explained to the police what had happened I was told to "break down the door and fling her out on the street." I was in tears and could not believe my ears. I ran back to Peter to see what I should do next. He was having great difficulty in getting access as the door was so heavy and thick and had a good strong lock. He mustered all the tools we had that might be useful, and I ran to phone the Embassy. They promised to try to get an ambulance, which was sometimes difficult as there were very few. Eventually the wood of the door split, it was still not easy to get in as Jovanka's body was lying against the door. We eventually managed to pull her out. She had cut both her wrists with a razor blade which Louisa kept on a shelf in the kitchen. I realised then that Louisa suspected what had happened when she saw the razor blade had gone! Jovanka had also banged her nose which bled profusely. She looked as if she were dead but I did not stop to make any tests, I treated her as if she were alive. At this time a tourniquet was the treatment for excessive bleeding. I quickly found two pencils and tore two strips from the bottom of Louisa's apron. She had been playing with the children in the garden but having strapped Christopher in his pram, she had sneaked back to see what was happening. I quickly applied the tourniquets to Jovanka's arms. She had bled profusely and the blood was beginning to congeal anyway. I tried to feel her pulse or her heartbeat but could find neither. The ambulance arrived almost immediately. Two men examined her quickly, covered her completely with a red blanket and told us to follow on or contact the hospital. Having made certain that Louisa was in a fit state to care for the children, we followed the ambulance to the hospital. We waited for what seemed an endless time when a doctor came to speak to us. He told us that although still unconscious, Jovanka was very much alive. He said that she had cut a place on each wrist which bleeds a great deal but which is not fatal, and that she had scars from having done it twice before. This was evidently quite a common occurrence in Belgrade at that time, although he also admitted that some people were not quite as skilled as Jovanka and they died. He shrugged his shoulders and held out his hands in a gesture that spoke volumes of the sadness and difficulties that existed. We were told to go home and phone later. It became obvious that Jovanka had contingency plans, that she was either very unbalanced or very devious. I felt terrible, I was guilty and confused because it was obviously our actions which had brought this about, but nevertheless, Peter and I were quite sure that we would not have her back in the house.

We had received an invitation for that evening to a very special formal dinner party at the Royal Netherlands Embassy and there was no possibility of cancelling it. Christopher's godparents had been posted to Djakarta and their Ambassador was having a farewell celebration for their close friends, twelve of us altogether. I had an appointment with Ivanka the dressmaker to try on and collect a new dress she had made for the occasion. I also had matching evening shoes to collect, which my mother had purchased in London, and sent in one of the special delivery Embassy bags. My morning appointment with Kosta had passed, so had lunchtime. Peter dropped me off at Ivanka the dressmaker's with a promise to return when I phoned. It was not until I was sitting waiting for Ivanka to bring the dress that I realised what a mess I was in. I had blood over my hands and on my dress, and also, I found out later, on my tear-stained face. Strangely I didn't care, I was quite numb. Ivanka behaved as if she had noticed nothing and I did not say a word. She tried on my dress as if everything was quite normal, I suppose she realised I was in a daze. The dress was one of her special designs made with material which my mother had sent, a new kind of printed black nylon voile, over- printed with silver. It had a wide sash and a stole of the same material. Instead of sewing the ends of the stole Ivanka had frayed them to about one and a half inches deep; she said it would look prettier on the fine nylon. I listened to her without a word. She placed the stole round my shoulders without apparently noticing all the blood and without showing any curiosity. The dress fitted beautifully, so she said, but she just wanted to press the stole with her iron, an old fashioned flat iron which went on the stove to heat. I suppose the tenseness of the situation caused her to forget what I had told her that nylon needs a very cool iron; this material had previously been completely unknown to her. We both saw the material shrivel into a big hole.

I had not been able to eat the delicacies Ivanka had provided for me, and I was already concerned about the time. The Embassy office would be shut and I would not be able to get my shoes which had been promised. Everything seemed unreal as I sat there watching Ivanka cut the shrivelled twelve inches from the end of the stole and start to fray it again... a long job. I can remember clearly the acrid smell of burning nylon, and Ivanka constantly murmuring her apologies. Peter arrived wondering what had happened as I had been so long. It was Ivanka who explained. I was in shock and could say nothing. Peter collected my shoes from the Embassy and returned to take me to the hospital. Jovanka was conscious and wanted to see us. I felt she was surely going to apologise, but no, her first words to us were, "Unless you have me back, I will do it again." With her blood still over me unwashed since morning I remember saying, "Then you will do it somewhere else because you will not come back to my house." That was the last time I saw her. I packed up her belongings and took them to the hospital.

Peter and I somehow got through the evening at the Royal Netherlands Embassy. I did try to explain what had been happening to us, but at that level and on such an occasion, no one knew what to say, nor were they particularly interested. Although I had washed my hair and done my best to look presentable and had passed Louisa's scrutiny I sometimes wonder what my appearance and my behaviour were really like. I know that I was in deep shock which showed itself the following day with the loss of our third baby.

Four weeks later when I was recovering from the miscarriage and resting on the sofa, Jovanka came to the back door, wearing a beautiful fur coat, according to Louisa, and asked to see me. Louisa came to tell me, but even before I answered, she said that she would tell her to go. She told me it was very unwise for me to enter into any conversation with her. Jovanka wanted Louisa to tell me that she had a very good job with a family from the French Embassy. Louisa told her never to come back again. I realised much later that my behaviour was not very Christian. In the circumstances it was really difficult to know how to deal with the variety of situations one encountered and there was very little help available. All I wanted at this stage was to be in my own home in England looking after my children myself. If ever there had been any glamour it had vanished. We had at least another eighteen months to face, or so I thought.

Chapter Four

Journey to England

It was now time to make new plans. We talked about going to England, but Peter did not have any leave until the spring. It was essential to find a replacement for Jovanka. With the onset of winter not only did we have to think about the work of keeping all the stoves going, but Louisa's rheumatism became worse as the weather became cold and damp and she was forced to do less than she wanted. I had spoken to my mother at length several times on the 'phone even though it was at that time quite expensive, but because I had not wanted to distress her more, I was unable to speak really freely about all that happened. I knew she was already worried about our situation, and she was particularly upset about my miscarriage. I wrote home regularly each week but felt restrained as I did not want my mother and father to know just how homesick I was feeling.

I had taken the miscarriage very badly even though I was only three months pregnant. I felt a great surge of grief and disappointment every time I was alone and could think about what had happened. Also there was quite a lot of resentment towards Jovanka, who had seemingly caused it. It wasn't until much later in life that I learned about loss and grieving, and the ministry there is for praying for a miscarried baby, naming him or her, and as it were baptising them, knowing and understanding that they would grow spiritually in their new life. We did this later, but at that time although I knew abortion was taking a life, a miscarriage, because of its inevitability, seemed generally to be dealt with as an illness, without the understanding of loss. It was also much later that I was able to deal with my hurts and resentments. They were building up and getting pressed down in my sub-conscious, hidden away for fear someone might know that sometimes I was near to not being able to cope. It was more difficult to get out into the mountains and surrounding countryside as winter came. Sometimes, except for important events, when the weather was really bad I was confined to the house for weeks at a time. Gerard was too small to walk in the deep snow, and one couldn't push a pram. Sometimes even the car was immobilised as we had no garage, and the car would freeze into the snow. Peter managed to get to the Reading Room and the Embassy by sending for an Embassy car, for which we had to pay.

It was through a friend in the Swiss Embassy that I heard about Fanni. She was thirty two, divorced and was looking for a secure happy home. She had no children of her own but seemed to get on well with our two. Louisa was slightly more of a problem as, being older, Fanni had ideas of her own. Louisa could be rather interfering, thinking that she always knew best. However they seemed to sort things out fairly amicably, although there was always a certain amount of tale-bearing. Fanni worked hard and quickly, and understood what had to be done. She could clean the house, wait at table even for large dinner parties, manage the children and supervise the regular coal deliveries. Coal was dark brown and was delivered in large lumps by dumping it onto the pavement outside the house. Albanian boys, considered in Serbia to be the lowest class, would then be employed to carry it down into the cellar. They wore white suits and hats and were always very polite. They were happy to talk if you addressed them first otherwise they would get on with their work quietly. It would take them all day to move a delivery of coal, and I remember being in true admiration when, during Ramadan, they would not eat or drink whatever you gave them. At dusk they would stand with perspiration dropping off them, even in winter, watching the sun go down with a cup of water in their hand. It was only by mutual agreement of the right moment that they would gently sip their water. We always had the same boys and I grew quite fond of them. We called them boys but they were really young men. It was my first introduction to Islam.

Our cellar had fourteen rooms in it but was used by us for storage only. One day we had a shock to hear from Louisa that water was rising up through a drain in the floor. On further examination it was found to be sewage. Without our knowing it all those months our drainage was by cesspit and not main drainage. This had also not been known by the previous tenants. Apparently there were cracks in the tank through which sewage had leaked for years, these had become blocked with the change of detergents or so it was thought... such were the standards of hygiene. However we seemed not to suffer too much. We acquired the services of a large tanker and two men who pumped out the cesspit regularly from then on. Milka, a vagrant woman who Louisa knew and sometimes fed at the back door, was pleased to receive payment for scrubbing out the cellar. The cesspit was situated under the front garden where Gerard had delightedly dropped stones through a grating learning to say "plop" in Serbian, which he could now speak equally as well as English, and was a real 'music-hall act' for all Serbian visitors to the house. He would never converse in Serbian with the English speaking people visiting us; he seemed to know clearly the difference. When eventually we returned to England, with everyone waiting to meet this bi-lingual wonder, we could not get him to say one word in Serbian. The only concession to this was a little rhyme which Louisa had taught him through constant repetition which he would say grudgingly...

> "Boubalasi nešto traži,
> Boubalasi Gerard da traži."

There were several occasions when Fanni threatened to leave us. We had been suspicious that Gerard could climb out of his cot, and back again, but had never seen him doing it. He well knew that the fire in the bottom of the stove was 'hot' and 'burny'. The door into the fire closed securely, so it seemed safe, and although the tiles did get hot there seemed to be no great danger. The fire was lit late afternoon and was allowed to go out, keeping the room extraordinarily warm until the following morning. The ashes fell through a grating and piled up into a cool mountain hidden from sight by a little door. We were awoken early one morning by a kerfuffle outside our bedroom. Fanni who had been cleaning early, heard movements from Gerard's bedroom, and went in to wash and change him, and get him dressed for breakfast. She opened the door and had a terrible shock. Gerard had climbed out of his cot and had quietly spread the cold ashes from the stove over every inch of the polished parquet floor that was not covered by the rug. Having finished his job to his liking, he had climbed back into his cot, and was 'reading' his book, having left a trail of dark grey ash over his hair and face and on all the bedclothes, whilst asserting to Fanni in Serbian, "not Gerard, not Gerard."

Another time, having been sufficiently scolded about touching the ashes, he found he could drive his cot round the room by standing at the end and jumping forward; fortunately the windows were safe so he could not go far, or so we thought. One day he manoeuvred the cot to the door and by clever calculations opened the door handle, driving the cot backwards, so that he could then open the door wide. Whether his intention was originally to come to our bedroom we will never know, but he saw the stairs, and decided on a much more exciting plan, even as a small child he was apparently fearless. There was an initial crash as the cot fell to the first bend in the stairs and then more banging and crashing as Gerard tried to get it round the corner. It was Fanni who was disturbed, frightened and angry. Gerard was unaware of the reason for everyone's alarm. I think we raised Fanni's money to get her to stay.

It was during this time that Louisa was really ill and had to stop working. When ill she developed a paranoia which was difficult for everyone to cope with. Most probably it was because she was so used to being in charge, and therefore saw anyone who was able to help and do a good job as a threat. She really believed that no one would look after us properly. We replaced her with a cook named Maria on the understanding that Louisa would return when she was better. Maria was a very different person from our first Maria, who still sometimes came to help. She was older and wanted nothing whatsoever to do with the children. She did a certain amount of cleaning rather badly, but was an excellent cook.

Whilst she would not serve at table for dinner parties, she did the marketing and prepared all the food to a very high standard. I had to be very careful not to upset her, and our food bills rocketed. We got into the habit of either borrowing a maid for dinner parties to help Fanni serve, or more often hiring one or two waiters. Toma who worked in Peter's office was a trained barman and waiter, and often helped us out; there was fortunately a set wage per hour. It was very usual at that time in Serbia for people to have two jobs running at the same time. One job was insufficient for the average family man. Even the leading Belgrade opera singer Valeria Heybal lived, by our standards, very simply. She employed a fourteen year old maid who came in daily to clean. We came to know Valeria when we were entertaining guests from England, most of whom we would never mix with at home. They were often film stars, well known film directors and leading journalists. It was difficult to explain to our Yugoslav friends that we were just very ordinary people in England; they did not believe us, because they saw such a high standard of household management compared to local standards.

At this time the consulate in Sarajevo was closed down. As promised I was offered first choice of the furniture and furnishings. By this time we had our villa furnished fairly comfortably, but we were still in need of stair carpet and curtains for the rooms downstairs. The curtains from Sarajevo were beautiful. They were deep ruby red, and inter-lined with very heavy wool blanketing. There was also a great length of almost new red stair carpet. This was initially very exciting. The stair carpet was fixed with no trouble and great efficiency by one of Peter's office staff and it looked superb. The curtains were much too long, even for our large windows. I was not short of recommendations of 'professional' people to alter them. Ratko, Louisa, Fanni and many others all knew an excellent 'Majstor' who would estimate and carry out a wonderful job. It took me a long time to learn that each was trying to find employment for their friends and acquaintances. Times were really hard for the locals. The Serbs were shameless and persistent; they could all turn their hand to anything, some were skilled and some weren't.

I spent many hours watching men, clean and dirty, trying to measure the windows in an effort to determine the amount of shortening needed so that these beautiful curtains would hang properly and pull open and shut on the runners and cords. I narrowed it down to the one who at least understood what I wanted, or so I thought. There would be no problem he promised, "Everything would be 'u redu'." ...in order! In my uncertainty, I decided to let him have only one curtain, knowing and already understanding that the sale value of even one curtain would be high. Word had spread like wildfire. People were still phoning and coming to the door, promising me their service and great skill, to the death. Having already experienced so much difficulty, I decided to go and supervise the procedure before the scissors were put to the material, and I was so glad I did. The man I had trusted was actually a shoe mender with no idea of needlework. He had unpicked the stitches at the bottom of the curtain, folded the edge up to the 'more or less' required length and when we arrived was just in the process of machining the six thicknesses of the materials, including the two thicknesses of blanket interlining, with his thick 'leather' needle. I almost could not believe what I saw. I removed the curtain as politely as I could, leaving the poor man insisting it would all be 'u redu'. I was learning the hard way the lesson which I should have learnt from earlier experiences. The Serbs generally would say anything to please you without any consideration whether they could actually carry out the task in hand. The most important part for them was to say "Yes," if that was what you wanted. They seemed to have no shame in what they were doing and did not mind the failure. It was always one's own fault for being unappreciative. After some further searching and disappointments I altered the curtains myself carefully cutting out the blanket lining to the correct length and mitring all the corners. It took me ages as I had to sew it all by hand. There obviously were those in Belgrade who could do the job efficiently, but finding them was too difficult. When the story was told later I was recommended to an upholsterer who was evidently superb at his job, but fortunately I did not have a further opportunity to try him out.

When Louisa had been taken ill, before we employed the elderly Maria, word had passed round that we were looking for a good cook, who was prepared to do some cleaning, and occasionally help with the children. We were at dinner with the BBC correspondent and his wife. They were leaving Belgrade and they had an excellent cook. She had not only cooked the dinner we ate, but also served it at the table. She was a very presentable person. She also had seen us and talked with us and was very pleased to make an appointment to see our villa and meet our children. She arrived on time, and I spent over an hour taking her round the house and explaining everything in detail. She was very keen and we arranged that she would start work on the Monday of the following week at 9.00am. Monday morning came and I had prepared very well for her so that there was no backlog of work. I waited until 11.00 am. Patiently, thinking that something had delayed her. I then phoned our friends to see what had happened to her. I was astonished to be greeted with great surprise by our friend. I was told that she had returned home from the interview with me and said that the job was not suitable; she had found the house too large and anyway preferred a position with no children. When I asked to speak to her, she was quite unperturbed. She just told me what he had said, that the house was not suitable and that she preferred not to work with children, with not even an apology. I don't think I ever got used to this characteristic; I became very untrusting of almost everyone.

We had yet another fright with Gerard at this time. Fanni had left the front door open for a moment while she swept the front step, believing that Gerard was safely occupied. It was only when she had finished the step that he was found to be missing. We searched the garden, the road, and the house, calling and calling with no response. Not knowing how to proceed, I was just about to phone Peter at the Embassy, when there was a knock on the door. A lady had found Gerard striding alone down the main tree-lined street which led in the other direction to President Tito's residence. This road was the route which we took to the Embassy. She had asked Gerard where he was going, in Serbian. He had replied, "Idem u Ambasada, videču moy Papa." ("I am going to the Embassy to see my Daddy.") Fortunately, the lady although not knowing Gerard, knew that there was a house in Suvoborska Ulica which belonged to the British Embassy. She had the kindness and sense to walk back with Gerard, who was slightly disgruntled because his plan had been foiled. Nevertheless he was delighted with his welcome home.

It was after this event that we found Fanni had disappeared one morning. She had flown quite silently in the night with all her belongings. The only items of ours which had gone with her were some rolls of Andrex toilet paper which we could buy in the NAAFI. Local toilet paper was rather like thin cardboard. It was natural to think that Fanni felt there was too much responsibility with two lively children and a great deal of entertaining. I wondered if she had quarrelled with Maria, but no, Maria was as mystified as we were and they had never been close anyway. Fanni rarely spoke about her circumstances. I was led to believe that she had no relatives in Belgrade, even though she sometimes stayed away for a night when she was off duty. She had told me about her broken marriage, evidently her husband was known to all as a womaniser, and one day when he came in complaining his meal was late, she had thrown it at him and started divorce proceedings. Divorce was easy, and the divorce rate was high. Many of the older women, both those working in the Reading Room office and those we knew in other walks of life were divorced. I had been very pleased with Fanni, she worked well and although her manner could be brusque, she needed understanding, and was really very affectionate. She served at table very well and did not mind how hard she worked clearing up and sorting things out. I knew I would find it hard to replace her. By cutting down on entertaining, paying old Maria more money to light the stoves and keep them going, and paying our other Maria, or Greta another maid we knew to baby sit when we had to go out, I decided to try and manage. My fear was that our old Maria would get fed up and leave.

Three weeks passed. I was really busy, taking on more and more of the housework, looking after the children completely, and still trying to be presentable as a diplomatic hostess. I refused all day-time invitations which did not include the children, and when Maria had her day off, I could barely manage. I was just about to give in, and start looking for another maid, when there was a knock on the back door. It was Fanni, in a mood of deep repentance. Would I ever be able to forgive her and have her back? She would pay me for the toilet rolls she had taken, which were now used! It appears she had fallen in love with a Turk from Sarajevo who was sometimes in Belgrade. He seemed, unusually for a Turk, to have money and had promised her a good life if she would marry him. She had gone to Sarajevo with him where he had kept her in a small hotel until their wedding plans were made. After a quiet wedding she had moved into his house, to find that she was wife number two. The first wife was not only in residence, but very much in control; Fanni was horrified, angry and disillusioned. She had immediately packed her bag and returned to Belgrade. Needless to say I welcomed her back with open arms, as she determined through her tears never to trust another man.

As spring approached, Peter and I started to plan our journey to England. It was decided that I would travel alone with the boys a month early to give me time with all my family, and Peter would follow on when the time came for him to take his leave. Maria wanted to be set free from her job as she had decided she was too old to go on working. Fanni decided that she would be willing to stay on alone and look after Peter and the house while I was in England, and then take paid leave for four weeks until my return. However, this was not to be.

I was rather apprehensive about flying to England with two very

active young children, one aged two years and ten months, the
other fifteen months, especially as we had to change planes in
Zurich, with some time to wait. There were many jokes about JAT,
the Yugoslav airline; the aircraft were second-hand, and did not
have a good safety record, however, there was no alternative. With
all my farewells made, Peter took us to Belgrade Airport. Two
seats had been removed in the front of the plane in order to
accommodate the children in comfort. I was able to lie them down
for a sleep, and extraordinarily, they loved it, and were no trouble.
The air hostesses made a great fuss of them. There were not many
passengers on the flight, and I was very relaxed. When we arrived
at Zurich I was met by two Swiss hostesses. They helped me with
the children and settled me in the airport lounge to wait. Gerard
immediately went off to look through the wall of glass where he
could see the planes taking off and landing and within seconds he
was out of sight. Those round me were very kind, promising to look
after my bags, filled with baby needs, while I retrieved him. The
children had missed their meal on the plane, and it was doubtful
if it would have been suitable, anyway. Christopher although
very mobile was not actually walking on his own, and was very
heavy to carry. I made a rein with my belt so that I could keep
Gerard near me. I managed to give them something to eat, and we
occupied ourselves playing some games, and watching the planes.
Eventually it was time to board the plane to Heathrow and my
excitement was mounting; it was only one hour on the Swiss
Airline. I had imagined it would be the epitome of comfort as
everything I knew of Switzerland was perfection. Every seat was
taken and although Gerard had a seat to himself I had Christopher
on my lap. No one seemed to have any time to help me. I was left
to alter the size of the safety belt for Gerard and strap him in, and

when it was time for tea to be served, I found it almost impossible to manage. The time was so short, each one of the hostesses was very busy, hurrying to get everything done before landing, and I had no room to move.

We landed on time and somehow I managed to get off the plane and collect the luggage. From the customs room I could see my dear father and my sister Margie waving. I was struggling with Christopher in my arms, dragging Gerard on my belt tied round him, trying to push our luggage in a trolley, holding on to my handbag. I ran forward and handed over the children, hardly stopping to say hello. A customs officer reprimanded me and called me to order, saying that the children must come through customs. However he had seen my plight and relented, leaving the children where they were and quickly signing me through with some deft strokes of his chalk. I was in tears of joy and exhaustion. I stayed for the first week in my mother and father's flat in Staines. It was quite difficult for me because while I had been away they had moved out of the house in Purley which I had lived in for so long. Our own house was still rented, and I could not have access even to just see it without the presence of the agent. I felt quite strange in a district which I did not know at all. However, my sister lived nearby, and they all stopped at nothing to make me welcome and comfortable. My parents were so happy to see their two grandchildren, and we soon settled down. After about a week I moved with the children to my sister Josie's house. Cyril, her husband, had been out of hospital for some months or so, and could walk a little with two callipers. He also had a wheelchair and what we knew as a buzz-box, a three-wheeled invalid car, now, I am sure, known as a car for the physically disadvantaged!

During the previous week, Josie's two children Madeleine and Marion had not been well, so we had not seen any of them. It was found that they had measles, but not very badly. It was the custom then to put children together if they had measles so that each could catch it and then put it behind them, so this is what we did. As Madeleine and Marion recovered Gerard became ill. He gradually got worse and the doctor recommended that he went to hospital. He could not eat and became very thin; I was very concerned. He was taken by ambulance to Waddon Isolation Hospital. This was a large old fashioned forbidding looking building, which has now been demolished. It was approached from the gas works, through a tunnel under the road across waste land by the power station; Ikea and Valley Park has now been built on this site. The consolation was that the staff were wonderful and very caring.

Chapter Five

Christopher

I visited Gerard every day in the hospital. He was in a very large ward, full of children with measles, about forty altogether. That year 1957, there was a severe measles epidemic. My sister Josie, in trying to accommodate us comfortably, had moved out of her double bedroom, and Gerard and myself had shared the double bed, whilst Christopher slept in the cot, which had been kept since Marion moved into a bed. Marion was exactly three, just two months older than Gerard, and Madeleine was six years old. We had great hopes as Gerard was recovering, that Christopher would escape the disease. He seemed well and full of life. It was Wednesday and we had been reassured that Gerard would be home by Saturday. Quite suddenly during the evening Christopher became unwell. We called the doctor the following morning, and he was with us by lunchtime. He thoroughly examined Christopher who by now was looking quite ill, and not eating. Guessing that he would take the same course as Gerard, the doctor told us not to worry, that Christopher would most probably get a little worse, and then start to get better. He would come in and see him again on Monday morning.

During the day Christopher became worse, and his temperature was high. Naturally we were all concerned. It was difficult to know whether to hold him and give him comfort, or to let him lie still in his cot and be cool. We did both, staying with him all the time. I was beginning to think it would have been wiser to have stayed in Belgrade. Although I had spoken to Peter on the telephone, I had not wanted to worry him unduly. My sister, Josie, was a great strength, and looked after Christopher while I went to the hospital to see Gerard. My loyalties to them were strained as both needed me. Gerard was jumping about in his cot trying to drive it. He was already sleeping in a bed before we left Belgrade, and felt he was far too big to be in a cot, he wanted to run about. The doctors wanted to keep him just another day, as he had been very ill and they were carrying out certain tests. I was very happy about this as I had watched other mothers removing their children from the hospital because they were not satisfied. Conditions were not ideal, but I felt sure the care was first class.

During the evening on Thursday Christopher became worse. Josie and I comforted each other with the reassurance that the doctor had said he would get worse. His temperature was very high. I bathed him gently on a towel in his cot and tried to get him to drink. He was very ill. Eventually he fell into a sleep, and I tried to sleep. I was awakened during the night by a strange sound in Christopher's breathing, a moaning sound. I had not nursed a really ill child before; I was desperately worried but kept telling myself the doctor had said he would get worse before he got better. I crept in and woke Josie and together we lifted him out of his cot. We were very uncertain, trying to get him to take a drink and wondering if we should call the doctor; neither of us wanting to share what we were really thinking. We continued to bathe his forehead with a cool cloth, taking his temperature, and soothing him, but by 5.00am. I knew I must send for the doctor. Doctor Doust came immediately, he took one look at little Christopher, listened to his chest and asked if he could use the telephone. He ordered an ambulance to come 'emergency'. He then phoned the hospital to confirm that they had a place, telling them that an oxygen tent would be needed. I remember at that stage thanking God we were in England because in the Belgrade hospital there was only one oxygen tent in the children's ward and there was always a waiting list and of course many children died. I had been in the children's ward with a grieving mother, so I knew this at first hand. Our doctor explained that there was no time to lose, that Christopher had developed complications and was very seriously ill, but in an oxygen tent there was every hope. He suggested that I telephone my husband in Belgrade and advise him to get the first plane he could. The ambulance arrived and I did not know whether to go with the little bundle the ambulance men carried gently down the stairs, or whether to stay and phone Peter. I was still in my dressing gown. I quickly got dressed and was ready by the time they had given Christopher oxygen. The ambulance had come quickly, it was now almost 6.00 am... 7.00 am in Belgrade.

I was not sure whether Peter would still be monitoring the early morning news sheet at the Reading Room or whether he might still be at home. He might have made an early start at the Embassy. By 7.00 am all of Belgrade was at work. He might even have started the trip to Niš in southern Yugoslavia, the journey he had planned to make while I was in England. I could hardly think. I felt sick, and my stomach was turning over. Surely my lovely little Christopher could not die. I knew I must first go to the hospital, but phoning Peter was also urgent. I remembered the conversation

I had had with Lady Roberts, our Ambassadress, on two occasions, one of which was just after Christopher was born when she had visited me at home. She said a wife's first duty is towards her husband. If she has children she has to choose for her husband, even at the risk of leaving her children or sending them to boarding school. This was in answer to the statement I had made when she asked me if I had visited the monasteries in Southern Yugoslavia. This was a trip some people made even though they stayed in very primitive conditions, exploring parts of the country which were quite untamed. There was no possibility of making this trip with babies and we had not wanted to leave the children more than was necessary. Lady Roberts had no children so perhaps this excused her view. I definitely did not agree with her, and was sure each situation needed to be examined on its own merit. Little did I realise how much I was to be put to the test during this time.

When I contacted the Embassy Peter was not there but they promised to find him and ask him to contact me immediately. I did not give them the reason as I wanted to explain to him myself. I just told them it was urgent. I gave them our number to save time, in case Peter did not have it with him; it was not a number we knew automatically. Peter phoned almost straight away, I explained to him the seriousness of the situation, and without asking too many questions he said he would leave as soon as possible. I knew, as he did, the difficulties involved. One started planning days in advance for any journey out of Yugoslavia. It was not possible just to leave the country at any time, permission and visas had to be obtained, and this sometimes took days. It was the Ambassador who took control on this occasion. A visa was promised by 3.00 pm, money was obtained, and the necessary papers organised. The problem was that there was no plane out of Belgrade until Monday, only a military plane, which would have taken Peter to Berlin, but this was already over-subscribed. Not even the British Ambassador could do anything about that. Peter packed a case, paid Fanni, filled the tank of the car with petrol, and set out for a non-stop journey across Europe by road, leaving a colleague to phone to say he had left. We did not know where he was and he did not stop. He guessed that whatever was happening he still had to get home and he had a very adventurous journey.

In 1957 there were very few motorways across Europe; even an apparently short distance on the map took many hours, winding over the mountains. Peter arrived at my sister's house in the early hours of Monday morning. What a reunion that was. We went straight to the hospital, and Peter thanked God to find that Christopher was at least still alive... in the oxygen tent... but alive. The doctors and a consultant were there with Christopher, even that early trying to find exactly the cause of his deteriorated condition. I had sat beside Christopher for much of the time on Saturday and Sunday watching him struggling to breathe. Evidently he had a very rare type of measles, called haemorrhagic measles, but it had been explained to me that this was not the real cause of his illness. There was something else, a complication that no one could understand; therefore it was difficult for them to know what treatment to give him. Peter and I stayed with Christopher a while, just watching him struggle. Gerard was already back at home with my sister, seemingly quite recovered. Peter was exhausted and fell into a deep sleep, having seen Christopher, and I felt a certain amount of peace and relief to have Peter with me and to know that he was safe. The next three weeks were a nightmare and Christopher remained on the danger list. We visited the hospital taking it in turns to look after the other three children, all with Josie's help. In all this Josie was a tremendous support. Her husband Cyril at this time was working and was amazingly independent, even though he had many difficulties; he also was very quiet and supportive. I always felt he had a special kind of wisdom. He was only to be with us a short time; he died quite suddenly the following year of an aneurism, not related to his poliomyelitis in any way, although the doctors evidently knew that death could happen at any time. Cyril had never been very strong. At the beginning of his marriage he had suffered from nephritis, a disease of the kidneys.

We watched Christopher lying so helplessly in his cot wired up to a drip, screaming when anyone in a white jacket or nurse's uniform came near him. He was being tested for tuberculosis and meningitis as well as other illnesses. The lumbar puncture he had was excruciatingly painful. After this the nurses and doctors made a plan to visit him in mufti if they had to open the oxygen tent for any reason at all. This was the only way they could approach him without screams of fear as he recognised the uniforms. Otherwise he would just lie listlessly, very often with his big dark eyes open. Every scream and cry would leave him weak and almost unable to breathe and his temperature remained constantly high. We spoke to the consultants, but they could tell us nothing, only that they were changing the drugs every few days to try and bring his temperature down.

Christopher had shown no sign of recognition for Peter or myself; this was very, very painful. I longed to pick him up and hold him, and to have him know who I was. Never at any time did I feel it was anybody's fault, as all the nursing staff and doctors were very caring and never at any time did I want to take him out of the care of the hospital. I was so grateful that someone else was looking after him, with skills that I did not know. I never felt critical, or thought they were doing something unnecessary; I just remember being very grateful. Sister Cullen was the sister in charge and she had become a close caring friend. All the other children who had been in the ward had gone home leaving a skeleton nursing staff. Christopher remained listless in his cot covered by the oxygen tent alone in this cavern of a ward. It all seemed hopeless. I remember finding prayer extremely difficult, but had tried in the only way I knew. Then came the dreadful day, Friday, when Peter and I were summoned to a meeting with the senior consultant and Dr Lenahan, the doctor in charge. It was four o'clock in the afternoon; they both looked very glum and serious. We could tell the news was not good. They explained that there was a mystery; they could not find exactly what was wrong with Christopher, and his condition had deteriorated. They could find no way to bring down his temperature so the prognosis was difficult. They did not expect him to live through the night. We were silent. What could we say? There were no words. Everyone in our church in Purley where we were well known as a family was praying. The school children were all praying. My tears had nearly all been cried, but they still ran down my face. Peter put his arms round me and I knew I did not understand. This could not happen to us, it only happened to other people.

We went home to take our news to Josie and Cyril, tucked Gerard into bed, and returned to the hospital. Sister Cullen was on duty, and after a while she came and sat with us in our lonely vigil. I was crying, and she put a hand on my arm; she said "You are a Catholic and I am only an Anglican, but haven't you got something you can bring like a medal, something to show you believe?" Of course! I had Christopher's baptismal medal, given to him by his godparents Ied and Hein Schaapveld. It was solid gold, and they had been very upset on the day of his baptism because the medal ordered from Holland had a slight mark on it. I had to admit this was difficult to see, but they had insisted on sending it back to be replaced. So careful was I with this medal that although I always kept it pinned on Christopher's little vest, I had removed it in the hospital in case it was lost. The greater meaning of faith behind it had escaped me and it shows the state of my faith at this time. Peter and I rushed back to Josie's house to get the medal and returned to the hospital. Sister Cullen pulled a length of bandage from a roll and put her hand down to find the scissors hanging from her pocket by a ribbon; I can remember it all exactly. She snipped off a length of bandage, put the end into her mouth to moisten it and threaded it through the medal and went over to open the oxygen tent where little Christopher was lying. "Please don't open the zip" I pleaded knowing that every time the tent was opened Christopher coughed and fought for breath. "If it's going to do any good it has to go inside." said Sister Cullen with great authority. She unzipped the long opening on the oxygen tent, lent in and tied the bandage inside, so that the medal was hanging over Christopher's head. "Go home now and have a good night's sleep." she commanded. There were no facilities for anyone to stay the night in hospital in those days unless they were a patient, everyone was encouraged to go home. Peter and I lay side by side in Josie and Cyril's double bed, holding hands, with Gerard now in a little camp bed beside us.

I cried and cried and I remember the prayer I prayed... "Dear God, I promise you, that if you really want Christopher to be with you, I will let him go to you, without being bitter and resentful. I know you will look after him."

I suppose we must have slept because it was 8.30 am, when the phone rang and woke us up. Peter and I fell out of bed and down the stairs. This was the call I had been dreading. Josie was listening from the kitchen, too afraid to answer on our behalf. We were sure that it was the hospital with the dreaded news and I could not bear it. It was Sister Cullen's voice; Christopher's temperature was down to normal, he was out of the oxygen tent and breathing normally. Now I can say "Praise God," ...then, I am not sure I even thanked God. We were dressed in seconds and went to the hospital. What a miracle; it was true; there was Christopher standing in his cot having eaten a dish of cold custard for breakfast. It was most probably all they dared give him. I picked him up and cuddled him, but I think he was not very sure who Peter and I were. He had eyes only for Sister Cullen and the nurse on duty. By 4.30 in the afternoon he had been seen by the consultants, at least from that hospital, although we knew that consultants were called in from elsewhere; it was unbelievable. Christopher was eating normal food, laughing and playing, as if nothing had been wrong. The doctors were as amazed as we were. I knew that God had answered Sister Cullen's prayer of faith; but strangely, I felt frightened within myself. If God was this close and had heard my prayer and knew me, he must know everything about me. This after all was what I had learnt from my childhood but I had never really believed it to be true in a practical sense. There were many things I did not like about myself and I certainly didn't like God knowing about them. I had been brought up to keep my life right for God, to be a good girl, go to Mass on Sunday, say my prayers, which I always found difficult and unsatisfactory, and I was assured I would go to heaven. I had been very chuffed when Canon Denning our dear Parish Priest in Purley had said to me one day, when Gerard was a baby, and I had been telling him how difficult I found it to pray, "Paulette, every time you put a pin in your baby's nappy with love, it is a prayer." However, in the depths of my being, this sounded far too easy to me. I suddenly felt an impostor, hypocritical and false. I felt that God would now find out the truth about me. I am not sure what I thought would happen. I experienced what I think Adam and Eve must have felt in the Garden of Eden after they had eaten the apple. I wanted to hide from God. Although I knew that he had really been present, it was as if I was struck dumb. I left everyone else to say what a miracle it was, and how wonderful that all the prayers had been answered. I was very quiet about it. The consultants, doctors and nurses were all equally amazed, and could offer no explanation. They were sure there must be some other reason. Peter and I sadly did not have the courage to tell the story of the drama of the previous night; I think I was afraid of being laughed at and Sister Cullen also said nothing to them. But between the three of us we knew that God had intervened.

I had been brought up in a strict Roman Catholic atmosphere. My father was headmaster of the local Catholic elementary school, in which my two sisters and I had received our primary education. I certainly had learnt all about Jesus, and knew every Bible story, at least from the New Testament, and many from the old. Miracles were strictly for the time Jesus was on earth except for Lourdes, where we all knew that some people were actually cured.

Even as a small child I had loved going to church; my mother sang in the choir, and I used to sit on the top step of the iron staircase which led up to the choir loft, right beside the organ bellows. Sometimes I would stand beside her, just able to see over the wooden edge of the loft, down into the church. It was wonderful, a really privileged position; I could see everything that went on, and enjoyed trying to recognise each person from behind. I knew much of the music from constant repetition, and would often join in; no one seemed to mind. Sometimes I would be with my mother and father in the main church. My father had a loud and not very musical singing voice. He thought all church music was sung too slowly so he was always a little bit ahead of everyone else and I found this very embarrassing. If I tugged at his sleeve and tried to slow him down, he would tell me to "pay attention". The fact that he was also my headmaster put me in a difficult position. There was no favouritism at school and if I was naughty, talking in class when I shouldn't or perhaps even being cheeky, I would be sent to him. There was a big deep step outside his room and if I knocked and he had someone with him, he would say "Wait," and I would sit on the step until he came. If it was only a minor misdemeanour, he would let me off with a strong warning, but I can remember him several times giving me one stroke of the cane on my hand, saying that it hurt him more than it hurt me. I loved my father dearly and wanted him to approve of me. By the age of nine I could answer all the questions by rote in the catechism; this was required knowledge for everyone at school anyway.

I had a little altar at home with two little vases on it and a statue; it was made of white semi-circular wood. Whether it was actually mine I don't know but I used to tend it, when I remembered, putting fresh flowers and arranging things; sometimes lighting the little candles, but that was discouraged by my mother as being dangerous. I also sometimes played games with my sister Margie, like doctors and nurses, shops, and priest and server. I was usually the server unless in some way I had gained her favour and she allowed me to be the priest. We would dress up with garments from our dressing-up box, and use a glass for the chalice. We went through everything the priest did at Mass usually with a few arguments, and shouts of "I'm not playing any more."

At seven I made my first communion; this was a day we all looked forward to. This was the day that Jesus would really be with us and I really believed it. My mother made a lovely white dress for me to wear, and we bought a veil and a wreath of white flowers. I was very upset because I wanted a long dress because Pat McCrory had a long dress, but my mother said it was too expensive, and Pat McCrory was an only child. Anyway Mummy said it was too pretentious, but I still wanted it. I could never get the wreath and veil to stay in its place as my hair was straight and slippery, rinsed with vinegar every Friday night. Even a year later when the Archbishop came to the parish to confirm all those who were ready, my dress still fitted me. I can remember how pleased my mother was. I was very young to be confirmed, but I could answer the questions although I still had not mastered the art of keeping my veil on. Absolutely no one knew the dark secret that I carried with me. It was just after my first communion and I had already been several times into the confessional box, a dark secret place where you told the priest what you had done wrong. I don't think I really understood about the being forgiven bit, but I knew it was supposed to be good. With me my sin was almost always that I had been disobedient. I can hear my father now saying, "Be obedient, go now, do as your mother tells you." or "Do as I tell you." We had a list of sins to look at, but I had rarely read anyone else's letters, and although I was sometimes envious, I didn't then really know what it meant, so I stuck with what I knew. I thought that God would understand, as I had learnt that he was omniscient, meaning knowing everything, and omni-present, which meant everywhere, but I sometimes forgot this.

It was such a time that I forgot about God when my mother was having friends to high tea. It was a Saturday, the table was laid with the best china, a set of 'Queen's Green' porcelain. Everything was in place, except the sandwiches which my mother was making in the kitchen. Fruit salad was in the best glass bowl, the Victoria Sandwich, filled with home-made raspberry jam and cream, a plate of cakes from the cake shop, only ever bought when visitors were coming, and the jug of 'Bel' cream with its bakelite screw on handle and pourer. This cream made from butter and milk at blood heat, forced through a special little machine by pump action, was my mother's speciality, and we all loved it. The silver spoon was already in the jug as the cream was particularly thick that day. One spoonful, I could just manage it easily, not even a drop spilt to give me away... straight into my mouth. Delicious! Why stop at one? Who would ever know, if I was quick? I returned the spoon to the jug for a second spoonful, and had just put it in my mouth when my mother came in and caught me red-handed. I couldn't make an excuse, I couldn't deny it. I wondered what my punishment would be; would I be excluded from the table for tea altogether? No it was much worse. My mother lent over me and said how disappointed God was with me and that on Saturday I must confess to the priest in confession that I had stolen a spoonful of cream from the table. I knew of course that it was worse, it was two spoonfuls. I was miserable all the week wondering how I was ever going to say this in the dark of the confessional box. I knew from what I had learnt that I was actually talking to God but it still had to go through the priest. It was alright if it was Father Patrick because he was a friend of mine. He was a rather happy Irishman and I felt he might understand. He had bought a raffle ticket at the parish garden fete for a rather beautiful doll with long fair ringlets. He sought me out and promised that if he won, the doll would be mine. He won and I named the doll Patricia after him. I even took her to the priest's house to have her baptised properly but Father Louis just laughed and made fun. I also displeased my mother by cutting off Patricia's curls. What if it was Father Louis or Father Julien in the box on Saturday? Both were rather severe French priests. Father Louis would approach me sometimes in the play-ground and ask me if I had been good. Whether I said "Yes" or "No" he would say "Hold out your hand." I would then get what he thought was a playful stroke across my hand with the black inch wide leather strap all three priests wore round their waists, two lengths of which hung down in front. It really hurt but I didn't ever have the courage to tell him.

Saturday came and my mother did not forget, although the incident had not been mentioned again. I wondered whether my father had been told. I really loved my father and I did not want him to know what I had done as I wanted to please him. This always seemed to be an impossibility. Even if I wanted to get him something for a present perhaps for his birthday, and asked him what he would like, he always said "Peace and quiet." This was always out of my reach.

I crept into the dark box when my turn came in the church; my mother was waiting a few rows behind. To my horror it was Father Louis. We went through the preliminaries... and it came to the time that I must confess my wrongdoing. "I have been disobedient Father"... a long pause... "Anything else my child?"...another long pause. I just could not bring myself to tell him about the cream. What if priests did talk about what they heard in confession, and he told my father; he was often in my father's room at school. I did a quick calculation and said "Father, I stole a penny."... "You stole a penny eh? From whom did you steal a penny, my dear?" I had not reckoned on being cross-examined. "From my mother," I lied. "From your mother eh? From her purse?" "Yes." "And what did you buy with the penny you stole, eh?" His thick French accent not disguising for me any word. I was in tears but kept them very quiet. "I bought some sweets, Father." "Oooooh, so you like the sweets do you then, but you must use your own money for sweets and not steal from your mother eh?" By now I knew he had recognised my voice. All the times flashed through my mind when I had been to my father's room after school to cadge a ha'penny or even a farthing, and Father Louis had been there. A penny was more than I ever had at once. You could buy quite a lot with a farthing. "So are you sorry for stealing from your mother, eh?" ....a long pause..."Yes Father,"... and it was over. Three Hail Mary's to be said, and an act of contrition. I knew that however forgiving God was, that I was now beyond his reach. I had lied in confession. I hated what I had done, but saw even less how to get out of it. For some time while it was all fresh in my mind, I tried hard to be very good so that I did not have to go to confession, but the damage was done, and after a while I relegated this whole incident to that black place in the back of my mind, which, hopefully, I thought,

God can't see. It was the beginning of knowing God as a God to be feared, not the loving and forgiving God that I now know him to be.

There were many occasions in my life even after my marriage, when I really tried to sort things out with God. Try as I might, I was always convinced that I was not forgiven; not only not forgiven, but beyond the possibility of being forgiven. I tried both in and out of the confessional box, but could never find anyone who could hear me out. More often than not priests were even more condemning, and I hated going in the box. One day, years later, a Catholic priest came to take a service at St. Andrew's Church of England school where I was teaching. He was very understanding and was teaching the true gospel of forgiveness and reconciliation not only with others but with one's self. I had no opportunity to speak to him on that occasion but knew where he was from. It was St. Gertrude's parish in South Croydon. I did not have the courage to see him personally outside the confessional box, but I found out the times of confessions. He was most understanding when I told him my story and suggested I came each month to talk with him at the same time. He assured me that as I said sorry to God, I was forgiven, but I did not believe him. He was making it too easy for me. At this time Catholics were not allowed to see a priest for confession outside the confessional box and he did not suggest that I did this. When I went back with great expectation and excitement after a month I found that this priest had been moved. At first I did not know where, but eventually found that it was a parish too far away for me to visit. The black place in the back of my mind where so many things that had hurt me were stored became so full that every now and again it would overflow, causing me to experience hurts quite unrelated to my present life. I did not know how to deal with this. My method was to shut it down more tightly and to get on with life in the best way I could. I became quite a perfectionist, and this sometimes got me into trouble with other people who were more easy-going. I also became critical of others, without necessarily expressing what I felt. I was angry and irritable on occasions, without understanding why, but giving out on the top surface that everything was okay.

To our great joy Christopher maintained his newly found good health. The hospital kept Sister Cullen and a small group of nurses on duty, even though at first Christopher was the only patient. Later he was joined by a little coloured girl named Audrey, who was about the same age. Christopher was the centre of attention and greatly loved. It was my sister who gave a party for all the doctors, consultants and all who had been involved with nursing Christopher and I remember even the trivialities of that evening. Josie and I were both qualified Home Economic teachers, and we had shared in preparing a really lovely buffet supper. We felt extremely grateful both externally to the hospital and Sister Cullen, and internally to God and for all the prayers. We had made some little balls of cheese choux pastry, fried in deep fat. One of the doctors said to me, biting into one of them, "These prawns are really delicious". I remember smiling an affirming smile; they did look like prawns fried in batter. We had decided that to make prawns would be far too expensive! Everyone was very happy. Although inside I knew that God had intervened and that Christopher would now be quite alright, I was unable to talk about it. The doctors and consultants concerned held a conference and decided that because Christopher's case was so extraordinary, they would have to keep him in hospital under observation. They were afraid there might be some hidden illness which could burst out again. They could not give any definite time-table and this caused us some concern as we had to make decisions about the future. In reviewing the situation and talking about it together, Peter and I decided with no hesitation at all, that we would give up our diplomatic life, take back our house in Purley and resume life in England. We both realised at that time, that had we in actual fact, been in Belgrade, Christopher might not have had a chance. Now I realise 'That with God all things are possible.' Anyway this turned out to be one of the best decisions we have ever made. Peter had at least four more months to complete before he could be released from his tour in Yugoslavia. My sister Josie persuaded us to go back to Yugoslavia for a month, have a little holiday and then close down our villa and send our chattels back to England. It was decided that we would go back together on our own. Peter thought it would be easiest for him if he lived in one of the hotels in Belgrade when I returned to England. Josie promised to look after Gerard, and visit Christopher in hospital as we could get no firm answer from the hospital as to how long they would keep him.

In fact he was there for another two months, (three altogether), before they were satisfied with his good health. I found the terms of my month's return to Belgrade very difficult, leaving the children was not easy and we had to make contingency plans in case Christopher was discharged from hospital within the month. Josie was busy enough with three young children and she was concerned that she would not manage with the four of them, especially as Christopher was just starting to walk. It was one thing to visit him every day, another thing to have total responsibility for him. The hospital authorities were very helpful and because of the strange situation they had a whole ward open and cleaned, with hardly anyone using it as there was no more infection, the measles epidemic finished as quickly as it had started. They gave permission for my sister to take Marion and Gerard to visit Christopher in the afternoons when Madeleine was at school.

It was a very painful time for us after all the joy. Peter and I said our farewells and set off on our journey once again across Europe by car, taking a different route, and aiming to make a little holiday of it. We found our friends in Belgrade very supportive. Fanni had looked after the house well with some help from Louisa, who insisted she had done it voluntarily but was quite pleased when we paid her. I managed to keep out of the parties for the most part except those that were given particularly in our honour. We packed up the house completely and had our goods containerised and shipped back to England. We settled Peter in a comfortable hotel, and I once again said my goodbyes. It was really difficult leaving Peter but I knew I had no option. I returned to England on the Orient Express, which turned out to be a very exciting journey and I took up my new life, staying again with Josie and her husband, visiting Christopher every day, and getting the tenants out of our house, which would take us into another story.

Little Christopher had no idea who I was when I returned. He was adored by Sister Cullen and the nurses who had been kept on in the 'measles' ward. Christopher had one loyal companion, the little black girl Audrey, who also had suffered from measles. There was a heat wave that year in England at this time. I spent every afternoon with Christopher out on the grass in the shade of the trees. I never knew what tests they did on him, if any, but he seemed healthy in every way. He was quite happy to play with me and walk, and gradually began to reach out to me when I arrived. Although Sister Cullen tried very hard to release Christopher to me she was still caring for him most mornings and early evenings, until the night nurse came on duty. As it was so hot she would put cool water in the bath and let him play there while she watched, and he loved this. As soon as I arrived she would disappear so that Christopher was not distracted away from me. I know that it was a painful time for her. I was already settled in our own house when the doctors felt it was safe to discharge Christopher. What a happy day that was for me, although I missed Josie's company and all her help. One never really knows what goes on in a child's mind; whether Christopher remembered I was his mother or whether he lovingly accepted me again I don't know. I do know that whatever he experienced leaving Sister Cullen and her staff, they missed him. I took him back several times to see them until they closed the ward, and Sister Cullen visited our home for dinner when Peter returned from Belgrade.

There were many events that took place in my life, both through inner healing and my outer journey before I could speak freely of the wonderful thing God had done for us all in healing Christopher. I was then able to truly praise him and thank him. Most of our Catholic friends recognised the miracle of Christopher's healing without any difficulty. God had answered Sister Cullen's prayer but it had not really been my prayer. All I had done was what she had said I was to do. All I knew was that I had been willing to let Christopher go to God with love. I think that also was only because I saw no alternative. I was unable to talk about the deeper meanings to anybody. In fact when I tried to talk about what I thought God had done, I felt paralysed. I felt sure that God would punish me for all the things I did not like about myself and other people, nothing very enormous, but lots of things that I did not feel comfortable with. I felt ashamed of myself before God, the all-powerful God who knew everything. My mother and father were over the moon, thanking God for all those who had prayed. I knew that I was really afraid of His power. With all my Christian education I had failed to see clearly what Jesus' death had meant; this understanding was to come much later, but God knew about my self will.

I had been told as a child and an adolescent both by my mother and father and my sisters that I was strong willed, although I never seemed to get my own way. God knew about my desire to have everything perfect, wanting to do things well without ever achieving that perfection, and experiencing great frustration. He knew about my bouts of anger, the times when I felt low and unfulfilled. He knew about my lack of love for the difficult people that came into my life. I suppose I did want my own way. How was it that Christopher's wonderful recovery should have affected my life so much? I was on one hand so happy, but on the other felt my memories had been stirred. I felt uneasy with the person I was; I wanted to be different so that I could be friends with God. There was no one I could speak to and the whole subject caused me great embarrassment; there was no one who could possibly under-stand the movements within me. Why was God so close for Christopher and yet seemed so distant for me? I longed to be totally at peace. It was many years before I found the beginning of any answers to my questions. I did sometimes try to pray, but I always thought my prayers were fairly unsuccessful, and that it was unlikely that God actually heard them.

There was something which was very important to me, which had now changed, but the memories lurked, and I knew that I was unforgiven. I had hated my sister Josie, who was so good to me later, particularly until I was about thirteen. Josie was nine years older than me. She had been like a second mother to me, often being left completely in charge. I really had hated her when I was young. She was always right. My mother used to trust her with things that I knew I would never be allowed to do. She was bossy and dominating, and if my mother and father went away, she was very strict. I thought things would change when she went to college when I was nine, but things got even worse. We had a holiday in Belgium and I remember it well. It was 1938, the year before the Second World War started. We stayed in the Hotel Digue in Oosduinkerke. The first few days were bliss. Margie, (who was four years older than me), and I played on the beach running over the sand dunes with bare feet in the sun, screaming when we trod on one of the large black shiny beetles which hid under the surface of the sand to escape the sun. We ate all our meals in the hotel and the food was really exciting. It was my first time abroad and there was a lot to learn. We had rabbit with prunes, delicious steaks served with fine french 'chips' and salad, and terrine made from all sorts of things. Even the enormous Macaroni Cheese served individually to each table was out of this world. How could they get it to taste so delicious? Josie followed on later with her best friend Maureen, who was her life-long friend. I think she had been staying with her in Ireland. Almost immediately they were left in charge whilst my mother and father went to stay with friends in a big country house in Courtrai. I had a real feeling of being threatened. Josie would say to me "I'll tell Mummy," and this for me was a very powerful statement as I knew whatever had really happened would not be believed, and that Josie's word would be taken as true. We really continued to enjoy our holiday but I was very aware of Josie's very firm discipline, and her unbending rules. I knew that I had to be very good, or I would get a bad report when Mummy and Daddy returned. Now in later life, Josie had become my best friend. I saw her kindness and her great willingness to help. Our relationship had started to improve when I was fourteen but changed quite dramatically at the time of her marriage. She knew that I had cut the hair of several friends at college, and as she now treated me more as an adult, she asked me if I would cut and set her hair for her wedding. She had very curly hair and did not like going to the hairdressers. I was really happy to do this and it meant a great deal to me. I felt somehow as if I had been accepted. Later, I used to go over to Plumstead where she was living and look after Madeleine when she was a tiny baby in 1950. Cyril was not very strong and sometimes was in hospital. If I stayed the night Josie could go and visit him. I was so pleased when she confided in me.

Chapter Six

Nutfield

Change came for me in 1939 when I was ten, three days before war broke out. We had already packed the trunk when war was threatened in 1938 after our return from Belgium ready to move to the country. There was a great deal of unrest, and then Neville Chamberlain met with Hitler in Munich and managed to bring about a truce by giving into some of his demands. This truce was short lived and during August 1939 the situation in Europe became serious. Although I was only ten years old I was aware of there being war between China and Japan at this time, also that there was war in Spain. Even though I had listened to my father talking about the First World War, it was all remote. My mother and father had been married in October 1916 when my father had three days leave. They had spent the afternoon of their wedding day visiting my Uncle Ray in hospital. He had been badly wounded by a shell which had hit and killed the man next to him in the trenches. His face and head and the side of his body were damaged and remained disfigured and one ear was completely deaf. He was only 20 years old.

The seriousness of the situation escaped me to begin with and life became very exciting. There was a big move to get children into the country in case London was bombed. Many of us from my school were evacuated by train. Because my father was headmaster, my mother accompanied him as a helper. I can remember being lined up in rows with children from other schools as well. We all had large identification labels sewn on us, so that if we got lost we could be taken to the correct location. No one seemed to know where we were going. We were each given a carrier bag containing food for the day and we all carried a small suitcase with our clothes. As well as this we had our gas masks. These were in a square cardboard box with a long piece of string for a strap. Some of us had a more sophisticated case made of a kind of oil cloth, with a strap that went over the shoulders and head which the box fitted into. We had been told to carry our gas masks wherever we went. There was a great fear that Hitler would use gas to kill us all. We had to practise wearing our gas masks for long periods of time and they caused much discomfort. After what seemed a very long journey we arrived at Caterham Station, which for me, being a London child, seemed to be deep in the country. We were then bussed to South Nutfield. The village hall was put at our disposal and everyone in the village who had any spare rooms was obliged to take evacuees. My mother and father and other helpers, some of whom I knew well, were busy placing the children in the homes available.

A girl named Sheila Harrington, younger than myself, had attached herself to me. Her mother, who I knew my mother did not approve of, had asked me to look after her. I had no idea my mother was relying on my sister Margie and me to stay with her, so that we could all live somewhere together. Somehow without my mother knowing, Sheila Harrington and I were whisked off to the Bristow household still holding hands. Mr Bristow was the village baker, he was small and thin. What I remember most about him is the wonderful way he could eat a herring, or indeed any fish with bones. He would delicately slice his knife through and lift out all the bones at once. To me this was the most amazing thing I had ever seen. One day I asked him to teach me how to do it, but I could never manage it. He also brought a bag of small doughnuts home with him every evening. They had a house in Trindles Road. Mrs Bristow was a large lady with a big ruddy face; she was very kind and a real country housewife. I had seen her picture in books many times, or so I thought. Their only child named Eric was eighteen, and he was delighted to have some sisters, if only to have fun teasing us. Life had become so exciting, it was unbelievable. The mood changed a little when my worried parents knocked on the door later that evening. Sheila and I had eaten, unpacked, explored the house and garden, and were washed and ready for bed, literally in our pyjamas. Mrs Bristow was really surprised as she had no idea I was the headmaster's daughter and that my parents were with me. My mother was very upset because she had wanted us all to be together. Margie had also gone off alone and was settled in 'top' Nutfield, a mile up the hill, in the school house, with the headmaster Mr Denning, who was to share his school with my father. I remember thinking that this was very kind of him. I think my mother soon realised that to extract me peacefully was going to be too difficult. It was much later when I began to feel homesick that I understood why my mother and father wanted us with them.

Sheila and I had a wonderful time, playing in the fields at the back of the house, talking to the animals, and climbing trees. Our new mother seemed very reasonable as long as we stayed within sight of the house. It was a new world. Eric took us under his wing trying to teach us billiards on the small table in the back room. The schools were on holiday, and I remember the day war was declared on the 3rd September standing round the crackling radio, listening to the announcement by Neville Chamberlain, but I still did not realise what it all meant. On my birthday the 12th September the Bristows made a lovely party for me, to which I invited my best friends and my parents. Mrs Bristow did everything she could to make Sheila and myself happy, but there were some things that she could not change that we found difficult. The toilet was outside across a little yard. It was fine in the daylight, and was so different that we didn't at first mind, but as the nights became darker and colder, we found this very nasty. The weekend after my birthday Mrs Harrington arrived to visit Sheila, sweeping in, in full flood, with Sheila's two older sisters, Joy and Violet. They were both singers and on the stage, and one of them was engaged to an American 'big band' leader, although no one had ever heard of him. It was obvious even to me, that Mr and Mrs Bristow had not experienced anything like this in their lives, and of course I hadn't either. Joy and Violet were like dolls that mustn't be disturbed or touched. They were very made-up and very dressed up, with elaborate blonde hair styles. They had nylon stockings from America, and very high heeled shoes. A strong scent filled the room, and Mr Bristow and Eric retired to the back room to the billiard table. There was hardly room for us in the kitchen which was also the dining room, even without the men. I don't think there was a Mr Harrington. I heard nothing about him anyway. Mrs Bristow served tea beautifully. She must have known they were coming because she had it all ready with the best china which had flowers on it and a gold edge round the top of the cups. There were some of the special cakes from the bakery as well as sandwiches made with cucumber and a tin of salmon. She needn't have worried so much because Joy and Violet just had a cup of tea. Sheila and I ate as much as we could and Eric finished it all off when they had gone. The visit was not a great success. Mrs Bristow tried hard to make conversation but it was impossible. I understood then why Sheila had such pretty underwear. I had already complained to my mother that I didn't like wearing brown school knickers all the time. After I had seen Sheila's I was even more adamant. Sheila tried to lend me some of her pretty green silk French knickers, but as she was two years younger than me and on the small side, they quickly split. Whatever happened I don't know, but before I started at the County School, Mrs Harrington came one morning, packed Sheila's clothes and took her away. We vowed to be always friends, but I have never seen her or her mother since. I think it was to do with the toilet across the backyard. It was really quite clean, but had a distinctive smell, and there were quite a lot of spiders around the white distempered ceiling and walls, hanging in their tiny webs. Sheila was terrified of going out there in the dark and always wanted me to go with her. The day Joy and Vi visited, I had guessed from their facial expressions they had not been impressed with the facilities.

I travelled to Reigate County School on the train from South Nutfield station to Reigate via Redhill wearing the brown pleated gym slip that had already been bought for me to start at the Notre Dame Convent in Southwark in September. This caused me a great deal of upset as I always felt I didn't belong. A special exception was made for me because I was an evacuee. The rest of the school wore slim-fitting navy blue pinafore dresses with white blouses. Economy was high on everyone's agenda.

It was at this same station in June of the following year, that we went to take food, drinks and fruit for the soldiers coming back from Dunkirk. There were both French and English of all ranks, in great disarray. The trains must have stopped by arrangement. I have no idea where the troops were taken to, or what happened to them. I only know that it was the first time I started to understand a tiny bit of what war was really about. It affected me deeply. Although none of the soldiers was badly wounded there were many blood soaked bandages on arms and heads, although all were able to walk. I wanted to help them all. It was from this time that I started to take more interest in what was going on. I began to realise that there was a real world outside myself, and that there were a lot of people who needed help.

When Mrs Bristow went into hospital to have gallstones removed, a new home had to be found for me. It was not at that time possible for me to go to live with my mother and father. I went to live with the Patersons whose home was the lodge of Brandt's estate in top Nutfield. Mr Paterson was an under gardener. The Brandts were a wealthy family who owned Cape-Nor, an enormous mansion and estate, right in the centre of the village. They had taken in twenty evacuees from my father's school. Mrs Skinner, a close friend of my mother and father, and my sister Josie were two of the helpers who were put in 'the big house' to look after them. They were given a very large room and not very much in the way of facilities. Josie remained a close friend of Mrs Skinner up to the day she died. There were many difficulties, both with the children and with the household. When Josie returned to her college which had been evacuated to Shrewsbury the children were moved into other houses where the people were more amenable. The servants in the Brandt household had found it too difficult, and made that quite clear. Mr and Mrs Brandt hardly had anything to do with the evacuees themselves, and there was a lot of resentment.

The Patersons had a year old baby named Shirley, and this pleased me a great deal. They also had a dog called Toki who became my best friend. Mr Paterson's name was Cecil, he was a very gentle type of man. I never knew what Mrs Paterson's first name was because Cecil always called her 'dear'. In the evening he would put on big white gloves to cover his brown gnarled hands, and knit. He was sometimes knitting for himself beautiful 'Fair-Isle' patterns which were very popular at that time, but mostly he knitted the ribbing for 'dear's' jumpers that she made as a means of extra income. She knitted very quickly, and sometimes wanted me to go to Redhill on the bus to get her more wool. She wanted me to do this one day when I had arranged to take a picnic with some friends from school who lived near. We had planned to pick some primroses and go 'bluebelling' which at that time was exciting for me. She told me that I could not go with my friends, and that I must do what she wanted. I was very homesick and felt nobody understood. I had to do a lot of jobs in the house and there were strict rules that I had to obey. Although I saw my mother and father on Sundays at Mass, and often went to lunch and tea with them afterwards, I did not see so much of them as when I was at the Bristows. The Sunday Mass which my father had arranged in the village hall was open to anyone from the village as well as the school. Father Crowley the assistant priest at Redhill came especially, and we made the altar from beer crates, covered with a sheet. My mother and father were living in another big house called Glebe House, but they only had two rooms and the use of the kitchen. My mother was trying to negotiate another bedroom so that Margie and I could live there as well. The only room that would be suitable at the 'service' end of the house to which we were all relegated was the day nursery, which was sometimes in use for the grandchildren of Mr and Mrs Douglas, the owners.

At this time I longed to see my mother. I knew she could sort it all out. I was very unhappy. It seemed an age to wait until Sunday, but I did not know what to do. I did not dare to completely disobey Mrs Paterson, and I did not know how to get in touch with my mother. I was not sure what power Mrs Paterson had over me, but I was quite afraid of her being cross. Every night when I arrived home from school I took Toki for a walk down Crown Hill by the house. I had strict instructions to go there and nowhere else, and I was forbidden to go in the direction of my parents' house. This night I had made my plans. I would go out as usual waving to Mrs Paterson through the window as if I was going on my usual walk, and slip round the house and go the opposite way from usual to where my mother and father lived. There were two ways to reach Glebe House, one was fifteen minutes walk from the main road down a long drive, and it would take at least ten minutes along the main road to the top of the drive, the other a shorter cut through the churchyard along a dark drive with high laurels on either side (which at dusk became alive with swooping bats, which sometimes touched you,) then through a lych-gate, and across two fields. This was the route we usually took. I put in my pocket a pencil and some paper in case time ran short. I remember wishing that I had a watch so that I would know the time exactly. I was very hopeful that I might meet someone I knew who could take a message, even possibly my mother or father themselves, which would be wonderful. It might be Mrs Bennet the chauffeur's wife or their son Donald who was a year younger than me, though he was not likely to be out on his own at this time as he had diabetes very badly. The two gardeners rarely went out, and certainly not on foot across the fields. They were two brothers, Jack and Will Shaw. Ruth and Jack lived in one of the two cottages by the big house, next to the Bennets, and Will and Alice lived at the top of the drive. Ruth was an invalid and rarely went out, so my chances were thin.

I reached the lych-gate and suddenly felt panicky. It was much further than I usually walked with Toki, and I began to be afraid. I could see the house across the fields and knew that I would not have time to get there, see my mother and get back. I wrote a note as best I could. "Dear Mummy, please come and see me P." There was not room for my whole name. I put it half under a big stone, right in the path of the lych-gate. Someone was sure to see it; I was worried that it was not very legible. I had been called Baby by everyone who knew me well since I was born, but I never addressed myself as Baby. It happened because I was the youngest. I hated being called Baby but I was fourteen before I had the courage to make a stand to be called by my proper name and refused to answer to Baby. I turned and ran all the way home. Yes, Mrs Paterson had noticed I had been a long time. What had I been doing? Had I been talking to strangers, which was forbidden? I told her that I had been further then usual on my walk. She scolded me and told me never to do it again as she had been worried. I had not thought through the result of my actions. Mrs Bennet had found my note, put two and two together, and guessed it was for my mother. My mother on reading it thought something terrible had happened, showed it to my father, and they both came immediately. Of course the story came out and I was in tears. I told the whole story of not being allowed to go on the picnic because I had to buy wool in Redhill. I can remember exactly the wool I had to get; it was Paton's twisted pale blue and white 3ply. Mrs Paterson was left pleading her innocence, denying that she had ever made me do anything against my will and looking to Cecil to back her up and defend her. He was obviously on my side as he knew how strict she was with me, but was afraid to say too much, as she treated him the same way.

The result was that I went out with my friends and many of the strict rules that had been made were changed. My father said I was to be allowed to go and see them at Glebe House whenever I wanted and that with due wisdom she was to allow me to do this. I found out afterwards that they had never previously come in to see me without making an arrangement because Mrs Paterson had shown her disapproval at their unexpected arrival. It was difficult for them to make an arrangement as they were both so often out visiting the other children and seeing that they were being looked after properly. There were long distances to walk, with no other transport. Some of the evacuee children were quite difficult to look after, and people couldn't cope with them. There were reports of boys fishing with their gas masks and chasing sheep, trying to catch them and ride on them. Although I was scolded for giving my mother and father such a fright, I felt really loved and wanted. My mother made urgent enquiries with her hosts at Glebe House, telling them clearly of the situation, and my sister and I moved into Glebe House almost immediately. This was the start of what seemed to be a charmed life for me; it was wonderful. I walked up the drive to the main road that ran through the villages to Redhill, to get the bus to school, I would cross to the other side and although there was no bus stop there the bus driver would always stop for me to get on. Sometimes I went to school with my sister Margie and sometimes I left home earlier and went on my own. During August and September we would sometimes wake up really early, and walk the fields at the back of the house, picking the mushrooms which grew at that time of the year. I would wash mine and cook them in milk very gently with salt and pepper, and on school days put them in a glass jar with a screw top, and take them with a spoon to go with my packed lunch. Going out really early before anyone was up was wonderful. It was often still dark and we would take a torch, then we would watch the sun coming up. The White Hills made a backdrop for the beauty of the many fields and lanes which formed the view from our bedroom window; there was hardly a house in sight. There were cows in the field in front of Glebe House and I spent many hours naming them and talking to them without any fear, even putting my arms round their necks; they didn't seem to mind.

My happiest time was when my father said to me "Do you want to come for a walk tomorrow?" This meant a packed picnic lunch and a long walk across the footpaths and lanes and a climb up one of the hills. He knew I liked walking, as he did. He had belonged to a group of men before the war started, called 'The old Crocks' who went out hiking together at weekends. I loved being alone with him; he talked to me about the first world war, the trenches and the terrible times; he repeated again how my Uncle Ray had been blown up by a shell and the man next to him killed, and how he was scarred with big pits in his face from the shrapnel wounds.

He would tell me again how he and Mummy had been married on the 14th October, 1916 and how he had worked in the mobile laboratory just behind the lines in the First World War, making sure there was clean drinking water for the soldiers who were fighting. He told me of the fear and the terrible conditions, the mud and disease, the sadness and death. I learned the names associated with the First World War like Ypres, Lille, Passchendaele and the Somme. He also spoke to me of the people he had met, both during the war and before it when he visited France regularly. He spoke fluent French and this had helped him enormously. His mother, my Grandma Nagle, had been a governess to a wealthy family in France, Count and Countess Milly in Berzé la Ville, when she was young. My father not only knew the family from his visits when he was a young man, but their friends, and also the priest at the church became a close friend and Daddy would serve his Mass every day during his visits to France. This was interesting for me as I knew my grandmother as a rather difficult lady who was strong minded and always thought she was right. I remember her in a long black dress with her hair in some way wound closely round her head. She wore a bonnet-like hat and carried a black crocheted 'Dorothy bag' with crocheted black strings that went over her wrist. She died when I was fourteen, deaf and blind, fighting her way to church in the early hours of the morning through heavy rain in the dark. She went every day to the 6.30 am Mass at her local Catholic church in Lewisham. She would get up and go regardless of the right time. It was known that she sat on the church steps until the priest came and opened the door. The day she died she was crossing the main road, and failed to see or hear an oncoming tram, the driver did not see her until too late, even her large umbrella was black. She was taken to hospital and died later that day. It was a blessing and a relief for everyone as she would not receive the help she needed and was extremely independent. She was 89 years old.

During these walks with my father, I felt like an adult. I received none of the usual criticisms or comparisons, none of the usual corrections, like "Stand up straight, girl." or "Say your words properly" or "Walk properly". He became my beloved father who I knew really loved me; I cherished these times. It was during this time at Glebe House, that Princess Pat's Canadian Light Infantry came into all our lives. The Canadian soldiers were living in many of the large houses which had been taken over, one of which was known as 'Bloomers'. It was the house at the end of the pathway lined with high laurel bushes, which ran along the back of the churchyard. This was always our way home from the village. I was free to go out and there seemed to be little restriction on me unless there was a reason. My mother helped run what was known as the canteen in the evening, opened especially for the troops, serving food and drinks. I made friends with a group who ran a mobile canteen of a different nature. It supplied sweets, chocolates cigarettes and non-alcoholic drinks. I was twelve when I first met them, and they appointed me as their mascot. They would occasionally let me ride with them, which was against the rules, but they supplied me most days with chocolate and sweets which were very strictly rationed for the English. There was no fear from my mother and father that I talked to them and there was never any trouble in the village from any of them, only perhaps a little drunkenness now and again. My mother used to say they were lovely fellows, and they were.

I used also to spend time with Alice and Will Shaw. They loved me going in to see them at any time. She at first was not able to have children and was very upset about this as she said she would be too old, although to this day I have no idea how old she was then. One day they broke the news to me that they were going to have a baby. This for me was very exciting. I used to help her pick raspberry leaves to make raspberry tea, which she was convinced would help her have an easier birth; they were real country people with broad accents. Their family had originated from the West Country. I loved being with them and they numbered amongst my close friends. Between them and Winifred Booker at school I learnt a great deal about life. Will used to tease me when I talked about what I would like to do when I grew up. He would say, "Don't you worry my darlin' you'll be married by the time you're nineteen."

There was another company of Canadians who built a road for their own use, I think it was in case of invasion. It was called Canada Road and this went from top Nutfield southward, the name has now been changed. Margie and I also made friends with some of these soldiers; I was twelve or thirteen and my sister four years older. She liked me to go with her as a kind of chaperone I am sure. As the road they were building got longer so we had further to walk. Strangely, for some reason we were not encouraged to befriend these Canadians. I guess it was because their work was ordinary labour and dirty, or perhaps it was because my parents didn't know them. My father had given me strict instructions not to ride on their machinery, the tractors and bulldozers and lorries, which they sometimes had to take through the village. We used to duck down as we went through the village in their lorry in case anyone saw us who might tell tales.

Eddie MacIntaggart was the one that Margie liked, and Irish was the one who used to talk to me. It was all extremely harmless, and in actual fact it most probably did me a lot of good. They were great fun and always treated us with great respect. One Saturday we set out to see them when the road was nearly finished. We found it was almost too far to go, and we realised our friendships were coming to an end. As we took a short cut across the fields, on the opposite side of the village from where we lived, going south from the house, a German bomber came over very low and dropped a stick of bombs in a line quite near to us. When we heard it coming we threw ourselves to the ground. We had been too far from the village to hear the air-raid warning, if indeed there had been one. The bombs fell into very soft earth and consequently caused no damage at all except to leave fairly large craters. We ran and examined the one nearest us before turning tail and hurrying home. I think they were aiming for Redhill aerodrome, which was quite near. Our main concern, although we were very frightened, was that our mother should not know where we had been. I don't even now understand how our parents disciplined us, but we seemed to be trusted, which trust we obviously sometimes betrayed. I remember having great freedom for hours on end; however there were very strict rules about being home for meals, and being home in the evening for bedtime, which we always were.

We often experienced bombing even though we were supposed to be in a safe area. One night an unexploded bomb fell in the field at the front of Glebe House. The air-raid wardens came and told us to get dressed. We were taken up to the village and spent the night in 'Little Dormers' guest house, the owners, the Rudkins, were friends of ours. Another time we were in the village when the air-raid warning went and Mrs McCarthy took us into her cottage which was next door to the Crown Inn. We lay down on the floor under her front window as we listened to the bombers going over; if a bomb dropped near and the window was blown in the glass blew over you and you were less likely to be cut. The McCarthy's later won some money in the Irish sweepstake, and he bought a stable with some racehorses and also some horses for teaching riding. I went for riding lessons at their stables with Josie sometimes after we moved from Nutfield. Although she was still a bit bossy, I was closer friends with her than I ever had been before. I think it was most probably because we weren't living together in the same house.

When we looked across the beautiful countryside from Glebe House on a quiet day, it was hard to believe that there was a war on, but at night from my bedroom window we could see the fires from the bombing of London, lighting up the sky with a red glow, silhouetting the White Hills, which looked black and ominous. We also watched many dog fights during the day, between the Spitfires and Hurricanes, and the Messerschmitts, which took place over the fields and hills. Sometimes we would see one of them spiralling down leaving a trail of black smoke. My father was a member of the Home Guard and on these occasions he would don his uniform and go quickly on duty, in case he was needed. I suppose my parents must have been very worried about what happened to us, but I did not experience any feeling of over protectiveness. The Douglas's, who owned Glebe House, employed a cook, a butler and a maid at the beginning of the war, as well as the gardeners and the chauffeur. Mr and Mrs Hirsch, the butler and cook, were Austrian and had been at Glebe House many years. When I went to see my mother and father, in the early months of the war, I spent a great deal of time, as it were, below stairs. We were very much relegated to the servants' end of the house; evacuees were definitely placed in the servant category by the gentry. I think I gained quite an interest in cooking from watching Mrs Hirsch. She would make the pastry for Apfelstrudel and pull it and shake it until you could see through it. There was a big Aga cooker fuelled by coke and Mr Jack Shaw the gardener used to come in every morning and every night to look after the Aga and the central heating boiler. I soon got to understand the mysteries of the Aga as there was no other means of cooking. It was not long after the beginning of the war that two men came to the house and arrested Mr and Mrs Hirsch; it was a terrible day. They both cried and pleaded but to no avail; they had to pack up all their belongings and were taken to an internment camp. We all cried, and I remember feeling a great injustice was being done. My mother was very upset for she had come to know Mrs Hirsch very well as they shared the same kitchen, although my mother was always very careful not to cook when Mrs Hirsch was busy. They had got on well and were fond of each other. Mr Hirsch was very pedantic and did not like people to be in his way. Fortunately he was often working in the butler's pantry which was through the green baize door. He had black hair greased straight back from his forehead, and a little moustache. In the evening he wore a black suit with a black bow tie. In the mornings he wore a kind of striped jacket, often with a big white apron round him. I was never quite sure what he had to do in the mornings. There was a hatch from the butler's pantry to the kitchen through which he sometimes shouted orders to his wife in German, and she would run straight away, and quickly carry out a job for him. When he was off duty he would sit quietly and was ready to be nice to us, sometimes even helping us with our games.

My mother always had to ask Mrs Douglas for permission for us
to visit, before we went to live there, so I always felt I could easily
be in the way. I never saw Mr and Mrs Hirsch again after that
terrible day, or knew what happened to them. Ada the maid who
was Welsh cried for days, and never really recovered from the
shock. Mrs Douglas had never learnt to cook or even tried to cook
in her life. She used to talk to my mother about this great
disadvantage and my mother sometimes helped her when she was
struggling to even make a cup of tea. This happened particularly
when Mrs Bennet was off duty. Mrs Bennet was called in to fill
the gap, and life certainly started to change for both Mr and Mrs
Douglas. Ada could only manage so much work, and Mrs Bennet
herself only knew very ordinary cooking. Mrs Douglas often used
to come and watch my mother cooking and try and take some
lessons from her. Donald Bennet and I used to play in the kitchen
cutting out puppet theatres from cornflake packets, and making
puppets. We would sometimes give a performance for anyone who
had the patience to watch and listen. Donald and I and sometimes
a young nephew of the Shaw's called Tony, who came to stay in the
holidays, would play in the fields and at hay-making time would
be allowed to help. Sometimes we would play in the barn. It was
great fun; we could jump from a kind of gallery into the deep hay
beneath. The barn only had three sides, one side was open, or
perhaps it had a door which pulled across, I can't remember. One
day Donald produced a magnifying glass which had been swapped
for some of my chocolate with a boy in his class. Donald was not
allowed to eat sweets or chocolate because of his diabetes, but he
had to carry some with him or some biscuits, in case he had what
we knew as a low; I didn't know what that meant. He showed us
how, by letting the sun's rays shine through the glass you could

actually set fire to a piece of paper. I had never seen anything like this before. We all were very excited fighting over who could have the next turn. Getting more and more daring until the sun had gone down behind the barn. We all went home for our supper and to bed as usual. Imagine my horror, when we were awakened by unusual noises, engines running and loud voices, to see flames from the area of the barn; I was terrified. I had said nothing at home about the magnifying glass as I think we most probably knew it was a dangerous game, but none of us had reckoned on setting fire to anything that mattered. My parents made us go back to bed when everything settled down and first thing in the morning we heard from Mrs Bennet that the barn was burnt to the ground. No one knew if we had been seen playing in the barn the day before although it was a known fact we sometimes did. We had decided at a hasty meeting to deny any knowledge of what had happened. We were terrified when individually we were cross questioned by Mr Jack Shaw, Tony's uncle. We had been seen in the barn, so we all said we hadn't seen anything unusual. It seemed that we were believed as no more was said to us. I felt terrible guilt as I was also the oldest one of the three. The first thing we did was to take our fishing nets to Martin's pond, another exciting place where we often played, and Donald threw his magnifying glass into the water as far as it would go. It was decided by the powers that be that the hot sun had caused instantaneous combustion. I remember not understanding quite what it meant, but felt it was best not to take too much interest. I knew in my heart that we had caused the fire.

Sometimes when Mr and Mrs Douglas were in residence I would help Ada do the work in the bedrooms. I helped her make the beds, and clean. It was a new experience for me to see the beautifully furnished rooms with everything in place, just like a museum. Without Ada I was forbidden to go through the green baize door. When the family was away which was quite often, I would feel the whole place belonged to me. At these times we were allowed to play tennis on the grass court, which was sometimes kept in very good condition, and sometimes quite neglected. We also could explore round the two large lakes, one drained into the other through a sluice gate. I was afraid to go round the lower lake because it was very overgrown and you could hear the snakes dropping into the water as you disturbed them. One day we saw an adder, with black and yellow V shapes all the way down its back. I was quite afraid to go to the lakes on my own in the summer, in winter it was different, you could see where you were going more plainly because the undergrowth had died away. When the weather was very cold and the lakes froze I borrowed skates, I can't now remember from whom. We had to be very careful because the ice became very rough and sometimes it was too thin. One day my sister Margie came home and said she had found a better lake for skating, it was smoother and more fun. We went there together with her friend Eileen to investigate. Margie was much more daring than me, she skated right across the lake, which was the other side of Redhill, and went straight through the ice and got all her clothes wet. She had to travel back on the bus with us like it with everyone looking; I remember being very embarrassed. My mother was very cross with us for being so careless and irresponsible; fortunately the lake had not been very deep. As far as I remember Margie did not suffer any further consequences except we were not allowed to go there again.

During all this time I went to church on Sunday morning with my family and the children from my father's school that were still living in Nutfield. There were also people from the village, some who had previously been going to St Joseph's church in Redhill and others who suddenly remembered that they were Catholic; we were a strange mixture but I really enjoyed it. I loved everything to do with going to church. We would sometimes go to Benediction in Redhill on Sunday evening and walk home afterwards, it was about three miles. Sadly I never imagined myself in any way close to God. I knew that everyone else was when they bowed their heads or sang. I would sometimes watch my mother when she was praying in church, and wondered what she would think if she knew about all my dreadful lies. The thing is that once you have done things that you reckon in your own mind are unforgivable, it doesn't seem to matter if you do some more, and this is what happened. I stopped trying to get good grades at school. The subjects I was good at without doing any work I continued to do quite well with and my marks were not too bad. Nobody seemed to notice I was barely working; in other subjects I was really failing badly. I was friends with a group of very clever girls and also some who didn't care too much about their work, so I always felt I was in good company. On Friday afternoon we had what was called activities and several of us joined the Greek Dancing class. We had to make special flowing dresses in our needlework lessons. If Friday afternoon was fine and not cold we would go out on the front lawn. It did not take us long to notice that our teacher who came to the school only for this lesson never called a roll. Once we were outside we could slip into the area known as the shrubbery which ran along the inside of the front wall. This area was forbidden to all but the fifth and sixth forms; it was thickly wooded with trees and shrubs. We would quickly change into our clothes which we put in our satchels, and slip out of the front gate which was completely hidden from view from the school; we were never once caught.

We all received a report at the end of each term which had to go home to our parents for a signature. I was adept at doing both my mother and father's signature. My sister and I used to practise them for fun without any ulterior motive. For two terms I was so ashamed of my report in some subjects that I was really afraid for my parents to see it so I signed my mother's name and no one noticed. My mother and father were quite happy to accept a yearly report. I think the fact that we were at war altered everyone's way of thinking. I felt at that time that my parents were glad if we were all safe. My sister Margie had already been moved to another school in Redhill because she was not working at Reigate County School. She wanted to be a nurse and my parents were afraid she would not pass her exams with a high enough grade to qualify. It was more important apparently for her as she was four years older than me. I was too ashamed to have this happen to me so just kept my head above water, hoping that no one noticed. Things were fairly difficult at this time, we had many air-raids and we spent quite a large proportion of our time in the Reigate caves, an entrance to which was opened especially in the school grounds. These caves extended under the whole of Reigate. To begin with it was great fun. Lessons were abandoned and we sang many songs and played games. The sand was thick underfoot, and the smell was strong and musty like an old cellar. After a while it was found that the vibrations from the singing were causing sand falls from the roof. In some areas this was quite considerable. Several areas were shored up and we had to sit still on benches set along each side of one of the hundreds of tunnels which was allotted to us. We took our books with us and lessons were resumed. Even here we quickly learned that if we went in first and sat furthest away from the teacher, she would not be able to see what we were doing. We would sneak off, sometimes two, sometimes three of us, and go exploring. This was absolutely forbidden. The tunnels were complex and I believe in times gone by, people have been lost and died. At least that is what we were told. I was never the leader, I was too afraid, but I would follow. We had to unhook a chain which cut off the dangerous areas or as we found out areas where other people had access. There were many entrances to the caves, and they were very securely monitored. We would plot our route remembering which way we had turned, it was like a maze. One day we came across beds of mushrooms which were possibly being grown commercially, but we didn't dare ask anyone. It was towards the end of the summer term, when I was almost fifteen, that many changes took place.

The school for all but the examination classes closed very early for the summer because of the frequency of the air-raid warnings, and the fact that the caves were becoming more and more dangerous from predicted and actual sand falls. Josie was teaching and was living in Purley with an old school friend named Joan Mortelman, whose father had been at college with my father. They had a house in Purley. We knew the family very well. My mother and father had visited and thought Purley would be a pleasant place to live. Almost all the evacuees had returned to London, and I learned that they realised, as parents always seem to, that I was doing very little at school. They sold their house in Honor Oak Park to the senior teacher at my father's school, to whom they had rented it when he was bombed out of his own house. He had been running the school in London for those children who had not been evacuated. A house that was suitable in Purley was quickly found, and without my knowing very much about it although I had visited Purley once, we packed up our entire belongings, said goodbye to Nutfield and all our friends, and moved. My mother and father had booked me into school, not the Notre Dame convent at Southwark, where my sisters had been before the war, and where I should have gone in 1939, but the Ursuline convent at Greenwich. I was to start at the beginning of the winter term in September.

I had no friends and was very lonely. The people next door invited us in the day we moved. We had no electricity and we could not find anything we wanted to wear, we felt really scruffy because their house so was beautiful. Mr Ralphs had been Chief Education Officer in Hong Kong before he retired, and their house was filled with Chinese treasures, many stored in glass cases and shown off by perfectly placed concealed lighting. The carpets were thick pile and the atmosphere was very opulent. Mrs Ralphs had Parkinson's disease and she could do very little, but Mr Ralphs had prepared some dainty snacks and coffee, and we were soon hemmed in by occasional tables, unable to move. My sister Margie by now had gone to a London Hospital to start nursing training. I think we all wondered that night how we would cope with our neighbours. They seemed quite removed from the reality that we knew. They spent the evening praising their wonderful only son Edwin who was away fighting in the east. He was a commissioned officer in the army.

We soon found out there was a young people's club which met

on Sunday evenings in the church hall, which was really a hut. My mother and father approved because it was attached to the church so I went to introduce myself and found that there were seven regular members, five boys and two girls, all older than myself and all working except one of the boys who was still at school. It didn't seem to matter that I was a year younger than the youngest. They quickly accepted me and took me under their wing so we became great friends. We went hiking at the weekends, and sometimes went to church socials in the district, sometimes to the cinema, and on Sunday evenings we played table tennis and danced to a gramophone; if anyone felt like organising, we played games. Everybody seemed to be talented, and we entertained ourselves with no problem. Very often others would join us, mostly friends of the boys. This group became a very significant part of my life and my mother was very happy for me to be friends with them because they were all Catholics, and she came to know most of their parents at church. Nevertheless, I was very bored during the daytime. I sometimes did some sewing, going to London and buying remnants of material, and making a blouse or a dress, which I enjoyed, I did some knitting, and helped my mother a bit.

One day when Josie was staying with us, I was pouring out my heart to her, telling her how bored I was, when she said to me "Why don't you get a job?" I was astonished, but although I was sure I did not have enough education to do a job, it seemed a wonderful means of escape and I saw it as a way forward. There was also another strong pull to this idea. If I could find a job in London, I could travel on the 8.04am train to London Bridge which some of my new-found friends travelled on. Although I was only fourteen, it was then within the law to leave school at that age. My spirits rose, but I knew that my mother would not approve of this idea. Josie and I decided not to say anything until it was settled. We scoured the papers and soon found an advertisement by Barclays Bank. They needed young people to train as comptometer operators. The training was in London for three weeks, and then the trainee was appointed to a local Barclay's bank. Letters were written, under Josie's guidance, and they were signed and sent. Within no time at all I was accepted without an interview, and was due to start on the training course the following Monday. The first hurdle was to tell my mother and father. My mother was horrified. Her plan was for me to complete my education at school and college; her main aim was to provide security for all three of her daughters. She was very angry and determined to stop me going. The office was at Goodge Street so I would have to go to Charing Cross Station and get the under-ground to Goodge Street. My father was more equable, he was inclined to believe that if I was allowed to try I would get fed up and leave but in my heart I knew I would not. It all seemed so exciting; at last I was going to grow up. I had worked everything out, and the 8.04 to London Bridge would get me there in time. There was no fast train through to Charing Cross in the morning anyway. All my friends thought it was a great idea. I determined that nothing was going to put me off what I had planned. My mother was displeased with me and verbalised her anger, but I blocked out her words. I had some money saved in the Post office, and I drew out sufficient for a weekly season ticket and to buy something for my lunch. I trusted that my mother would give me a dinner in the evening. She was very upset and the atmosphere was tense. Monday came and I was up early to meet my friends at the station. I had my clothes ready and a shoulder handbag which had been given to me as a present; I felt very grown up. I presented myself at Barclay's training centre in Goodge Street. I was a little disappointed as our 'office' was screened off at the end of a kind of warehouse. It was rather dirty and certainly not romantic. I had never learned to type, and this was obviously a disadvantage. The supervisor Miss Hinckley, a rather severely dressed middle-aged lady was not very pleased with my progress the first day, but I was not put off. I made friends with one or two people, mostly a year or two older than myself. We bought a sandwich and a cup of coffee for our lunch in a snack bar and my first day was wonderful. No more school and thirty five shillings all to myself at the end of the week, to be increased by five shillings when I was trained. Absolutely wonderful!

My mother was so angry when I arrived home that I really wondered how I was going to cope. She had however kept me a dinner, which was on a plate over a saucepan of hot water. I thought she could not possibly be going to put me out of the house. My father sat in his chair and said nothing. The following day was similar; I met my friends on the 8.04 and told them all that had happened. In the evening my mother was still cross, going on at me and nagging. The only difference was that I felt Miss Hinckley was picking on me rather a lot. There was no comparison with other people as we were all at different stages of training and I was the only newcomer. She questioned me in a loud voice across the shambles of the office where we were all sitting at our machines... "Miss Nagle, if you didn't learn to type, did you never learn to play the piano?" finishing with, "Use your fingers more quickly, you're very slow."... in what I took to be a slight Scottish accent. I didn't like her, but after all it was only for three weeks. My difficulty was that if I hurried, I typed in the rows of figures incorrectly, and then when I pressed the star which confirmed correct addition, it wouldn't work and I had to start again. It was very boring but I was very determined. Obviously my piano lessons hadn't helped me. My mother was equally angry in the evening, and my father silent except for the usual greeting, as if nothing had happened.

I went early to my room and wondered if I could keep it up for three weeks. Josie had gone and I felt very alone. The third day Miss Hinckley hardly left me alone, breathing down my neck and showing me new methods and things I must do when I was sure I had not mastered the first properly. I began to think perhaps I was in the wrong place after all. I comforted myself with the fact that after three weeks I would have my position in Barclay's Bank with no one to bother me. In the evening when I arrived home, everything was different. My mother was nice to me; she even asked me how I got on and my father was less silent. I did not dare tell the truth about how I really felt. That was most probably what they wanted to hear. By Friday evening when I had really come to dislike Miss Hinckley in every way, both her voice and her manner, even her appearance, she called me into her office, just before we were due to leave and chanted "Miss Nagle" in her sing-song voice, "we are so sorry you will not be coming in on Monday, your mother has telephoned to say you are going back to school, here is your money for the week, and I do hope you get on well." I had no words. A mixture of anger and relief filled me. My mother had played a crafty trick on me, but I was amazed how pleased I felt. No more boring days, with Miss Hinckley scolding me. Never again would I have to sit in this noisy smelly place with all these rotten machines that I didn't understand and didn't even want to. No more days just sitting, only being able to move if you went to the toilet and even being reprimanded if it seemed to be too often, and no more having to listen to "Remember Miss Nagle, you are in business now, not at school."

My mother was waiting for me with dinner and a smile but I was not pleased with her, and she certainly was not going to experience my relief. However, she made a good suggestion. "Why don't you spend your money on some food for a party for your friends? I'll help you get it ready." I telephoned my best friend Betty from Reigate County School who was now at the City of London School for girls. She was coming anyway in the evening to stay for the weekend; she had already met all my new friends. We made a lot of telephone calls from our house, and we found ten people who could come. Betty and I went to Sainsbury's on Saturday morning and bought slices of cold pork pie with boiled egg in the middle, salad vegetables, rolls and butter, fruit, and two quart bottles of cider. My mother helped us lay the table with her best cutlery. It was just large enough to seat everyone, pulled out to its full length. We used her best tablecloth and it all looked superb. She also gave us a quart of beer for the older boys. All the boys drank beer but she did not know this. We made up individual plates of food, on the best china, and it looked lovely. My mother helped us make the fruit salad and she made some of her now famous 'Bel cream.' It was the best party ever. My mother and father went out to play cards with some friends at the beginning of the evening, telling us to stack all the plates etc. in the kitchen. When they came home they washed up everything between them.

I had learned my lesson, and was really pleased to be good friends with my mother again. When she took me to the convent just before the term started, Mother Mary Henry Pendleberry the headmistress said to me. "Your mother tells me you have had a little adventure in the holidays, is that right?" I thought it best not to comment and sat very silently, she was a very awesome lady. I started school at the end of September and settled down with enthusiasm. My mother and I often laughed and joked in the following years about my job with Barclay's bank. When later in life I saw the comptometers rattling away, before the computer age, I was always grateful to my mother for her love and wisdom, even though I could not recognise it at the time. In years to come I saw that God worked like that, with wisdom, love and patience, through many people although I thought maybe my mother interfered with the process a bit. I never knew if my sister owned up to her part in my adventure. If she did, it was sorted out privately without my knowledge.

Chapter Seven

Amazing Grace

After Christopher's wonderful recovery, we settled back in England very contentedly. Peter returned to his job in the Central Office of Information and we moved to a larger house the following year for the birth of our third child Clare in 1959. When Clare was eighteen months old it was again my sister Josie who encouraged me to go back to teaching. I had been teaching at the Ursuline Convent, where I went to school, for the three years prior to my marriage. I had been requested by the headmistress, who was then Sister Anthony, to take up a position there as soon as I had completed the three years at college. It was seven years since I had stood in front of a class and I felt quite nervous at the prospect. We engaged an 'au pair' girl from Austria using a Croydon agency, her name was Erika and she was a seventeen year old gem. She stayed for thirteen months and was the first of a stream of au pair girls who came for the next ten years or so. I found a position as a part-time teacher in a local Church of England school, St. Andrew's, which was very convenient. They were so in need that they even changed the timetable to accommodate me so that I could teach every afternoon, this boosted my confidence enormously. I stayed at St Andrew's School for the next nineteen and a half years. This was a very happy and productive time. As well as the cookery programme I was able to create my own timetable which included relationships, marriage, conception, development, birth and care of a baby, as well as many other aspects. Fourth-year boys and girls enjoyed this course. I also witnessed and enjoyed the building of a beautiful new school.

It was during 1961 that my mother died. She had been ill and depressed for a long time, and I did not know what to do to help her. She had been in and out of hospital and could not seem to get any better. My sister Margie lived nearest to her and visited her and looked after her washing and other personal things. I was an hour or more away by car and as we only had a motor caravan, which Peter took to London each day, my visits were limited to the weekend. I felt sometimes that Mummy was so ill that she wasn't interested in anything, even ourselves or our children. Daddy had great faith and looked after her wonderfully. It was a very sad time and I wanted her to be the same as she always had been; I found it very difficult to cope with the change. During the summer of that year Peter and I and the children went on holiday to Devon, to a small hotel with Margie and Josie and Margie's husband Norman, and their children. Either we phoned my father each night or he phoned us, to give us news of my mother. I think we could tell from my father's voice that Mummy was worse, but Daddy was determined that we should not come home before the end of our holiday. We drove back from Devon on the Saturday and arrived home late as the traffic was very congested. We went to the hospital on Sunday to see my mother and although she was very ill, and had been given the sacrament of the sick for the dying which then was only administered if there was little hope of recovery, she was remarkably lucid. I held a cup of tea for her to sip, and she asked me about Clare and the two boys, and I felt she was just like the mother I remembered. I had found her illness really difficult to bear and I had felt helpless and useless. It was my sisters who had taken control. That night at midnight Mummy died, very peacefully. At the funeral my father said to us as we were crying in the car on the way to the cemetery, "Why are you crying? Mummy is happy now and in the best place, where is your faith?" I have never forgotten these words and although I grieved a lot with and without tears, those words stayed with me.

In September 1962 our fourth child Paul John Alexander was born. Alexander was my father's second name. I had Paul at home, and the story of his birth is told in a later chapter relating to our family doctor, Kelly Tighe. Paul was a lovely baby, very good natured and happy. All the children had been good, but I think that Paul's good nature was partly due to my previous experience of having children. I took maternity leave and returned to school in the New Year of 1963. It was in this year, and the following year that I had what I recognised to be two clear encounters with God, direct answer to prayer, that left me in no doubt that God had his eye on me, not only that, but he continued to pursue me. By this time I was sharing my teaching with a colleague Jeane Spriggs, with whom I became close friends. We worked well together doing one full-time job between us. We shared and planned our own syllabus the whole time I was at this school. In July 1963 Jeane invited me to go in and see her second year exam results. We were teaching Home Economics in an old house which was fifteen minutes walk from the main school, and this group were mostly boys. The class had been doing a cookery course and some of them were very talented. Jeane had told me a little bit about them over the months and as they were going to be my pupils the following September I was more than interested. I had a little chat with each pupil as I went round the room. There were two boys in the class from a local children's home, Shirley Oaks, now the site of a private hospital and a housing estate. Their names were Alan and David. Alan had come top with excellent marks. As I stopped to speak to Alan I felt a great ease in talking to him. He was a real London cockney, and in spite of the wide difference in our ages and the fact that I was teacher and he was pupil, we had a special rapport, and I think we both knew. In talking to Alan much later about this, he also experienced it. He told me that he and three others from Laburnum Cottage where he lived at Shirley Oaks were going to Switzerland for their summer holiday, and that he was looking forward to it very much.

I came to know that he was one of a family of five children, whose mother had left them when the youngest, Sylvia, was six and a half months old. The eldest boy Philip was already at our school in the fifth year and I realised when I heard the family name that I knew him slightly although I did not ever teach him. That August when Paul was eleven months old, we went to Spain in our carefully adapted motor-caravan. Peter had altered the back so that Paul had a safe cot between the two back cupboards and behind the rear seat. Its main feature was a wire window inside the back door which opened upwards, allowing Paul to see everything that was going on when we were stationary, but it also allowed a draught of cool air over him when the weather was very hot. It was a superb innovation. Every spare place in the vehicle was filled with disposable nappies, and tins of baby food, as well as the usual tins of meat and butter etc. for the rest of us.

We had a really wonderful holiday with all our children and a close friend of ours named Dennis, who was Peter's 'best man'. I thought no more about school until we started again in September. The third-year class worked very well, they were cooperative and keen. Alan, who worked very quickly, would, without invitation, stay after class had finished at the end of the afternoon to help with the many sorting out and clearing up jobs that accrued. On the whole he worked on in silence, but when it came time for him to go, he would talk to me about his family, and his hopes and desires. He hardly ever saw his father and it was obvious that he would like to. His mother came to the children's home very occasionally on Sunday to see him. The rest of his family except Philip lived with him in Laburnum Cottage with Miss Farrell, who looked after them with a variety of assistants. Philip was in a cottage for older boys. There were other children as well in Laburnum, about twelve altogether.

After a few weeks I had the idea that it might be good for Alan and David to come and spend a day with our family. When I suggested it to Peter everyone approved and Dennis agreed to come to lunch and help us. The two boys had exact instructions to get to the house and I was assured by them that they would be given money for their fare. They were to arrive at twelve thirty for Sunday dinner and we planned for them to do some special cooking which I knew they would both enjoy. The day came and all our children including our au pair girl Sabina who was from Berlin, were very excited, and were looking forward to meeting their new friends. However, one o'clock came and went, one thirty came and went. I decided to phone the children's home and find out what had happened. It was difficult first of all to get through to the right place, then I spoke to someone who was looking after Laburnum Cottage while Miss Farrell was off duty. She knew very little of what was happening. She did, however know that Alan was ill and was in the sick bay, which was in another part of the grounds. She did not even know David who lived in another cottage. I managed to get through to the sick bay and received permission to see Alan. We could not understand why no one had tried to telephone. We ate our dinner very quickly and piled into the motor caravan leaving Paul with Sabina. When we arrived at Shirley Oaks we had to pass through a security check at the entrance Lodge where we were directed to the sick bay. Shirley Oaks comprised twelve or thirteen different cottages all named after flowers. There was a Community Centre where parties were organised and larger events held. It was like a little town. We eventually reached the sick bay to find Alan in bed and evidently in the middle of a bad bilious attack. The nurse in charge thought it had been brought about by nerves. Alan had evidently been looking forward to coming to see us and was very disappointed. He had not been able to phone himself and no one had found our phone number. David had felt unable to come without Alan. I learned a great deal that day. I had presumed so much from Alan's confident behaviour. He was desperately upset and thought he had missed his chance. I found out later that he had never made a telephone call in his life, and had not known how to deal with the situation. Because someone fairly new to the establishment was looking after the children in Laburnum cottage, it had not been apparent to her that anyone needed to be notified. David actually often went to stay with his aunt in London but Alan never went anywhere. We weren't allowed to stay long with Alan but planned that they would both come and see us in two weeks. He had to stay the following Sunday in case his mother came. Alan and his family would wait at the gate every second week, until the time for visitors to arrive had passed by. Sometimes she came and sometimes she didn't.

Everything worked out well the next time. We prepared especially nice meals and everyone who was old enough, (that was everyone except Paul), did some cooking. We played some games and took the two boys home just in time for bed, tired and happy. During the lesson the next week when there was a quiet moment and no one listening Alan said to me "Will I be able to come again?" It was just a few weeks before half term. I already knew David was going to his aunt. I remember saying that I was sure he would be able to, thinking that I would ask Peter if he could come and stay at least one or two nights over half term. Peter agreed that it would be a good idea. I planned to put Alan in the room where our two older boys, Gerard and Christopher were sleeping. They all seemed to get on well, even though Alan was older. One of our boys would be quite happy to sleep in a sleeping bag on the lilo and let Alan have his bed and I saw no problem. I invited Alan and he was delighted to accept. His only proviso was that if his father invited him for half term, he would have to refuse our invitation. As he said this I could see that it was wishful thinking as his father never invited him. The only time they went to stay with him was for one night at Christmas. Alan longed to be with his father who could do no wrong in his eyes. I did come to know that his father was living with Ann, who was a very kind person. She had actually taken on all five children when she first moved in with Alan's father. She had a daughter of her own and the work and strain was too much for her. She had a breakdown, and all of the children had gone to Shirley Oaks. Alan's early memories of his father were not good; he had been punished with the strap at the age of seven and remembered it plainly. He thought he must have deserved to be beaten. He had no clear memory of home before this, only rows and punishments. His father was in the Territorial Army and Alan loved him, he was Alan's hero.

I phoned Laburnum Cottage to find out how we would set about making our invitation known. Miss Farrell said she would have to speak to Alan's Welfare Officer as the social worker was then called. I still saw no problem ahead. It was when I received a letter from Mr Nelson the Welfare Officer, asking if he could come and see me, that I began to be slightly concerned. An appointment was made, and Mr Nelson came to visit. He was a pleasant, friendly man, who knew Alan well. He wanted to inspect the room where Alan was to sleep, as well as to see the kitchen and the living rooms. I took him to the boys' bedroom which was clean and reasonably tidy, and I explained to him my plan. It was a horrible moment and I felt so totally inadequate. He explained to me that the only way that Alan would be allowed to come and stay was if we had a single room for him alone, with a permanent bed with proper sheets and bedclothes, not a sleeping bag. My spirits dropped. We did indeed have a spare bedroom, and we had a bed which Peter's mother had given to us. We had just bought twin beds for the boys' room and had not had the money for anything else. Each month we were just in the red at the bank, and although we lived quite well we had no spare money. Mr Nelson said that he was really sorry but he had no authority to allow a child in care to stay in a house without the proper arrangements, and that even if I managed to get sorted out, time was short, as half-term was almost upon us. I was desperately upset as we seemed to have made all the arrangements, even planning what we were going to do. It had not entered my head that my house would not be suitable for a boy who had almost nothing. To begin with, I felt angry and cheated. I knew that I could not just go out and buy blankets and pillows. It sounds incredible now, but we were on a really tight budget as far as capital expenditure was concerned and there was also quite a lot of pride in me as well. I was very resentful. I did not know how I could possibly explain all this to Alan, but of course, I had to find a way and he was very disappointed. As I took some time to think about it all, actually voicing my feelings quietly within me, possibly to God, I suddenly I had an idea, which I shared with Peter. I decided to pray very positively about the situation. I knew God did answer prayer, I was not so sure about *my* prayer. The prayer I intended praying was not going to be like the prayers I said in church by rote, or like those we had said at school when we had to go to chapel, they were going to be special, and I was going to kneel down, not at night in a routine of going to bed, but in the day time, so that I and God knew it was special. It had to be a prayer of faith; prayer at that time did not play a great part in my life, and I felt quite excited at the prospect. I think I had already started praying inside myself about saying a right kind of prayer, whatever that was supposed to be.

I chose my time, when all was quiet in the house, knelt down and found myself pouring my heart out to God. I was telling him how unfair it all was that this had happened, how resentful I was that someone with authority could come along and change all our carefully made plans. I told him that all I wanted was to give Alan a good half-term holiday, so that he could have a happy time like my own children. It was a good moan, but in my heart I felt God was listening. On the evidence that he had heard Sister Cullen, all those years before, I begged him to do something about it all. Afterwards I felt very at peace. We had become really fond of Alan and could see his desperate need to be wanted. He definitely felt rejected by his own family, but was proud and very self-contained. This showed itself in many ways; one was that he was unable to say 'thank you' to us at home. He was able to write it in a polite letter which he had learnt to do, and which was possibly supervised. He could also say thank you at school quite easily. When it came to the personal level of saying thank you, he found it impossible.

At that time in our church there was a kind of lottery running based on the football results shared with some other churches in the district. I paid a shilling every week to a friend opposite, and Peter and I sometimes had the job of taking the money and names down to Merstham where the scheme was organised. It was put into action originally to make money for church building and it came to an end as the churches realised that it was not a very good way of raising money to finance their needs, even though it was lucrative. That Saturday was an extraordinary day. I had rarely won anything, but that night I won the first prize of fifty pounds, which was quite a lot of money in those days. I did first say a big "Thank you" to God. I knew that it was his answer, although I have to admit that I was quite amazed at the speed and the method. I went straight to Allders in Croydon on the Monday morning, and bought two blankets, two pillows and sheets and pillowcases. What joy! I cleaned the spare bedroom with all the energy I

could muster. I made up the bed, and realised that I would not
have to disappoint Alan. I telephoned Mr Nelson and arranged for
him to come and inspect.

That half-term was the beginning of many weekends, weeks and
holidays that Alan spent with us and he became one of the
family. There were many difficulties which had to be overcome
on all sides. Both he and I can now laugh over the things that
happened, some of them not easy to deal with. One of the big
pressures on him was that he did not want any of the pupils at the
school to know that he came to stay with 'teacher', and that he
was living with us for six days in every week. The one proviso the
council made was that he slept in his cottage for one night in seven;
this kept his place for him. It was very difficult to keep this a secret
but Alan managed it, and although the Headmaster and all the staff
knew, and his brothers and sisters and the children in Laburnum
Cottage knew, no pupil, certainly in his own class, ever found out.
It was a secret kept in an amazing way. To this day I don't know if
Alan threatened anyone or whether it was by the grace of God. He
had a great dignity at school in the way he conducted himself and
he never expected any favour from me in my professional capacity.
He worked hard and treated me at school as he had before he
ever came to the house, although at home of course our relationship
was quite different. I began to think a lot about God and who he
was and how he looked after things. I think I most probably started
chatting to Him about my life more than I now remember, but I
still did not feel forgiven. I felt tolerated!

Life was going on gently, and in April 1964 when Paul was nineteen
months old and Clare was just five, we had some trouble with our

bathroom taps. It had been difficult to turn them right off, and the plumber from the Water Board came to help. In those days the Water Board sent someone at a phone call request with no extra charge, to give advice and put basic things in order, like changing washers and attending to leaks in an emergency. This man had been before to change washers, but this time his verdict was disastrous for us. He could not stop the water leaking from the bathroom cold tap, he said we would need new taps, but because so much water was escaping, he was bound to seal the taps so that we could not use them. However, that was not all. He explained that because the house had been built in 1906, and the piping to the bathroom was original, we would not only need new taps, but new pipes, and therefore a new bath and wash-basin. This was devastating news for us. Our budget was extended as far as possible and we could see no way that we could afford a new bathroom. With four young children, the youngest not yet two, as well as Alan, I could see no way forward. I bathed Paul and Clare in the kitchen sink, and took buckets of water to tip in the bath upstairs for Gerard and Christopher and Alan. We adults had to manage as best we could. It was not easy, and there seemed to be no end to it.

I said to Peter that I was going to pray. I chose my time and again knelt down. Somehow kneeling made me feel I meant what I was saying. I also thought God would know that it was special. Again I poured out my heart about all the difficulties, defending the man from the Water Board, explaining that it was not his fault and that in fact it wasn't anybody's fault. I did not ask for money and I could not see how God could work things out. I just asked him to please help us. I did not at this stage of my life think about praying these very serious kinds of prayer to Jesus. I realised that most Catholics never said the name of Jesus in conversation; they always called Jesus 'Our Lord.' I felt comfortable praying to God the Father for some reason, and found praying to Jesus more difficult. I saw God the Father as father and mother, an understanding being who must surely be approachable. I knew in theory that Jesus had died for me, but basically wished he hadn't because I felt guilty. I remember wishing that the Jews had been nicer to him. It was 1971, when I wrote the following poem and obviously still did not understand that Jesus had to die for us because it was the plan of God, because of his great love for us. This message from the gospels had not yet filtered through to me. I still had a great deal to go through before I began to realise how great God's love was for me.

JESUS 1971

I would have loved you Jesus, had I been there,
And seen you, God made man,
At your mother's breast in Bethlehem.
I would have helped you Jesus, had I been there,
On Calvary, King of Kings,
And tried to stop them killing you.
I would have knelt, dear Jesus, had I been there,
And seen you, risen from the dead .....triumphant,
At the tomb, like Mary Magdalene.
But now I am here, and so are you,
In homeless, hungry, orphaned, aged, ill.
I would have loved you Jesus, but just now,
Time is short ... floors to clean, dinner to cook,
clothes to buy... and still you wait.
Will you wait, dear Jesus, 'til I have time to love you?
Or will it be too late?

It was as late as 1975 when the truth started to be real for me. Although I had learnt off by heart automatically and knew in my head all these things, my heart had not known the wonderful thing Jesus had done for me.

It was Thursday of the following week April 15th 1964 at 7.15pm, rain was beating down, it had become very dark early and the thunder and flashes of lightning were frightening. Clare and Paul were fast asleep in bed, and Gerard and Christopher were watching the television in their dressing gowns. Petra, the current German au pair girl from Berlin had just poached herself an egg and made some toast, as she had eaten a main meal at midday. She had left her egg above the stove to keep hot while she went in to chat for a moment with the boys, and tell Christopher that he had another fifteen minutes before bed. The remainder of the dinner, a beef casserole that I had cooked for the children and myself was keeping hot for Peter, who had just arrived home from London. Toffee our dog was cowering in her bed, terrified by the storm, when suddenly there was a deafening bang, an explosion like a bomb, then terrible crashing and rumbling. The lights went out and all the things on the gas stove blew across the kitchen. I ran to the hall amidst clouds of dust and smoke, the ceilings were down in the hall and over the stairs. Petra ran out from the sitting room holding her hand on her ear, to say the television had blown up but that the boys were alright. I tried to scramble up the stairs over the slabs of plaster and wall, to get to Clare and Paul. I ran first to Paul who was in a large cot in our bedroom quite near the window. The wind and rain were blowing through the window frames where the glass was missing, but fortunately the glass had blown outward. Paul was covered with pieces of plaster. I

thought at first that he was dead, I quickly lifted him up, and
he stretched and groaned, and I could see that he was okay. He
had been covered tightly with blankets and only his head was
exposed. I put him back quickly and ran into Clare's room. Her
bed was well away from the window, but again all the glass had
blown outward; it was the ceiling at the window end of the room
that had come down, the area over her bed was intact. She was
deeply asleep and unhurt. I ran then to see what other damage
there was, I had seen fires burning. There was a large fire in the
floor outside the bathroom; I was just in time to stop Petra pouring
a bucket of water over it, she did not understand about the danger
of water and electrical fires. I suppose somewhere in my past this
had penetrated my mind. I told her to take Gerard and Christopher
to safety outside the front door, and make sure that someone had
dialled 999 to call the fire-brigade. I ran to get the heavy bedspread
off my bed and flung it over the fire, but it wasn't entirely
quenched, it was burning fiercely. Peter was running up the stairs
with our only fire extinguisher which we kept in the motor-
caravan. He sprayed it over the fire outside the bathroom and over
the fire burning in the wall. They were immediately extinguished.
He ran up to the third floor to Petra's bedroom where there were
two storage rooms and reported the roof and joists and doors were
damaged and that there were many little fires; it was as if we
had rehearsed our movements. There was absolutely no panic.

At this moment, the fire-brigade arrived, just three minutes
had passed. They had heard the explosion and were sitting on their
fire engine, waiting for an address. I think about four people had
phoned 999 as soon as they had seen which house was damaged.
The fire brigade were marvellous. They went in an orderly manner,

from top to bottom of the house putting out all the little fires that had started, another one turned off the electricity and the gas, which unbeknown to us was of course leaking everywhere. I wanted to wake the two younger children and take them out of the house, but I was advised that as long as we did not light a live flame, the danger was now over, that it was better to let them sleep than frighten them. The fire officer in charge posted one man on the landing. He stayed the whole evening between the two rooms, doing nothing but watching the children were safe, ready to call me if either awoke. He assured me he would not leave them.

Neighbours were arriving with storm lamps and blankets, everyone wanted to help. Our neighbour Connie, who lived opposite and who we knew very well, (she had been with my mother when I was born) took charge of our lodger Mr Mitchell, whose room in the front was the worst damaged. He was very dazed. The fireman in charge took control and allowed no one into the house. Another tipped out the dustbin and started clearing the rubble from the stairs into it so that they were made safe to use. The dust was beginning to settle and Peter went to search for our insurance policy to see if we were insured. We had no idea whether we were or not. We had never considered that this could happen to us. The sudden thought of losing everything we had and not being insured was terrifying. Peter found the policy quite quickly with a torch, and by the light of that and a storm lamp we could just read the small print. We were insured for an act of God, whatever the words actually meant, we knew that everything would be included. What a tremendous relief filled us. I remember thinking was this in actual fact an act of God? Then I remembered the bathroom.

I ran up the stairs which had now been completely cleared of rubble, consulted with the fireman on duty at the top of the stairs, who assured me that the two small children were still sleeping peacefully, and went along to inspect the bathroom. It was devastated. The ceiling had come down and the plaster was off the walls. The washbasin was cracked. Was this really answer to prayer? Could it be possible? If it was, then we would surely be alright. God would look after us. After all, no one had been hurt, although Petra did admit to a slight burn on her ear, where the gas fire had blown out an enormous brief flame. I called Peter and he came to look. Had my prayers indeed been heard? If so my relationship with God had become a very serious business. The chief fireman explained to us that we had been struck by what is known as a thunderbolt, which is a ball of burning gases. It had been seen circling over the hill and then suddenly swooped down on our house, skidding over the roof and trying to earth itself unsuccessfully through the television aerial. It can evidently enter the house through a minute space, which one of the firemen thought to have been a window frame in the front bedroom where Mr Mitchell was, this was next to our front bedroom where Christopher was sleeping. It had hit the electricity system through the light switch in Mr Mitchell's room and the switch adjoining it on the landing. It had exploded there blowing the switch across the room and embedding it in the opposite wall. The brickwork was completely blown away and burnt. The result of the blast throughout the house was like that of a large bomb.

When Mr Mitchell had come to us as a paying guest to help with our finances about four years before, there was already in the room a Della Robia plaque of Mary, the mother of Jesus. I explained to him who this was and asked him if I could leave it there. He had told us that although he wasn't sure even whether he believed in God and certainly knew nothing of Jesus, he was quite happy for it to stay. He was a bachelor of high principles and routine habits who lived quietly. He was very good to the children. He was a skilled fisherman and took the boys, including Alan, fishing. He made them fishing rods which were beautiful, and was always interested in the children's progress. We were all very fond of him. On this day he told us that he felt he had had a miraculous escape from injury because of the plaque and what we believed. The whole ceiling had come down like a pancake, except a tiny circle where he was standing. He had felt the light switch whiz past him. Connie arranged for an ambulance and he was taken to hospital for a check-up, glad to be alive. He was discharged that evening and went to stay with Connie.

There was a flurry of activity as the gas and electricity board representatives arrived. We were amazed at the speed at which everything was taking place. All gas and electricity was disconnected from the mains. The local council were actually having a meeting and could not be persuaded to leave. It was suggested that we move out into a hotel and everyone seemed to think it would be best, but Peter and I felt strongly that the worst was over and that it would be wisest for us to stay. The boys' room was not too badly damaged, only the windows had blown out. Our neighbours next door had opened their house for the use of the phone, and the Salvage Corps were on their way. I was not quite sure what the Salvage Corps' function was in a case like this, but I was soon to find out what a wonderful group of men they were. There were twelve of them. They went through the house removing rubble and clearing up. They removed all the glass from the broken windows, sweeping up the glass outside. Then they covered the areas where the windows had been with strong material fixed to frames which they made to size. Rain was still coming down by the bucketfull and continued to do so all night. They opened waterproof sheets and covered the areas in the attic and in Mr Mitchell's room where already the carpets and furniture were soaking. It was not until after eleven o'clock that the local council could be contacted. It was evidently their responsibility to cover the roof with tarpaulins where the tiles were missing, to alleviate the damage from rain. One of them did call to say they could do nothing until morning, but they showed no great interest. By this time the major excitement, if you can call it that, had died down, and Gerard and Christopher were tucked up in bed, having explored the fire engine and asked many questions even though they were in their dressing gowns. To begin with they were shy of standing outside the front door, later they forgot what they were wearing.

We had managed to contact my sister Josie, who had been out for the evening. When she saw the damage she was shocked and upset, but by now we had become a little used to what had happened and were feeling hungry. Petra, who was a lovely supportive girl, said that she was going to find her egg and toast, which she did amongst the dust on the kitchen floor. She washed the poached egg under the tap, (we fortunately still had water), she brushed the dust off the toast and sat down at the kitchen table to eat it. We laughed and laughed. Peter and I ate the remainder of the cold casserole and vegetables, as of course we were unable to heat it up. The house was seething with people doing jobs, and all we could do was laugh. I think it was a tremendous release of tension. The Salvage Corps were finishing off their jobs and were ready for a cup of tea which we made on a little camping stove. We all sat in the kitchen, with a pile of quickly made sandwiches, by the light of electric light bulbs strung on a flex and taken from the electricity main outside the house. We laughed and joked and listened to many stories told by the Salvage Corps who went through the house gathering chairs so that we all had somewhere to sit round the kitchen table. What had seemed like a terrible nightmare seemed to change. I had felt when the crash first came, that we would never recover, it all seemed so terrible, but now, things within me had altered. I saw a challenge to get on with what we had, and be grateful that no one was hurt. The house seemed relatively unimportant for the moment. I felt very supported. Peter put his arms round me without saying anything, and I felt a new era had begun, without being able to put it into words.

When the men of the Salvage Corps realised that the local Council were not going to cover the roof that evening they returned at midnight with large tarpaulins which they spread out in the house where the rain was coming through. Petra made us laugh the next morning because a man had come into her large attic bedroom with out realising someone was there, had looked around to see the extent of the damage and need for keeping out the rain, using a torch. In other circumstances she would have been terrified. Her room at one end was open to the sky with no door. She was a wonderful character, and she helped us a great deal. She was a very calming influence on the children. Clare and Paul slept all through that night and in the morning Clare clambered over the rubble in her room running into our bedroom, saying "Mummy, come quickly, some one has made a terrible mess in my room, but it wasn't me!" She was amazed and quite disappointed to know that there had been such a lot of excitement, and she had heard nothing. The boys were not slow to tell her of the fire engines and the Salvage Corps. She was just five years old.

After this, there followed two years of work on the house and its surrounds. From the first day we knew who our true friends were. They came daily with what we needed, hot dinners, suppers, chocolate cakes and scones. As people came in they would sit round the kitchen table with us in the dust and mess and laugh and talk and eat. With the pressure of housework off my hands, my life somehow seemed easier. I continued my part-time teaching, from the first day, and the children went off to school, nothing stopped. We all kept our clean clothes covered in the sitting room which was fairly clean as the ceiling had not come down. We changed there immediately before we went out of the door. In this way we could present ourselves to the world in a normal kind of way. Not only had ceilings come down on that particular night, but on the following Sunday morning, just before Peter's father arrived, we were getting ready to go to church and Paul had been sitting in his pram by the back door, waiting for us to go. I had just lifted him out and brought him through to the main part of the kitchen, when suddenly there was a terrible crash. The whole of the ceiling in the area by the back door, that had originally been the scullery, and which now contained the washing machine and the boiler, came down at once, causing not only a great noise but tremendous dirt and dust everywhere. On Monday we had an inspector to examine the remainder of all the ceilings to see if they were safe.

He recommended that several areas were pulled down until we reached the stage of having them re-plastered.

There was much work to be done before then, and for a long time we had eighteen men working in the house, all from different areas of maintenance, some laying new gas pipes as the whole of the system had to be replaced, some replacing the tiles which were destroyed on a large area of the roof and carpenters replacing the roof joists that were split and putting a new door on Petra's room in the attic, which had completely blown out. Petra spent her time washing through the house, with a bucket of water to try and keep some of the dust under control, which was continuously dropping through the slats in the bare ceilings. She would then make tea for the army of workmen who made the kitchen their own in the day. When I was at school she looked after Paul and took him for a walk. The children were amazingly adaptable to their new kind of life. Washing had become less important and the kitchen sink was very useful. We all got used to quick wash-downs. Somehow the pressures of living had changed, and the change because it was a challenge was exciting. It was a whole year before I had any kind of reaction, and then the doctor said it was delayed shock. I felt tearful for nearly three weeks, and then it passed. I remember that first year as one of the fruitful years of my life. Alan was often with us, and during the year he helped Peter pull down the ruins of the old garage which had caught the blast and build a new one. Then they removed the wreckage of the fences and built walls from concrete bricks which Peter made. We were a hive of industry.

Eventually after several weeks we were ready for the plasterers. They were two very skilled men, one the master and one the mate. They worked very quickly and very efficiently. They set up scaffolding wherever they were working and it became exceedingly difficult to get about the house. We had to make a plan with them each day to make sure we could manage. One day they set up scaffolding across the landing after I had put Paul in his cot for his morning sleep, not realising that he was there. When Paul woke up he would always call out so that I knew he was ready to come downstairs. When I heard him there was no way that I could get through the scaffolding. One of the men picked Paul up and threaded him through the scaffolding poles, and passed him down the stairs to me. Paul thought it was great fun.

As we sorted out the cupboards in the house we realised more and more how many things had been damaged and broken. Peter's mother had given us a set of fine china for a wedding present, including soup cups on saucers, dinner plates and side/tea plates, cups and saucers, vegetable dishes, coffee pots and teapots, etc. as well as a set of beautiful cut-glass drinking glasses for all occasions. These glasses were my pride and joy. I vetted who washed them up if we used them, and preferred to do this myself. When we were abroad I was always afraid that one of our cooks or maids would break them. About a half of everything I possessed in glass and china was totally destroyed, and quite a lot beyond that was damaged slightly. I was surprised myself at my own reaction. There was a certain amount of relief that I didn't have to worry about it any more, a tremendous feeling of thanks-giving that no one had been hurt, and a quite new feeling of freedom. We could already see that whatever happened we would eventually have a new bathroom, and that fact continued to amaze me. We had to wait until the plastering had been done, and then to wait for the certainty of the insurance money, which actually came through very quickly. We had to prioritise the work because inevitably one's claim, however bad the damage, is never fully met. A lady in the parish named Mrs Townson, who we all knew to be wealthy but who lived a good simple Christian life, visited us. Before I was married I had sung in one of her music groups that gathered informally at her house and my mother had known her well. She came to the house to ask if we were insured. I am sure she was ready to help us. She was always very unassuming, but very caring and generous.

Our Parish Priest, dear Canon Denning was a tower of strength. He arrived the morning after the disaster with a bottle of Bailey's which he said he had in his cupboard, a gift from someone, and insisted that we sat down together and had a drop. I had quite a job to find some glasses at that stage. He also gave us a substantial amount of money from his own private account, which he said was for immediate things I needed. Several people sent us gifts of money, including another priest friend Father Geoffrey Burke (now Canon), whom we knew very well.

Gradually as time passed and we began to get organised again, I realised that I was changing. No longer did I hold on to wanting to show off my very best skills at dinner parties, spending hours preparing food which would be eaten in one hour, and forgotten. I preferred to be with people and spend time with them, without so much emphasis on doing everything perfectly. This did not mean that on special occasions I was not able to throw myself into something wholeheartedly but that there was much more balance in my life. I was more easily satisfied. I was very grateful for what

I had, especially the relationships that I had. Although I kept the remainder of my beautiful crystal glasses and enjoyed having them in the cupboard, I actually bought some cheap glasses which I enjoyed using. If things were broken it was unimportant. I could say that it doesn't matter, and mean it. Life was less pressurised. Our bathroom was eventually finished, we were able to change it round, and have it as we wanted it. I was able to thank God for his great goodness to us all, for sparing our lives, and for our friends and relatives and for our new bathroom. As I look back, these years were very formative in the growth of my relationship with God. I began to know that he really knew I was here, and that he cared a lot about what happened to me and us, but I still did not feel forgiven.

Chapter Eight

A New Life

Our life moved on very pleasantly and apparently happily for the next ten years or so. There were the usual difficulties and arguments. I always felt things could be better than they were, and tried hard to achieve this, sometimes at the expense of other people's peace. Certainly I tried hard to do everything well. Many times I was too tired, or drove other people at the rate I felt they should go but on the whole life seemed good. However I still felt my inner turmoil, wanting things right within myself but not being able to change, and wondering always if there was more to life than I knew.

Alan left school and went to the Technical College to train as a chef, where he met Judith, who was later to become his wife. He worked as a chef on one of the merchant shipping lines, as well as in one of the television studios. He later joined the police force where he became a chief inspector. Gerard and Christopher were being educated at Wimbledon College, Clare at St Anne's Convent, and at eight years old, after a family conference, it was decided to send Paul to Donhead Lodge which was the preparatory school for Wimbledon College and was actually situated right opposite the college in Edge Hill. Even thinking of sending Paul to a private school went against our basic principles, but there was a good reason, and we wanted the family to know that there was no favouritism. Wimbledon College had changed its status with the new education laws and started secondary education at thirteen. The college was also in another county. Paul was at a school which completed primary education at eleven years. Fortunately because the College wanted to keep families together they were willing to accept our boys following on from Gerard, who had entered at that time quite legitimately. Christopher promised that he would look after Paul on the journey until he was sure of what he was doing. The journey was quite long and complex, but it did not take Paul long to master the train times and routes and he was soon quite independent.

Each year we had several holidays in our motor caravan, the old Volkswagen having been replaced by a second hand 'Auto-sleeper.' At Easter or half term we would go somewhere in the British Isles, and it would always be according to the length of holiday time that Peter had left. He had a very generous amount of leave, in fact six weeks each year not counting week-ends. The 'Auto-sleeper' was equipped with its own toilet and kitchen with water supply for three days. We always arranged our summer trip abroad to coincide with one of Peter's many visits to Europe. He would go to his conference or festival, and we would camp nearby, then we would have our family holiday, or sometimes the programme would be reversed, especially when he had to be in Venice for the Film Festival. Arranging our holiday like this meant that Peter could stay with us instead of in a hotel. He was always given a set subsistence allowance for his trips abroad wherever he went. It allowed us an extra holiday time.

Getting ready for the summer holiday, which was usually six weeks long, was a major task. We started buying supplies and collecting what we needed well before we were due to leave. Each person had a place for their personal things, games or books, or writing material. We fitted out the motor caravan so that there was a place for everything that we might need. We carried enough tinned and packaged food so that apart from bread which we bought before breakfast every morning we could be quite independent whilst on the move. We made delicious meals from tins of meat and vegetables, packets of potato, and packet and tinned puddings. We collected new ideas during the year, sometimes from books or magazines, and sometimes from friends who also travelled like us. We often went away for weekends during the year, and met up with other motor- caravanners. The favourite pudding to this day was an apple upside down pudding. Some butter and sugar was melted together in a large deep non-stick frying pan. Then a large tin of apple was added and heated in the large teflon frying pan which had a lid. A packet of Green's Victoria sandwich mix was then made up according to the instructions and poured on top of the apple. The lid was put on and it was left to cook on a low gas. We usually served it straight from the frying pan, but of course it should be turned out. Served with custard or ice cream this was always a favourite. While we were travelling we all slept in the motor caravan which meant putting outside and underneath out of view the large and heavy tent poles for our extra large tent, which we only erected for long stays. The tent was carried in a large laundry basket which fixed onto a roof-rack over the 'cab'. The long roof pushed up to make two full sized bunks on either side so there was no other room for a roof-rack.

During this time we came to know Europe very well. We explored Pisa and spent three weeks on the Isle of Elba, after a week by Lake Locarno where Peter attended a conference. We also stayed on the Gargano in Southern Italy and for several years went to Venice for the Film Festival. The fact that Peter was paid and given expenses for these conferences and festivals was a wonderful bonus, because he was happy to live with us, camping in the tent and motor caravan nearby. Our stay in Venice always took place after we had been on holiday for a month in Croatia in the former Yugoslavia, either on the Istrian Peninsular or in Novi Vinodolski. This name means New Sweet Wine, and we loved it, (the place and the wine).

The only other luxury we took when we were going to Venice was a large suitcase, wrapped in waterproofs, and filled with our evening gear and smart clothes for all the children. The Film Festival required a smartening up of our appearance. It was amazing how we met and mingled with all the stars and journalists, having lived like gypsies in our swimsuits for a month. I took a very nice wig which was very similar to my hairstyle, so that I could wear it when I came off the beach and had to be presentable in the evening, it was like magic. Transformation had to be speedy. We told few people at the festival that we were camping. The children would go to bed in the motor caravan, and we would park it by the back entrance of the festival cinema on the Lido. Peter would slip out every now and again to see all was well. Gerard and Christopher were by this time very responsible and we felt we could trust them.

On occasions we would all go together to the festival films and to daytime receptions. Sometimes, 'retrospectives' were shown that the children loved, like Charlie Chaplin or Laurel and Hardy. Peter and I also went to the mainland for evening receptions. We would then leave the children in the tent with a friend who we had made there. Sheila was the sister of a well-known journalist who had been disowned by her family because of her vagrant lifestyle and spasmodic drinking episodes. She never returned to England because of her dog, and travelled along the north coast of Africa and around the Mediterranean countries in her converted land rover. I used to cut her hair and help her in various ways and she in turn was very happy to help us and to be accepted as one of our family. People were very kind and willing. Whether we were innocent or foolish I don't know, but I would not leave the children like this now.

In Venice we travelled to and from the mainland in the canal bus, the vaporetto. Being in Venice was a great education for all of us and we loved it, wherever we were we enjoyed exploring the treasures and reading the history. In those days no one was 'belted' in a car, and we never thought about safety, only to say a prayer for protection before we set off. The Lord was looking after us because we never had even the slightest accident. In the afternoons when we were travelling, I would prepare tea for the children while we were going along and get the young ones ready for bed; they would be asleep before we stopped for the night. We would then transfer them to the bunk when we pulled off the road at a suitable place to finally stop for the night. The two young ones would sleep top to tail quite comfortably on one bunk. Gerard would go in his sleeping bag on the floor with the case and the tent poles stowed safely under the van. Christopher slept on the other bunk and Peter and myself on the double bed, which changed into a dining room during the day. We never went into a camp whilst travelling. Sometimes Peter and I would stop at a Routiers restaurant for a meal and leave all the children asleep. We would be sure to sit in full view of the Autosleeper. Every now and again one of us would go out and have a peep inside to see that all was okay.

During this time we continued to go to church on Sunday wherever we were and we encouraged the children in their faith, in the only way we knew then, saying prayers, and explaining. As a family we talked about many things. I know that I was always very definite about what was right and wrong. I felt many pulls towards God in my inner being, but had no idea how to deal with them. I belonged to a group at the church called the St. Gerard's Society which met in small groups on Wednesdays, in each other's houses. It was for mothers to find help with the spiritual upbringing of their children. I found this a tremendous help because we sometimes would discuss things very fully and we would all think we were right. Then after thought and a few night's sleep I would re-think my ideas, sometimes completely re-forming them. We learnt from each other, and I know many areas deep within me began to be more free. We also developed deep friendships. I continued to teach at St Andrew's where I was very happy.

It was about this time that Peter and I became deeply interested in helping the 'third world.' We started a group at the church called the 'World Hunger Campaign', which became affiliated to the Catholic organisation CAFOD. It was launched with a talk by the well known ex-communist Douglas Hyde who became a wonderful Christian. The evening he came the church was packed. We collected the names and addresses of everyone there and set up groups who met and talked and thought of ways they could help. We passed information and books round the groups in folders so that those interested could learn more. Our parish priest Canon Denning was very supportive and celebrated Mass for us regularly once a month when the donations from everyone were brought together and blessed. At this time CAFOD was being run by Kieron More the film star. He came to visit several times and was surprised by the enthusiasm he found. We financed many projects in various deprived countries, and we would advertise them with beautiful paintings done by a young member of the church. We would organise speakers and had many fund-raising activities. There was not only enthusiasm but quite a lot of competition amongst the groups. This organisation fell apart when our dear Canon died. The new parish priest did not like money being collected independently, and decreed that 5% would be sent from the weekly collection to the needy. It became difficult to sustain interest in the World Hunger Campaign without the support of the parish priest, and it gradually faded away.

It was in 1974 alongside these events that many changes started to take place together which put into action a process which completely changed my life. I can look back and see that the Holy Spirit, who I know I received both at my baptism and confirmation was already at work and had been, although I couldn't see it at the time. I do believe now that we have to really invite the Holy Spirit into our lives as adults with a prayer of faith and surrender, but more of this later. I was talking to a friend in my St Gerard's group about my deep searching, and the fact that I did not feel forgiven by God, which I knew was not right. She suggested I joined another group to which she belonged as well, run by someone called Gwen which met in her house on Tuesdays. It was called 'Re-evaluation Counselling.' Four of us from the St. Gerard's group went together. Re-evaluation Counselling is a complex process. It is about either one-to-one or group therapy to help each person get rid of the rubbish in their minds, and to foster the knowledge that each of us is an important being, and therefore needed to see ourselves in a good light. There were methods and ground rules. As you entered in more deeply it became more complex. To begin with I found it very helpful. I relaxed in the company and soon lost my self-consciousness. It was not a Christian movement in itself, but many of the people were Christians. It was very much about listening to each other, and sharing time equally. If someone listened to you, you then listened to them for an equal amount of time. You were given a list of all the members and you could phone anyone and arrange time if you wanted to be listened to, but you had to repay it.

To begin with it seemed wonderful. One could cry, or be angry, sit in silence or yawn. Your allotted time was your own to do what you liked within reason. In the evening, which was controlled by Gwen, you might be with one person for some of the time, and then with two or three or perhaps four others, and then in the whole group. Nothing was too terrible to share; everyone listened and validated the other. Everything was completely confidential. Friendships other than counselling friendships were strongly discouraged. During this time, I cried a great deal. I never knew quite what it was about but I always felt better afterwards. More importantly I started to pray more than I ever had before. I prayed on my way to the group very particularly because I began to see that there was never an end to one's need in this group. One never seemed to get better, but always needed to go on. I felt that this could not be right. It seemed like a kind of drug. I eventually found myself not needing to talk, and when asked why, I said I thought it was because I was praying during the week. Some people did not like this and I could see that they had become addicted to that way of life, and were almost fanatical. It was just at this time that Gwen asked me if I would train to be a group leader; I had refused but she insisted on taking me to a large Re-evaluation meeting in London, before I finally made up my mind and she was quite sure that I would do it. This meeting affirmed me in my decision to leave the group, and two of the friends who had joined with me also left. Although I did not agree with the methods it certainly seemed to have helped me move on from where I was.

It was just at this time that questions were being asked in my St. Gerard group about the word 'Charismatic.' Something with this name seemed to be happening in the churches. Peter and I had seen the very end of a programme on the television in which we heard the words 'Catholic Charismatic Renewal.' These accompanied a picture of people sitting around in a room with their eyes shut, including a Franciscan priest with a guitar, which horrified me and made me feel very angry. I thought that this was something purporting to be Catholic, but that it was far from the truth. Peter and I decided that we must find out what it was all about with a view to opposing it. What I actually had in mind I cannot now remember! My friend Margaret was able to throw some light on the matter. She had a relative in Ireland who evidently 'belonged' to Charismatic Renewal, and although her relative said very little about it, she was very enthusiastic and very committed. As a group we decided to find out more, and our chaplain said Father Michael Gwinnell would be the person to invite to talk to us. However, unbeknown to us, a general meeting of our whole St. Gerard's Society had been called for the following Wednesday, at the house where our parish sisters lived, to explain Charismatic Renewal.

St. Gerard's was really a women's group, but Peter wanted to be present. We phoned the Sister Superior whom I knew well. She had helped me do the hand printing for the big 'World Hunger Exhibition' which I had put on a few years previously to take round to the churches and schools. Of course she said that he would be welcome. Peter and the two chaplains plus the priest giving the talk were the only men present.

The priest who came was not Father Michael Gwinnell but another young man also not known to us. He started by saying that when he was ordained he had been through a bad time and did not believe in God. He was aware that this was a dangerous situation but did not know anyone whom he felt he could confide in. He was afraid, particularly of letting people down, especially his family. He then went on to tell us that he had, apparently by chance, been introduced to a group of praying people, who met together every week, praying and sharing and studying the bible. He described how they had brought him to the stage when he could confess his lack of faith to another priest from the group who listened and understood. He told us of his great joy when he confessed, and how his faith returned. He went every week to this group, (which incidentally was in Godalming and was one of the first charismatic groups in England). He told us how he had been baptised in the Spirit, and could now speak in tongues. At this stage the anger in the group of women but also in ourselves was intense. When he invited us to ask questions, people were on the whole scathing. "Who would not be filled with joy having confessed disbelief in God?" "How could you be baptised again if you had already been baptised?" and so on. The young priest had no bible with him to back up his statements, but to his credit he persevered. Peter and I were perhaps the most angry. "What was speaking in tongues anyway, and how did you know that it was of God?" We argued and questioned him, poor man, long after the others had lost interest and were silent. I remember being almost rude in my vehemence and questioning and determination to get to the truth, which I erroneously thought that I knew. I was certain that here was something that needed investigation, not to believe it but to deny it. It was ten minutes to eleven when eventually this brave young priest spotted the 'Jerusalem Bible' on the bookshelf. He reached out for it, found the place, and read from St Paul to the Corinthians, a passage which I had heard many times but had never applied it to 'now,' and certainly not to 'me.'

"There are many different gifts, but always the same Spirit; there are many different ways of serving, but it is always the same Lord. There are many different forms of activity, but in everybody it is the same God who is at work in them all. The particular manifestation of the Spirit granted to each one is to be used for the general good. To one is given from the Spirit the gift of utterance expressing wisdom, to another the gift of utterance expressing

knowledge, in accordance with the same Spirit; to another faith, from the same Spirit; and to another the gift of healing, through this one Spirit; to another the working of miracles; to another prophecy; to another the power of distinguishing spirits; to one the gift of different tongues and to another the gift of interpretation of tongues. But at work in all these is one and the same Spirit, distributing them at will to each individual." (1 Cor 12: 4-11)

What a terrible, dreadful feeling I had. I knew I had been quite wrong. I felt completely humiliated. St. Paul had touched me where it hurt. How could I have been so ignorant and so stupid? I had heard this passage read in church hundreds of times, but had never listened to it with hearing ears or understood the value of it. This was the truth and I was hearing it as if for the first time. Peter also had a similar experience, and all we wanted to do was get out of the room. We left quickly saying thank you to the Sister Superior, but not before she took my hand and said in a very soft quiet voice with great kindness, "My dear, it's all about humility!"

Peter and I sat in the car for quite a long time without speaking, knowing that we had heard something that was very important. When we arrived home, we talked until 3.00 am. We needed to find out... but where could we learn more, where could we go? We felt really desperate, but I also felt very excited. To think you know it all, and that in your heart you know you are bored and unfulfilled, and then to seemingly stumble on 'more,' is exciting. I did at that stage feel that I had stumbled upon it, now I know that God led us along a path which we eventually followed, after we gave up our stubborn self-righteousness, or anyway, started on the journey to do so. We were guided by a young sister visiting the community in the convent where we had met. She thought there was a charismatic prayer meeting every week at the Rosminian Seminary near Guildford, which was led by a priest named Father Tony Meredith. We phoned up to find the day and the time, and were told that we would be very welcome. We were very nervous wondering what we were in for, and how it would be. We had absolutely no idea what we were to expect.

Our first surprise was that the place was seething with people, all moving in different directions, some knowing where they were going, some not sure. We introduced ourselves, and were asked whether we wanted to do the 'Seminar' which was in its third week. We said we didn't know. Reference was then made to Father Tony Meredith, who firmly said "No, not the seminar, please go into the room over the way." We found ourselves sitting in a room full of about twenty people, most of them sitting with their hands either open or in the air, raised. We sat and listened as people prayed in a way we had never experienced. They sang lovely songs and read Scripture for about an hour and a half, which seemed to pass in a flash. Someone shared his experience of what God had done for him. Then a final prayer was said and we were shepherded into a large hall where there were already more than a hundred people sitting round in two very large circles, one inside the other. We guessed this had been the 'Seminar' whatever that was. Tea and coffee were being served, and as I went to the table to collect ours, I had a most extraordinary experience. There was an elderly man who was dressed like a monk pouring the drinks. He looked exactly like my father, who had died a while previously. I immediately felt a great emotion envelop me and tears started to run down my face. As I looked more closely at this man I saw that the name tag on his habit spelt out 'Brother Cyril' and this was too much for me. My father's first name was Cyril. I cried and cried, and had to go and sit down. I felt terribly embarrassed, and wondered what everyone would think. Peter put his arm round me and of course, wanted to know what the matter was. He went to look at the monk to make sure I was not imagining things, and he was equally surprised. No one else took any notice of my tears; they just left us to get on with it. As my tears dried, another part of the meeting started. It was a time of petition, and everyone could join in and pray for their needs in turn. Several people prayed for members of their family, and one woman burst into tears. I remember feeling very embarrassed, but no one seemed to mind. Father Meredith gave a blessing at the end and shared some notices, and then came over to us and said that he hoped we would be there next week. It was a long evening, and by the time we got home, (the journey took nearly one and a half hours), it was nearly one o'clock. We were both working and we decided on the way home that however much we wanted to know about it all, it would be too difficult to go every week, and there must be something nearer if that was what we were meant to do. It was after this visit that I started reading the bible. I was led to the Acts of the Apostles first of all. I found it very exciting but was afraid of anyone seeing me with the bible. As soon as I heard someone coming, I hid it. Sometimes I would lock myself in the bathroom to read it quietly. The bible had in my experience only been studied as an intellectual exercise, following a syllabus at school. I had never known anyone read the Bible for sheer pleasure. I was afraid that even my own family would think I had gone crazy.

Almost immediately after this, during the same week, I had an invitation to go to a friend's house to hear a talk by Father Ian Petit, on tape. This friend had also been at our original meeting in the convent. The talk had been given at a convent in Chester where this friend's sister-in-law was a nun. There were five of us invited to listen, but I was the only one interested. I asked to borrow the tape for Peter to hear, and we copied it. It was wonderful. I knew that it was what I needed to hear. It opened up new vistas of life which made me feel very hopeful. Peter and I spoke a great deal about our experience, and about the tape, and found that many people were interested to hear it. We spent many evenings listening to it with people invited for coffee and a sandwich, sometimes as many as twelve at a time. They had only to show the slightest interest and they would get an invitation. We had no idea where we going, or what it was all going to lead to. At that stage we were quite happy for everyone to know that there was a lot more to God, Jesus and the Holy Spirit than we had previously thought. We didn't mind if they agreed or disagreed, we discussed everything, and asked for nothing.

About the same time as this was going on, we had seen an advertisement in our church newsletter, asking for a family to adopt a ten year old girl, who had no one to care for her. It was on behalf of 'The Catholic Children's Society' in which I had always had an interest. Clare read this and asked us if we would think about adopting this girl. She said she would share and help me with her. We talked about all the difficulties that might arise, but Clare felt confident that we could cope. Clare was the only daughter amongst three boys; I think she had longed for a female in the family. I sometimes wondered if the baby I had miscarried was a girl. However, when I replied to the advertisement, we were told that there actually was no ten year old girl. This had been used simply to attract interested people. They did however have a twelve year old Nigerian boy who needed a home, possibly only fostering for the moment. He had a mother in England and a father in Nigeria who did not want him. His mother was unwell and could not look after him. This was quite a shock to us, as it was Clare who really wanted a sister. I told them I would think about it and they sent someone to see Peter and myself to talk in more detail. I felt slightly under pressure as this was an entirely different proposition. I felt I would really like to help the child, but was very aware that there were others in the family I had to consider. By now the Nigerian boy had been told there was a possibility of a home for him. Gerard was already at University and Christopher just about to go to Cambridge. It was Paul who was going to be most concerned. On top of that Clare was very disappointed, and although she could see the need, felt that she would find it too difficult. As time went on, I also began to think that I would find another boy too difficult. It did not seem quite right for our family. It was with a great deal of sadness that I finally said that we would not be able to take this on. I wrote a letter to the boy and sent him some money towards his holiday which he was just about to have with the children's home. I think I felt that it recompensed for my feelings of guilt, perhaps also in the fact that we were discriminating against a boy. I remember feeling enormously relieved when the whole matter was settled, and I determined to be more careful in the future with what I thought I could manage. This incident was to take on a different perspective at a later time, when I learnt more about discernment, and doing the will of God.

At the beginning of September 1976 Peter and I were invited to Kranj in Slovenia, which was then northern Yugoslavia. The purpose was to set up an international film conference in Kranj in the same week the following year. Yugoslavia had not hosted a similar conference and the person in charge Gospodin Dukovič wanted to be sure that the hotel accommodation and theatre facilities were more than adequate. We had already met their representative in London, and it was arranged between Peter and myself that we would hire a motor caravan and take a holiday in Europe. Our Autosleeper had already been sold to an Australian family wanting to tour Europe and the British Isles. We could take in a week in Kranj staying in the hotel and reviewing the facilities. This all went according to plan. We travelled across Europe into Austria and across the Loibl pass into Slovenia. We stayed in the Kranj Hotel in Kranj for a week, trying out ideas and making plans, and were treated like royalty. The countryside in Slovenia is beautiful. We explored Lake Bled where diplomats of higher rank from Belgrade spent their summer, because the climate is more gentle in summer than in Belgrade. We explored the Postojna Caves and returned through Italy experiencing the tremors of an earthquake in northern Italy. We came back to England full of enthusiasm for whatever was to come. Having previously lived in Belgrade when Peter was seconded to the Foreign Office, we felt quite at home with everything.

Back home again, out of the many people who came to the house and listened to our tape, which was fast wearing out, we found eighteen who were willing to join us in starting a prayer group. We still knew no one to ask or to advise us, and we really did not know what we were doing. This prayer group met three times, in each others houses, losing a few people each week, as we struggled with prayer and reading the bible. One man said it was like a séance, another that it didn't seem Catholic. Others felt they knew it all already, or were frightened by the silences, and felt they had to do something.

A young priest had been coming to say Mass in the parish during a time of ill health with our own priests. He had a way of saying Mass which drew everyone in. It was just at the time when we were allowed to receive communion in the hand instead of having the host put on the tongue. Most people were opposed to the new idea, but this priest explained it so well and I felt he was really going to be the one to help us. I talked to some of the others about an idea that I had, and it was decided that I should approach him and ask him if he would come to our prayer group and start us off in the right way. There were about six of us left plus one or two who had heard about us and later joined in. The young priest was rather surprised, and without giving anything away, arranged to bring a group of people that he knew, who met and prayed. The day arrived, and we met in the attic of our house which had been the au pair girl's room, and was now once again transformed since we no longer needed an au pair. We started with coffee and biscuits, and were praying rather formally, whilst still eating and drinking. The evening then turned into talking and discussion. It appeared that this group had broken away from a larger prayer group, and were talking about visiting people in their homes and not just sitting praying. They were set on good works and action as well as spreading the word of God. There were some very dedicated people amongst them and we learned a great deal from them, but not about praying in a group.

We then heard that there were 'Days of Renewal' taking place at Digby Stuart Training College each month. We gathered together a carload or two, and found these most helpful. There was usually excellent teaching, sharing groups, workshops, finishing with a really lovely Mass in the beautiful chapel. It was at one of these Masses that I first heard singing in tongues. It was so beautiful. Peter was convinced for a long time that it had to be a Latin motet. About this time, we received a letter in a Hambro bank envelope, quite anonymously, announcing that 'Life in the Spirit Seminars' were starting in St Teresa's Convent/Nursing Home in Wimbledon, in the New Year 1977. We found this absolutely amazing. We had last heard about 'Life in the Spirit Seminars' when we visited the Rosminian Seminary near Guildford. We knew immediately that this was very important so we shared it with our prayer group which was still meeting in a different house each week, but was reduced to about eight in number. I found that I was crying quite a lot in the group, but could not account for the reason. It was as if things were going on inside me in spite of myself. I felt a great longing to have a relationship with God that some other people I knew seemed to have. I knew that I was searching and would never give up.

When the time came for the Seminars to start we arranged to take three cars. We could not quite fit in two, and one person could never come until later. For me it was an experience that cannot be described. I waited expectantly each week for Wednesday to come and I could feel that I was being fed in a way that I had never experienced before. While it was exciting, I knew that there were many things I had to sort out with God. I could see no way that I could do this. I felt sure that this was up to me and my own effort.

During this time my faith grew; each witness I heard tell of the wonderful things God had done, I really believed. After all I had experienced wonderful things in my own life, but somehow they were negated by the fact that God must know exactly what I was really like, even though he had been so good to me. I tried so hard to be different but couldn't seem to manage it. I was critical, I felt angry about quite a lot, and could be angry or speak sharply, particularly at home, without really meaning to. I longed to know that I was forgiven so that I could make an entirely new start. The week came when we were invited to speak with our group leader. My leader was Father Michael Simpson a very holy and Spirit-filled person, he was the priest who was giving the talks on most of the evenings and I had found his witness had stimulated my faith tremendously. After the talks he was always rather tired and I felt I would not be able to burden him with any of my problems. I realised then that he should not have had the responsibility of a group, it was too much for him. On the evening Peter visited his group leader, Monique, I went with him intending to wait in the car. She lived alone in a small flat, and guessing that I would go with Peter had prepared a little tray of refreshments for me. I sat for what seemed ages wondering what on earth they were talking about. I knew that I needed a priest for confession, but that was to come the following week, and I felt then I would need a long time and I was dreading it. When Peter seemingly had finished his talk with Monique, he said "I am just going round the block for a little walk," and he left me alone with Monique. He had obviously told her there was no chance of my having a one-to-one with my own leader, which I realised afterwards she already knew. I did not know Monique but had greeted her on a Wednesday evening, and knew of her reputation. I had no idea what to say to her, but she asked me questions in such a way that I found myself confiding in her a family secret which was not to do with me personally, but which I had witnessed and had indeed been involved in helping my mother through her distress by listening. My mother had sworn me to secrecy. This is yet another story. Peter's leader promised me it was totally confidential, and I was amazed how unburdened of that secret I was at that time as she prayed with me. I was later to go through more healing, but for now it was very releasing. As she prayed with me I felt so pleased that there were people who understood, without making any fuss.

The following week we were told that it would be good if we could go to sacramental confession if we were Catholic, or talk with our pastor if we weren't. This for me meant going in the confessional box which I dreaded. Peter went to 7.00 am. Mass every morning in St. George's Cathedral which was very near his place of work, and he knew the priests there very well. He knew there was a Mass every Saturday evening followed by confessions. He suggested that on Saturday we go to the Mass and then I could go to confession afterwards. I agreed, but when Saturday came I was in a terrible state, fearful and crying. I felt that no priest would be able to give me the length of time I would need. I estimated about four hours would be necessary to go through my life. I spent the afternoon in our bedroom and I felt very vulnerable. Paul and Clare knew I was unhappy and came in to try and cheer me up. I was unable even to begin to tell them what was really the matter. Peter was very supportive and told them I did not feel well, although of course now they know the whole story. It was a terrible ordeal for me, I so wanted to be at peace and to know for sure that I was forgiven, although my sins were not murder or adultery, really just a muddle in my mind; they seemed enormous to me. We travelled to Southwark Cathedral in the car. Peter was asking what exactly was troubling me, and was talking to me as I answered. Through my profuse tears I was able to say that:

1) I felt I was not forgiven, whatever anyone said to the contrary.
2) I found going into the confessional box too difficult. Without being able to see the person I was talking to I felt trapped and unable to express what I truly meant.
3) I wished that I could just sit in a room with a priest, and tell him everything that was troubling me.
4) I felt the rules of the Catholic Church were too rigid in many cases and not sufficiently compassionate, and that they should be altered to meet the real needs of the people, particularly when it was to do with putting your life in order. Anyone who could help me seemed too distant.

Suddenly we had arrived, although it was a 40 minute journey. I groped in my handbag for the little zipped bag containing my powder compact and comb. I felt totally dishevelled. To my horror I had left it at home. Still crying I followed Peter into the Cathedral which was already quite crowded and we sat towards the back. It was the middle of March and Peter had on his thick winter coat. I buried my face in his shoulder to try and hide the sound of my crying, which I could not control. Never in my life had I felt or behaved like this. I suggested to Peter that it would be better if I went outside. He merely told me to stop worrying about what people thought. We stood up for the gospel and suddenly, I held my breath and pricked up my ears. It was the story of the 'Prodigal

Son.' I listened to every word and heard it as I had never heard it before. We sat down and Father Clements (later Canon) who was saying the Mass, said, "Instead of the usual homily, my colleague, Father Tom Heneghan and myself are going to have a question and answer time between us to try and explain the new rite of reconciliation which is very soon going to replace what we have known as confession."

They asked and answered my four problems one by one, starting with "Why is it that so many of us go to confession but never feel forgiven?" Father Clements explained the whole story of why Jesus had died on the cross, and that he had done this for each one of us to take away our sins as soon as we were repentant. That it was by believing that this was true, not by anything else we could do, that our sins were forgiven He explained that our sins were already forgiven by Jesus as soon as we were sorry, and that the church just confirmed this in confession. The next question was "Why do I have to go into a dark box to go to confession?" The answer was, that in the future we could sit in a room with the priest or in a specially designed 'confessional' which would be like a little room. "In fact," said the Canon "we are starting work on one of the little chapels to do this immediately." He added that the 'church' had come to see that the rigid rules governing confession that for so long had been adhered to were completely changing, so that we would know that God loved us and because he loved us had sent Jesus to die for us, and because of His death we were reconciled to Him, the Father, to each other, and to ourselves.

As I heard this I felt a warm pink cloud envelop me. My tears dried and I felt my swollen face return to normal; my whole being was filled with joy. As the collection basket came by, the schoolgirl next to me looked at me in astonishment as I smiled at her, my burden had completely gone. I was literally floating on air, and my legs were very weak and wobbly. I didn't need to tell Peter, he knew what had happened. I said to him, "What shall I do? I don't need to go to confession, my sins have gone!" He suggested that I go to communion, and then wait until Father Clements came to his confessional box and go to him, and tell him what had happened. Peter also felt weak at the knees. I said to Father Clements that I was going through 'Life in the Spirit Seminars' and briefly told him what had happened. He was delighted and asked if he could override the confidentiality of confession and tell his colleague Father Tom. I told him that he could tell whoever he wanted. I felt so wonderful. As we left the Cathedral, we looked at the notice board to find that the Mass had been named 'The Lord welcomes sinners'. I remember that it was the 19th March, the feast of St Joseph.

Never since that day have I gone back to any of those former thoughts and feelings. The 'Joy of the Lord' and the 'Peace of Christ' has stayed with me even through the many traumatic experiences which I did not know were to follow. It was for me the day I became a Christian. I really knew that God loved me and only wanted good for me. It was the beginning of a deep change in my life and a new learning process in which the Holy Spirit directly and through other people was my teacher. Not only did I know for sure that I was saved, but that I wanted Jesus to be Lord of my life. I knew for certain that I could trust him. It was an entirely new experience. When we returned on Wednesday to the Seminar, it was the time to make a new commitment to the Lord, publicly.

We did this and I felt a sense of real urgency and pleasure. I promised that whatever the Lord asked me to do, I would do it and I knew in my heart that I was safe with Him. After this we were prayed with by our group leader and an assistant. Father Mike Simpson and Lisa Reynolds prayed with me. We waited in turn. It was a very big moment when hands were laid on me to confirm my commitment. Lisa placed me under the protection of 'Our Lady' in prayer, and Father Michael prayed that Jesus would constantly fill me with his love so that I could share it freely. He prayed also that I would have the gift of 'praying in tongues' which is a gift of the Holy Spirit which enables you to pray in the spirit without words, praising God and thanking him. It is also a very helpful gift when praying with others. It was a wonderful evening for me, I really felt that Jesus and God the Father and the Holy Spirit were very close and that I had nothing to hide any more. I started praying more than I ever had in my life, and it was so joyful.

On the Friday following, I was on my own in the evening, just sitting praising and thanking God for the wonderful thing that he had done in my life, when I found I could pray in a strange language. It was wonderful. No longer did I have to search for words which eventually seemed to run out, I could pray with no effort at all. I was so excited I could hardly wait for Peter to come in, he had been to a meeting with another member of our group who had also been at the Seminars. I remember feeling very shy, and at first did not want to say what had happened, although they both could see something had. We celebrated together in prayer and it was not many days before all three of us had the gift. It was a most tremendous release, and I praise God for this wonderful gift. After this day we had two more Seminar meetings and a party, and we continued to learn how to go forward and grow in our newly activated faith. Our little prayer group started to flourish, new people joined us and we grew together in love and shared deeply. We continued to go to the days of renewal at Digby Stuart College, and I continued to attend the meetings of my St Gerard group, which also was flourishing. Several of the members of that group were in the prayer group. This year of 1977 had already been and was to be a year when many things happened in my life which are very difficult to explain but I did not realise the full story until afterwards. There were many events which were interwoven; I could tell that the Lord was teaching all of us.

There had been one Sunday earlier in that year which was a very special day for me and I am sure it helped me on my journey. Father John a priest who sometimes came to say Mass at the day of renewal at Digby Stuart Training College preached a sermon about Jesus and Lazarus. He told us how Jesus had not hurried when he had heard the news of Lazarus' death. He had waited two days, although he was very fond of Lazarus and Mary and Martha and how before he did anything he prayed to the Father and waited for the right time. When Jesus and his disciples arrived in Bethany, Lazarus had already been in his tomb for four days. Bethany was not far from Jerusalem and many Jewish leaders had come to pay their respects to Lazarus and to Martha and Mary. Martha went to meet Jesus when she knew he was coming and scolded him for not having been there. She said he wouldn't have died if Jesus had come sooner, but added that even now it was not too late. She said "God will give you whatever you ask." Jesus said to her "Your brother will rise again." Martha answered "I know he will rise again in the resurrection at the last day." Jesus said to her, "I am the resurrection and the life, any one who believes in me will live, even though he dies; and whoever lives and believes in me will never die. Do you believe this?". Martha affirmed her belief that he was the Messiah. Then Martha returned to Mary and said Jesus would like to see her. She left quickly as Jesus was still outside the village. The Jewish leaders thought that she was going to Lazarus and followed her. When Jesus saw her weeping and the Jews, who had been comforting her, wailing, he was deeply moved, and asked where Lazarus was buried. When they came to the tomb, Jesus saw the big stone that was covering the entrance. He asked them to roll it aside. Martha was alarmed because of the smell; Lazarus had been dead for four days by now.

Jesus reminded her that she was to see something wonderful, the glory of God. He raised his eyes to heaven and prayed. "Father, thank you for hearing me!" Then he shouted, "Lazarus, come out!" Lazarus came out bound up in the linen grave clothes. Jesus said to them "Unbind him." Father John looked at us, and I felt he looked at me personally, and he said, "Jesus is speaking to each one of you now, saying "Come out of your tomb, and allow yourself to be unbound. Unbind each other" He is saying "John, come out, be unbound. Eileen, come out, be unbound. James, come out, be unbound. He is speaking to you. He wants you to hear what he is saying. Are you locked in your tomb, doing the same thing every day unable to break out to do anything different? Are you listening to Jesus? Can you hear what he is saying?" When I walked up the centre aisle of the chapel to receive communion from Father John, I was still thinking about what he had said, I put out my hands to receive from him, and nothing happened. I waited with my eyes half shut, and wondered what I was doing wrong. I looked up and saw Father John, his head leaning on one side, trying to read my name badge, which I had pinned on sideways. I said to him, "It's Paulette," and he said "Paulette, the Body of Christ."

No one had ever given me communion by name before. It had the most incredible effect on me. It was really personal. The whole story of Lazarus took on a different meaning for me. I have never forgotten this day. I found myself wanting to be called more and more out of the darkness and into the light of Jesus, whatever that was to mean. I already believed then that God loved me so much that he only wanted the very best for me and that life does not end here but goes on for eternity, and that he wants us to start eternity now, not when we die. I found myself hungry all over again for the word of God, and thirsty like the deer that searches for running streams.

The Jesus who I encountered at the Life in the Spirit Seminars through the love and teaching of so many people was at once wonderful and awesome but real. Not only had I committed my life to God, but it was tremendously exciting. Looking back on these experiences I realise that this was the very beginning of a long journey teaching me how to rely on Jesus and the Holy Spirit. I realised how Jesus spoke in parables that people could not understand, he did not spell everything out with a rule to obey although he gave us clear guidelines. Very often there are dichotomies in what Jesus teaches in the gospels and he leaves us to think about what he has said, and puzzle over it, and pray for the wisdom to understand. I realised more and more that the way God works is a complete mystery, and that there is more to what we don't know than what we think we do. The road more travelled for many is the road where rules are laid down and where our religion spells out what we must do exactly, to keep everything in order. The road less travelled is the way of Jesus; he shows us the way of unconditional love, loving without counting the cost. He loves us and draws us on, picking us up when we fall and starting us off again, teaching and disciplining us and showing us the way forward as long as we have an open heart and eyes to see and ears to hear what he is saying. A journey of learning 'til the day we die. During the following years life became very exciting. Our prayer group grew large and we moved to the Convent in Monahan Avenue for a few years until it closed down, after which we continued to meet on the church premises for several years. Peter with an Anglican friend formed a group entitled 'Croydon Evenings of Renewal'. This was ecumenical and met monthly in different venues in Croydon, mainly churches. A speaker was invited each month and we celebrated with praise and worship. We made many good friends from other denominations and everyone was welcome. This group disbanded in the late 1990's after 20 years or more. Fountain Trust was also flourishing during this time and we were fed in many ways through wonderful speakers and teaching. Peter and I were very involved in organising Life in the Spirit Seminars in our diocese and evangelisation generally. I personally was involved in the ministry of inner healing, at home and at organised meetings as well. Jesus is risen and alive!

It was not until 1994 that we felt the call to work mainly in our own parish church which seemed to be much harder.

Chapter Nine

St. Olave's

A little later in 1977, the year we had completed the Seminars, it was a Tuesday evening and we were at our prayer group in Opal Goldring's house. Opal has since sadly died of cancer, but without doubt is with the Lord. Our family doctor, Kelly Tighe, was in St Olave's Hospital, in great pain and discomfort with cancer of the spine, and those of us who knew him were praying for him. We knew little about his situation. I need to go back a little to explain the relationship that we as a family had with Doctor Tighe, and more particularly my relationship with him. He was known by everyone to be a very difficult man, but he was an extremely good doctor. There were many times that I had seriously considered changing to another doctor in the partnership, particularly to Dr Alistair Lees, who did eventually become our family doctor. When I spoke to Dr Lees about leaving Dr Tighe he asked me to consider it carefully because I would not find such a good doctor anywhere. I really believe now that this was not just loyalty. Our experiences with Doctor Tighe had been mixed. I had seen his good side, and I had also seen him behaving in a very rude, stressed and difficult manner. I had always presumed that he was an atheist, not because he overtly stated this, but because of his general attitude towards anything connected with God or the church. Our previous doctor had died between Clare's birth and the time when I was expecting Paul in 1962. My first big experience with Doctor Tighe was when I explained to him that I had booked into St Teresa's Nursing Home in Wimbledon for Paul's birth. (St Teresa's was the place where we had attended Life in the Spirit Seminars in 1977). I asked him if he would still be able to attend me there. He said absolutely not. He was very outspoken and left me in no doubt as to what he thought was best for me, to have the baby in my own home and to let him attend me there. My fear at that time was that I had not experienced a home birth. It was regular practice at that time for only the first baby to be born in hospital, but because I had been abroad for our second baby, and he had been very large, it was decided that my third baby should be born in hospital, although she was actually the smallest of them all. I had been persuaded to book in to St Teresa's by the wife of a colleague of Peter who was going to have her baby at the same time as Paul was due to be born. Doctor Tighe was very firm and definite about his views on a private nursing home, and sent me home to speak to Peter and make a final decision. He said the midwife would deliver the baby, but if there was any need, he would be there, and that he would look after my post-natal care as he had looked after the ante-natal care. At this time Peter and I changed our minds and trusted in him with no regrets.

I had been to see Doctor Tighe many times with the children or for myself for various reasons. He was always busy, impatient and fairly irritable. In all this his diagnosis was good and he was very straightforward. He came one day to the house to see Christopher, when he was about ten. Christopher had very bad abdominal pain. Doctor Tighe could not absolutely be sure what it was, but went back to his surgery, looked it up straight away and returned to tell me that the pain and illness would pass in three days, and to treat him with disprin. This was exactly what happened. He was afraid at first it might have been Crohn's disease. He was not worried by what anyone thought about him, and he knew what he was doing. Another time when Gerard was ill, just before he was due to be in his primary school play, I was continuing to tell Doctor Tighe the symptoms, and he said, very abruptly and rudely, "Please be quiet, I am examining this child!" You didn't argue with Doctor Tighe. Another time I was looking after a friend's three children and needed to take Clare to see him, I had seven children with me. I could not leave them alone in the crowded waiting room, so I took them all with me into his surgery. He was on the telephone when we entered and was obviously annoyed with the caller. He threw the phone across the room and shouted. I was terrified and wondered whether we should just go. However, he apologised and dealt with Clare very gently. There were many times that I remember, when, although he was brusque, if he saw one of our family was ill or in pain, he would be very kind and concerned.

There was such an occasion when Paul was about six and I was due to go with Peter to a conference in Holland at The Hague. The day before we were due to leave Paul suddenly had an extraordinary rash on his body. Our excellent French au pair girl Danielle, whom all the children loved, was going to look after the family during our absence with some help from my sister Josie. Doctor Tighe was sent for, and of course I had already declared that I would not go to Holland. Doctor Tighe diagnosed an allergy to nylon clothing, which had been brought about by the heat. He was very concerned that I should not put off my trip and promised me that Paul would be quite better in thirty six hours. I was still uncertain, and Doctor Tighe said to me, "Look, I promise you, that if Paul is not better, I will personally look after him and take responsibility for him. Go, and enjoy yourself with your husband." We were crossing the channel the following day on the car ferry when we were called to the telephone. It was Danielle and the family, to tell me that Paul's rash had gone and that he was quite well. We had a quick chat with everyone and I felt much better and ready for everything that was to come during the following week.

One day in 1976 I called Dr Tighe to the house because Clare was very ill. She had a very sore throat, no appetite and no energy. She was seventeen at the time. He examined her and said he thought she had glandular fever, and would confirm it with some tests. He sat and chatted to us both, and seemed in no hurry. He was extraordinarily quite at peace. We had not experienced this before as he was usually in a rush. Clare was especially pleased because, although he was often cross, we were all very fond of him. He even had a cup of coffee, which was unheard of. At that stage I knew nothing about his personal life, but afterwards was told at the surgery that we were his last call before he went into hospital to have a lung removed; he had cancer. We were very upset but could only follow his progress through news at the surgery as we did not know him on a personal friendship level. He didn't work again after that, and although the operation was successful, he later developed cancer of the spine and was receiving treatment in St. Olave's Hospital in Bermondsey. I felt very sad about this and decided to really pray for him. On this particular Tuesday night in 1977 at Opal's house we started by praising God as usual and sang, and we then followed the theme that arose, studying the bible, and praying spontaneously. Towards the end we always had a time of petition and intercessory prayer. While we were praising God at the beginning, I had experienced an overwhelming desire to ask the group for special prayers for Doctor Tighe. I felt what is known as a real burden of prayer for him, a feeling that it was very important. Everybody praised God in the most wonderful way, and one of the group who did not know Doctor Tighe had a picture of him in her mind's eye. She described him in detail and the description fitted perfectly. When I arrived home that night, I was moved by an incredibly strong desire to write Doctor Tighe a letter. It was as follows:-

My dearest Doctor Tighe,
I am so bursting with wanting to communicate with you that I don't know where to begin. In the thirteen months you have been away from us I have gleaned tiny pieces of information from the few people I know who are in communication with you, but I have been quite unable to write a personal letter for reasons bound up with a doctor-patient relationship and other things which I can only say now that since tonight are totally healed within me, or so I feel. I am now not ashamed to admit that I felt whatever I did would be an intrusion on your privacy. I envisaged visiting you and finding your family and friends and 1,199 other patients who love you, like we as a family do, and without considering you (I am now truly sorry) decided that I would find it too difficult. We meet with a wonderful crowd of friends on Tuesday evenings, although the word friend is totally inadequate, and last night I had the overwhelming desire to ask them to pray with me for you, and I feel the love and gratitude that we as a family feel for you,

flowing through me that I must tell you. I could never in my life have spoken to you about God, let alone Jesus, but since last night, I feel that this is the overwhelming love which Jesus shares with all of us, if we ask Him, and in some extraordinary way, the most wonderful thing of all, is to be able to write to you my innermost thoughts, and feel sure that in some way you will understand, and not think that I have gone cranky. We had a most joyous evening... because of you... in thankfulness for all you have done, and will be able to do. May I come and see you? If you can bear it, get someone to phone 01 668 4321. I will come and do whatever you want. If I hear nothing then of course, I will not come, but either way I can assure you that you will continue to have concentrated prayer, said spontaneously with love in Wimbledon, Purley and Southwark. I can only sincerely apologise to you for what I have failed to do, and offer myself entirely to put it right. How long it takes us to learn that we need each other. I could go on but I have said enough. Clare sends her special love; she often speaks of your kindness.
With love in Jesus,
Paulette Coldham.

I read my letter through quickly without changing anything, and put a stamp on it ready to post the following morning.

On the following Friday evening, I received a telephone call from someone I did not know. His name was Keith Stockbridge, a well known lay preacher in the United Reformed Church who was also a long term patient of Doctor Tighe. Keith had been visiting him on the Thursday evening, and had not only been told about my letter but had also read it. Evidently Doctor Tighe had cried and cried when he read it and asked Keith to phone me to ask me to visit. We were on the telephone for two hours. It was a most wonderful discovery for Keith to find out that there were people in the Catholic Church who not only met in groups to praise God and pray, but also prayed in tongues. He told me that although he himself did not have the gift, his wife Beryl had been praying in tongues for the last twenty years. She then introduced herself; Keith had called her to listen on the extension line. Keith was an extrovert evangelist and catechist, and Beryl was a very quietly spoken, contemplative, with a strong ministry of healing and quiet teaching. We had the most wonderful and exciting conversation. They invited us to go and see them and this started a deep friendship which was to continue through to Keith's death. We learnt a great deal from them both, especially from Beryl. She was not a strong person and she died early on in our relationship. She was a great loss, and Keith was never quite the same again after her death. She was a strong support to him.

Peter and I made an arrangement to go and see Doctor Tighe the very next day, Saturday morning. It was a wonderful occasion; he was so pleased to see us. The doctor wanted to apologise for all the times he had been so difficult, which he knew very well. He said he had been irritable for a very long time. It appeared then that he had been baptised a Catholic, which was a tremendous surprise to Peter and myself. He had turned away from God quite early in life, but now, wanted to return but did not know how. He was suffering very much with the cancer in his spine; he was lying on a bed which moved rather like a sandwich, so that he could be turned and all parts of him could be reached, and at the same time his back was protected. His spine was crumbling with the effect of the cancer. The pain was very bad, but he insisted he was a coward, which I never believed. He screamed out when they gave him his regular injection which was known to be very painful. It was terrible.

Peter and I visited Doctor Tighe every Saturday morning and I wrote to him at least once or twice a week. I have recorded some of my letters. He desperately wanted to know about Jesus and to learn to pray, and to receive the Holy Spirit. His family at that time were not Christian and he wanted Christian company to find out more about the things which had suddenly become important to him. I found an immediate rapport with him, which was extraordinary, considering the fact that he had been our doctor for so long and had for the most part in all that time, been very brusque and bad tempered, and had not wanted to be side-tracked away from his work in any way. We were soon all on Christian name terms. We asked Canon Denning to say Masses for Kelly's recovery. Prayers were offered as I had promised, in Wimbledon by our 'mother' prayer group who had led the Seminars under the care of Tim and Mimi Turner, by our own prayer group, and by the people who gathered at our Diocesan Day of Renewal at Southwark Cathedral. Canon Denning also made the great effort to visit, although he was still recovering from a stroke. He had very little use in his right hand and could only walk with a stick. There were special reasons too for these visits. Kelly Tighe had been troubled with night visitations from the evil one, which had greatly disturbed him. Canon Denning told the story afterwards to every one, how Kelly had shouted at the devil to 'bugger off.' Kelly Tighe never minced words. Having been dealt with in the appropriate manner these night visits ceased, and Canon Denning lent him the biography of the Curé of Ars which helped him a great deal. Kelly wanted to be well, not only to make amends for the ways he felt he had failed, but he had an exciting and valuable stamp collection, which he longed to attend to. It was just lying untouched, and stamps that he had bought or received before his illness were waiting for him.

During this time our relationship with Keith and Beryl grew close, and we kept each other closely informed of what was happening in our churches. Beryl introduced us to the oil of gladness, which is blessed oil for the use of lay persons, particularly in the Catholic Church where the Sacrament of the anointing of the sick may only be carried out by a priest. Keith Twynam, another friend of Beryl and Keith also visited Kelly, he was from the Baptist Church. We continued to attend the days of renewal which took place each month at Digby Stuart. There and also at our prayer times many wonderful things happened. At the day of renewal we would have a talk by an invited person, usually a priest, then we would have workshops on various subjects, followed by Mass, during which there would be time after communion for free prayer. There would be praying in tongues in praise of God, and very often there would be a specific prophecy in tongues which would be interpreted. (This was absolutely according to Paul's teaching in 1 Corinthians, chapter 12 vv 10 & 11, and chapter 14 vv 26-33). We would take a packed lunch and sit in sharing groups at lunch time. There were many things that happened during these weeks. One day the leader of Peter's seminar group, Monique, had a prophecy after we had been praying for Kelly:

"I am with you in your pain and in your joy. If you bear witness to me,
I will bear witness to you. Go out and take my Good News to the world."

Its meaning for me did not come clear until later. There was another
prophecy a little later at the beginning of July when we had again
been praying for Kelly : *"I will heal you with my love."*

So much happened during that summer of 1977. The Lord was
teaching me many things, and I know that it was his love that
flowed through me to Kelly Tighe. At the time I am sure that his
wife Janet did not understand what was happening during our
visits, and at one stage she tried to bring a group of spiritualists
to pray with him and heal him. We all prayed against this as soon
as we heard, and they were stopped from coming in a most
extraordinary way, without anyone actually speaking to them. I
sometimes spoke to Janet on the telephone, but I didn't ever meet
her at the hospital. She later became a Christian and when I did
meet her of course she then had understood what had been
happening.

Peter and I went to St Olave's Hospital regularly every Saturday,
where Kelly Tighe occupied a single side ward off the main Pasteur
ward. We both felt very privileged and usually enjoyed our visits
even though Kelly was so ill. All he wanted was to know more
about Jesus and to feel free to say what he thought. He was full of
questions and there were many things he could not understand. I
continued to write to him at least twice a week in between our
visits. He loved to hear everything that would help him to accept
Jesus as his friend and Saviour. There were one or two occasions
when he was in terrible pain, one when he had been moved for an

X-ray and another was the second week of August, when I visited on my own. Peter had another appointment and arranged to meet me at the hospital at 12.30 pm. Kelly was to have a very special injection. It was almost time for me to leave and so I said goodbye, and left him with the doctors and nurses. He knew what was to come and he was very apprehensive. He always said that being a doctor made it very difficult to be a good patient. I was waiting for Peter in the garden not far from Pasteur Ward, when I heard his screams. It was terrible for me and I felt helpless except for praying. I remember crying all the way home, although I knew that this did him no good. I did learn later to detach my feelings from those who were hurting, without losing compassion, and then found that I could be of more help.

Kelly had a time during August when his white blood corpuscles were not functioning. Fear of infection was great. For a while he was allowed no visitors and he went downhill very quickly. I think that it was during this time that he really called on God to help him in a new way. He had told me of the many days in the past, before being taken into hospital, that he had sat on a 'hard and lonely' chair with the bones of his bottom poking through. It was his description of despair.

During this summer there were many other things going on at the same time. During Gerard's first year at University in Nottingham he had met Celia, who was one year ahead of him. They fell in love and told us that they wanted to get married. Although we fully approved of Celia in every way we both felt that Gerard was far too young to take on the responsibility of marriage, especially as he saw the only way was to give up his degree and get a job. After a lot of soul searching he came to see our point of view and the pair of them managed to arrange with the University to go together to Spain as third year students, although Gerard was only second year. They were reading Spanish and French. Gerard had a tremendous aptitude for these languages, and his Spanish was already excellent. He and Celia taught English at different schools in Burgos. They had decided to save all they could so that they could make a trip to West Africa the following summer vacation for two months backpacking, which they succeeded in doing. Plans for marriage were put off until Gerard had qualified in 1977 when Celia would have her degree and have completed a B.Ed. As time for them to qualify and think about marriage came near they realised that getting a job was not so easy, and they decided to try and get jobs within weekend commuting distance and marry the following summer when they would have saved some money.

Gerard suggested that we go to Lourdes as a family to work for the last week in August and the first week in September. Gerard and Christopher had worked as brancardiers in Lourdes for several summers, and Gerard was sure that the Abri St Michel where they stayed would take Paul even though he would still not be quite fifteen, especially as Peter would be there. The Abri had a rule that all helpers must be eighteen. Clare and I booked into the hospital as helpers, willing to do anything.

There was a hitch when it was realised that Paul was not eighteen, and the Abri would understandably not change their rules. It was to do with insurance, and responsibility, also there seemed to be no work for that age group. We did not know how to deal with this new situation. Paul was very disappointed and said that he would stay anywhere and manage, but with all of us working it was not so simple. I was not able to leave him in Lourdes on his own.

It so happened that almost immediately two jobs became available for Gerard and Celia, which were very near each other; for Celia a teaching job in Winchester and for Gerard a post in Basingstoke with the de la Rue Company. Celia also had the offer of a very suitable flat with her job; they immediately decided to get married. It was then the middle of July. Celia wanted to be married in her Anglican 11th century village church, which was a stone's throw from her father's house, and where her family worshipped. It was possible to get permission as a Catholic for this, even then, but the Catholic partner was required to fill in a very demanding form on behalf of the other partner. Gerard refused to sign the form as he said both he and Celia were Christian and they would bring their children up between them as Christians. He saw no need to have to bully Celia because he was a Catholic. It was the words 'I will do all in my power to see that my wife...' that Gerard objected to. Without him signing the form a blessing from the Catholic Church could not be given. They wrote to the Pope, they visited their University Catholic Chaplain, and they talked at length with Canon Denning who had known Gerard of course since he was born. I found the situation very painful. It was as if the last bastion of 'the law' was being presented to me.

I was fully sympathetic with Gerard's view and agreed with him but desperately wanted him to be married with the blessing of the Catholic Church. It seemed an impossibility and I was desperately upset. All the people in our little prayer group were praying for the situation and Gerard even came and sat and talked with them and allowed them to pray with him. We were due to go to London and meet Celia's parents at the hotel where they were staying. I had been to the hairdressers, and when Peter met me, took me into the car and opened the bible at St. Paul's letter to the Romans, Chapter 8 verse 27 and I read:

'And God, who sees into our hearts, knows what the thought of the Spirit is; because the Spirit pleads with God on behalf of his people, and in accordance with his will. We know that in all things God works for good in those that love him, those whom he has called according to his purpose. Those whom God had already chosen he also set apart to become like his son, so that the son would be first amongst many brothers. And so those whom God set apart, he called, and those he called, he put right with himself, and he shared his glory with them. In view of all this, what can we say? If God is for us, who can be against us? Certainly not God, who did not even keep back his own son, but offered him for us all! He gave us his son, will he not also freely give us all things? Who will accuse God's chosen people? God himself declares them not guilty. Who then will condemn them? Not Christ Jesus, who died, or rather who was raised to life and is at the right hand side of God, pleading with him for us! Who then can separate us from the love of Christ? Can trouble do it, or hardship, or persecution or hunger or poverty or danger of death? As the scripture says, "For your sake we are in danger of death at all times; we are treated like sheep that are going to be slaughtered." No, in all these things we have complete victory through him who loved us! For I am certain that nothing can separate us from his love: neither death nor life, neither angels, nor other heavenly rulers or powers, neither the present nor the future, neither the world above nor the world below, there is nothing in all creation that will be able to separate us from the love of God, which is ours through Christ Jesus our Lord.'

I burst into tears and knew deep within me that whatever happened it would be all right, that I did not have to worry or be upset any more. I knew that I loved Gerard and Celia and wanted the very best for both of them as God also wanted the very best. I couldn't see how it would all work out but all the pressure was released. The following day Canon Denning called in to see Gerard to say that he had written a letter to the Archbishop stating the situation and asking permission to sign the form on Gerard's behalf with the appropriate lines deleted that we all found so offensive. He also added that he wanted an answer by return post. Permission was granted and Canon Denning duly signed the form. It was the following April that the Bishop's conference decided to abandon this form completely. We sometimes wondered if Gerard's action had spearheaded change. Gerard and Celia also had a sheaf of papers from the Pope, explaining all the ecumenical work that was going on and a lovely letter, wishing them a very blessed and happy marriage. It was as if the problems in our trip to Lourdes had been solved and of course all the arrangements were cancelled with some sadness, especially in Gerard, who had originally planned it all. Gerard and Celia were married at Bottesford Church on September 3rd 1977 with the full blessing of the Catholic Church, and all members of our families present.

On the evening of August 23rd, a new assistant priest had arrived in Purley to replace Father Pat McCarthy who had become Parish Priest at Chatham; his name was Father Ken Bell. It was two weekends after the arrival of Father Bell in Purley that I wrote the following letter from our hotel, in Bottesford, on the morning of Gerard and Celia's wedding, when we normally would have been visiting St Olave's.

3rd September

My dearest Kelly,

I need not say how lovely it was to see you so perky and apparently well last Saturday. We had spent the evening before with Keith and Beryl, as we hadn't seen them for three weeks, owing to their holiday and Beryl's illness. We really enjoyed their company. Beryl is so gentle, and she complements Keith from whom we have learnt so much.

I hope that you are continuing to feel better. We have missed seeing you today. If 'Sister' says it is okay may I pop in for a few minutes on Wednesday? I won't stop long, as I am sure you will have had lots of visitors. We are going off to Yugoslavia on Friday, as you know, so we will not see you next Saturday either. It looks as if we will be flying after all, which is easier, although the journey by train is far more interesting.

We started celebrations for Gerard's wedding over dinner last night. I had planned a quiet read and an early night, but Celia's family had other ideas, and they all came over to the hotel to meet us. We had a really lovely evening. The wedding actually takes place in the little 11th century Anglican Church in Bottesford, for which Gerard has had to get a special dispensation from the Archbishop, as it is Celia's own parish church. She is a practising Anglican... how complicated it has all become.

I am now taking a sneaky hour off while Peter has taken the boys down to lunch. They seem to be able to eat endlessly.

Clare of course is a bridesmaid. It seems as if it is all going to be very pleasant. We are to stay at Celia's house tonight, and they are having a large buffet lunch party tomorrow. I hope we all survive!!

I was going to send you last Sunday's Mass leaflet, but didn't bring it with me on second thoughts, because it was all about humility, which I am sure was meant for me and not you. There were some rather nice prayers after communion, I think one sentence was, "Don't listen to what others say, but communicate with me. (God)"

Anyway even that doesn't stop me writing. I just wanted to say that even though life has been fairly hectic, with far too much emphasis on material things, it is difficult to know how to be otherwise for a wedding, it seems inevitable that it must follow tradition, I have not once missed the fifteen minutes each day for special prayers for you that I promised.

If you have a set back and get impatient and feel disappointed, try and hand it over to the Lord. I personally have worked him very hard this week. On Tuesday before the prayer group I shouted at all the family, (not Peter). It was the first time for many months. We have sat and played cards, done crosswords together, and had a very enjoyable time together during the holidays over the last few weeks but they don't like to be hurried over their jobs. I was really sorry, because it doesn't seem to make any difference to them, and only upsets me. This is where praying together is so marvellous, everyone understands everything. Anyway we

are all very relaxed today, and believe it or not, the sun is shining, very brightly here.
All my love, and from Peter,
Paulette.

It was during the beginning of September that Kelly had a most wonderful conversion experience. Instead of asking intellectual questions all the time, he accepted what God had said through the bible and the church and through those who cared about him so much. His questioning stopped and his attitude completely changed. To pray and share with him was a wonderful experience, his faith was so strong. His belief was also that God was going to get him well enough to go home, even if it was only for a little while. His spirits rose, and he started to improve physically and in every way. Canon Denning, brought Communion each time he visited, and conducted a little service welcoming Kelly back into the church. Kelly was very happy even though he was still in pain. He started then to have Communion regularly from the priest who came to St. Olave's. I was able to promise him that the hard lonely chair would never again bother him, as long as he looked to Jesus for his strength.

During this summer Clare had been applying to the London hospitals for a place in their school of nursing. Since a small child she had said she wanted to be a nurse. There was one big difficulty, she had suffered very slightly from infantile eczema and as she started going for interviews this recurred on her hands. Each hospital refused to accept her apart from the London Hospital who put her through a series of tests. They promised that if it proved not to be eczema on her hands they would treat it and accept her. However it did prove to be eczema, and she was left at the beginning of September feeling isolated, with no prospect of anything that she wanted to do. She applied for several jobs as assistant matron in boarding schools, and in the caring professions. A position with Doctor Barnardo's was the one that she really wanted. They took her particulars and she sent a photograph, it was a volunteer situation with pocket money, looking after deprived and delinquent children, with the possibility of training after four months if she was suitable. Clare heard no more from them, but she wasn't interested in anything else. She said I will wait, I am sure they will get in touch. As all this was going on, the time was drawing near for our visit to Kranj in Yugoslavia for the international conference which Peter and I had prepared on the same week exactly a year before. We were due to fly out early on the morning of the 9th September, a Friday, for one week.

Chapter Ten

Barts

I had barely spoken to Father Bell, who was appointed to our parish as assistant priest; he arrived on Tuesday 23rd August 1977 and I was present at his first Mass on Wednesday morning in the main church. I sat with a friend, Frankie Brandt, and in case we disturbed Father Bell with our conversation after Mass we moved into the church porch. The light was on as it was very dark and pouring with rain. When he had finished his prayers Father Bell came to the porch and, hardly allowing us to introduce ourselves, he said that he thought the light should be out. I told him that I knew someone whom he had received into the church, her name was Alison Warne; he asked where I had met her, and I said that it was through 'Charismatic Renewal.' He retorted immediately "I don't like that and I don't want anything to do with it." Ignoring this I said how difficult I thought it must be for a priest coming to a new parish, Father Bell said "I don't expect to be here very long as I am waiting to be a parish priest." And that was it!

The next Sunday (28th August 1977), I was sitting in the church after Mass with an old friend, Mrs Gillson, (who died in 1994 at the age of 94). As we sat talking, the son of a dear friend of both of us, Mrs Harrington, a stalwart member of the parish whom I had known since I was fourteen, brought the news that his mother had died; she had just had a hip replacement and we thought she was recovering. It was a great shock to both of us and we were very upset. Father Bell walked down the church and said good morning to us. The next weekend the 3rd and 4th September Peter and I with all our family were up in Scunthorpe for Gerard's wedding. We found out much later that Father Bell had presided over the wedding of a couple from Purley, on Saturday 3rd September who we later came to know.

I need to go back a couple of months when I had an extraordinary experience on the 14th July, this was following a Parish Meeting where I had suggested that it might be a good idea to invite speakers from other denominations to speak to us in our church hall. Afterwards, Mrs Harrington had sought me out to say how upset she was with what I had suggested. She said it was putting Canon Denning down, and making out that he did not know enough. I told her that this was not my intention, and that I really didn't want to upset her or him. I explained that I felt it was sometimes necessary to say what you thought was right; then on the morning of the 14th July I was awakened very early and felt that I needed to write something. I put on my dressing gown, took my pen and a large pad of paper and wrote the following:

"In the peace and love of Christ, prayer changes things.

1)   You have been hand picked by God our Father, who knows every hair of your head.
2)   Jesus his son, who is one with him, loves you more than you can possibly imagine. He loves you so much that he just wants to give and give and give to you, and he has many gifts to give.
3)   You have got what none of us outside have ever got, and that is time.

4) You do not have to understand. He loves you just as you are.

5)   You do not have to try to be better spiritually, or nicer, or anything like that. Just relax, and know that He loves you.

Then all He wants you to do is to praise him for everything; and He means everything. It is easy to praise Him for what is good. Do that first. Then, this is where it gets difficult. Think through all these things that are less than how you would want them to be.
(These may not be accurate for you so you must do your own).

a) I am in very much pain.
b) I am confined to one place.
c) I am separated from my family.
d) I do not always agree with the way I am looked after.
e) I feel resentment for some people etc.

Go through them individually, and praise the Lord for each one of these. God can go back in time, and heal every hurt from the past, not only releasing you, but as you forgive, so others are set free."

I realised that I was writing these things, they were not for myself but for Kelly Tighe. I also had a strong desire to look up the saint of the day for the 14th July. My father had given me the full version of Butler's 'Lives of the Saints.' It was not clear from this whether the feast was St Camillus of Lellis or St Bonaventure. I knew nothing about either.

I then wrote four letters. The first to Canon Denning:

Thursday 14th July
My dear Father Denning,
Do you have any modern readable information about the

saints whose feast it is today? Am I right? St Bonaventure and St Camillus of Lellis. I want to find something out about them, or perhaps you can tell me where to go to find it.

The second thing is that Mrs Harrington, who is a dear friend of mine, was very upset yesterday. She told me that she thought I had been very hard on you, and that I had upset you by suggesting that Frank Cooke the Baptist Minister and Ministers from other denominations should be invited to speak, including of course Catholics, in the church hall. She said that I was putting them up as better than you, when you as the Catholic were the only 'right' one.

You know me well enough to know that the very last thing I would wish to do, is anything to upset you, and in my heart know that I have not done so, as you understand the reason for our wanting to investigate all possibilities of agreement, between the different denominations.

If I have in anyway said anything that was unjust, I am very sorry. Perhaps when you see Mrs Harrington you will put her mind at rest, or perhaps it is better to say nothing. I still repeat what I quoted at the meeting from Revelations, "The Spirit is speaking through the churches."

Thank you for all you are doing for Gerard and Celia,

Yours very affectionately,
Paulette

I received an immediate telephone call from the Canon, inviting me round to look at a biography of St Camillus of Lellis whose feast he said it was. Evidently St Bonaventure was now the following day, the 15th July. He was really interested in all that had happened to me and assured me that he was in no way upset, but that our congregation let alone the Parish Council were not ready to welcome speakers from the other Christian denominations. I borrowed the book and read it with interest.

The second letter was to Canon Clements:

Thursday 14th July

Dear Father Clements,

You will know who I am when I remind you that I came to you to confession, I think it was in March after the Mass "The Lord welcomes sinners." This was the week that I took part in 'Life in the Spirit Seminars' and came to you before being prayed with for the release of the Spirit. My main problem was that all my life I had the feeling that I was not forgiven. I could hardly believe it when in my deep distress, I heard you and your colleague, Father Tom Heneghan, asking and answering questions, all of which I had been asking my husband Peter on the way to the Cathedral that night. I found such joy on that day that my problem has completely gone. Thank you.

Will you please pray for Doctor Kelly Tighe, who is in St Olave's Hospital with cancer of the spine, and for his wife Janet and their two sons?

Yours very sincerely
Paulette Coldham

The third letter was to Father John:

Thursday 14th July

Dear Father John,

When you know that it is Paulette and not Lazarus who has just started to come out of her tomb, you will know who I am. When I came to my first Day of Renewal at Digby Stuart College, and heard your sermon on Jesus calling Lazarus from his tomb, I had then not even started 'Life in the Spirit Seminars,' which I followed through with Father Mike, who concelebrated Mass with you on that day.

Your sermon was never far from my mind, and when you gave me Holy Communion after saying my name, reading it from my label, I knew that the prophecy which was interpreted from the beautiful singing in tongues, was in some way meant for me to listen to. It was not until Friday 8th July that I realised it was perhaps for me to pass on.

There have been a multitude of intricate webs woven, which at the time I have not understood, and now perhaps begin to a little. Anyway, that is a very long story. I am writing to say thank you, and the Lord, for your gifts and the way you share them. God is indeed wonderful.

Would you please pray for Doctor Kelly Tighe, who is in St. Olave's Hospital with cancer, also for his wife Janet and his two sons?

Yours, I really want to say with love,
Paulette.

The fourth letter was to Kelly Tighe, enclosing the words that I had written with a brief explanation. It was on Saturday at our next visit to Kelly that he went through his thoughts in detail. He had been really pleased to receive my letter, and wanted his past to be healed. We praised God together through the healing of many hurts, both that had been done to him and that he had been responsible for. Kelly was amazed that healing of this kind was possible, and that he had not known that Jesus was Lord of the past; he was repentant like a lamb. After this he spoke to Keith about his inner healing and we all concentrated our prayers for Kelly's complete inner healing. I was beginning to learn that inner healing was more important very often than physical healing, and lack of it could be the cause of many ailments, minor and major. Jesus promised to heal. His promise is resurrection from the dead on the last day. I also believe that he wants us healed in our inner being now, so that we may share his 'Good News' with those who are open enough to hear it. When our inner healing is nearly complete, physical healing is more likely to follow, although we cannot understand how God works and why some people seem to be healed and not others.

God remains a mystery, and our human minds can never comprehend his enormity. Faith is his gift to us, it grows like the mustard seed, it is believing in the unseen and knowing Jesus as Lord and not just as Saviour. This involves the removal of self from the centre so that He can be at the centre with us at his feet, not only worshipping, but trusting and loving, with the trust and love that we receive from Him, in our openness and willingness. This is a long journey for us, in fact the whole of a lifetime.

It was about 3.00 pm on Thursday, 8th September 1977, the day in the Catholic Church on which we celebrate the birthday of Mary, the mother of Jesus, and a day which has become very special to me for many reasons; our cases were packed ready to be closed for the flight to Llubljana, the next morning; I had been to the hairdresser, and the house was in order and ready to be left. Christopher and Clare were staying in the house and Paul had already gone to his best friend Stephen's house for the week. (Stephen is still his best friend even though they are both now married with families). Clare had spent the day at Digby Stuart Training College where they were preparing for a residential Charismatic Conference called 'The family of God'. She was helping in the crèche where babies and children could be looked after during the talks and there were also groups for the older children; Thursday was a training day for all the helpers. Peter had agreed to go about 7.30 pm to bring Clare home. She had been promised a lift to get there on the Friday, and was sleeping there over the weekend. I was determined that I was going to be ready so that I could have an early night.

A friend, passing on her way home, called to say did we know that Father Bell was in hospital? He had been injured in an accident. We were very sorry, but the news really passed us by a little as we had quite a lot on our minds. It was 5.30 pm when we had a phone call from another friend Peter Butler who organised the parish newsletter; he was checking an insert we were making. He asked if we had heard that Father Bell had been knocked over by a car, and was in the intensive care unit at St. Bartholomew's Hospital. Peter had answered the phone, and said that we had heard some news about him. As Peter told me this news and went into the kitchen, I was transfixed in the hall beside the telephone. I heard a voice, whether inside me or outside me, I do not know. It said, "Go to the hospital and pray!"

Peter knew from how I stood that something had happened to me. At first I was unable to tell him, and I felt very tearful, but it was not because I was sad. I hardly knew Father Bell. I was sorry that he had been in an accident, but the voice had touched me, in a strange way. It was very clear and definite. When I eventually managed to tell Peter, he believed me straight away. Of course, I had no idea what to do. There was no way I could go to the hospital, relatives would be there and I did not even know Father Bell, yet I felt sure I was to obey; I did not even question that. Peter said to me, "Why don't you phone the hospital?" We had a set of old London directories and we soon found the number for Bart's. I got through to the Intensive Care Unit, and found myself speaking to the Sister in charge. I said I would like to come and see Father Bell. She asked me if I was a relative, I said "No." She then asked me if I was a friend, I said "No." She then said "Well who are you then?" I said "I am a parishioner." She was obviously astonished, and said, "Why do you want to come?" Without batting an eyelid or even having a care of what anyone might think, (I realise now that people must have thought that I was crazy)! I said "I want to come and pray!" With a great deal of patience she said, "Look, I am a Catholic, you can pray at home, you don't have to come." "I know," I said, "but I would prefer to come." "Then you had better come." she said with no more ado.

I looked to Peter for help for the next step. He was ready to go to collect Clare. He said "You'd better put on your coat and we'll go together after we collect Clare." I got in the car and began to see how this was an impossible situation. I felt suddenly very nervous after my extraordinary boldness on the phone. I was cold and shivery and quite sure I would not be able to carry out my instruction. It was really too difficult. All thought of our trip to Yugoslavia and my early night had vanished. When we eventually arrived at Digby Stuart College, we managed to find the room where Clare was preparing and she wasn't quite ready to come. We had seen a large group of people through the windows in the enormous sitting room which they had then, it has since been altered. They were sitting in a double circle praying for the conference. Tim and Mimi who had led our Seminars and were praying every morning with their family for Doctor Tighe were leading the group. Also present was Father Michael Simpson, who of course we knew, and Father Michael Gwinnell , whom we had not then met, but who now is a dear friend.

We joined in the prayer and eventually Clare came and sat with us. Peter leant over and asked Tim if they had heard about Father Bell's accident. News travels quickly and Alison Warne who had already heard the news was present so they had already been praying for him. When Peter told Tim that we were on our way to the hospital, we were invited to kneel in the middle, the two priests laid hands on us, and prayed with us, and asked us to carry to the hospital all the prayers from those present. My fears left me. I felt a confirmation in a very strong firm way of what I had been asked to do.

How many evenings in the year were there that this could have happened, when we were all just sitting at home, and certainly no gathering of people praying together like this. It could not be by chance. I had by now learnt that with God there was no coincidence; everything is planned by Him. It is we who do not always see and hear what he wants us to. This had certainly been true in my life. I knew that it was also very important to have confirmation by others of any word you received. Although I had been a Catholic since birth, I was a very new 'Christian' but some things had been imprinted on me, in an interior way.

Clare was very tired, and she slept in the back of the car while we went into the hospital to find the Intensive Care Unit. A priest and a lady were just walking along the corridor, and the night Sister in charge asked us if we would mind waiting as Father Bell had just had two people with him and had been anointed. We introduced ourselves to the priest who was Father Richard Plunkett and the lady, who were both from his previous parish Walworth in South London. We talked for about 20 minutes. It appeared that Father Bell had been knocked over by a car, which had stopped the evening before at 9.00pm but that he had not been identified until early Thursday morning the 8th September. He had severe head injuries and was not expected to live. His mother had received a slight heart attack when she heard the news and had not yet seen him. By now it was about 11.45pm. We said goodbye to Father Richard, and said we would see him again. We spoke again to the night Sister who said it would be wise if we waited a little longer. We sat on two chairs in the corridor and we prayed. I felt again this pink cloud of peace envelop me as I prayed, with no thought at all of our long journey the following day. A full hour and a half passed, and the night Sister came out to say we could now go in. Whenever I recall my answer to her I am surprised. I said to her, "We have done what we came to do, we don't need to come in." We wished her a good night, and went home. We didn't even so much as glimpse inside the Intensive Care Unit to see Father Bell. Now, out of sheer curiosity I would have liked to, but it was as if we were being guided, and I didn't even think about it. It is only in looking back that one realises so many things. We had just three hours in bed, and were up to catch our flight to Llubljana, and thence to Kranj. Although I prayed every day for both Kelly Tighe and Father Bell, my main thoughts were with Peter and the organisation of the conference. I was sometimes in charge of the wives of the delegates, taking them on trips and looking after them. They came from many European nations. I helped them, especially with shopping. As I had already lived in Belgrade I could speak and understand a little of the language. Pure Slovenian is quite different from the Serbo-Croatian language then spoken in Belgrade, but in Slovenia both are understood. It was an enjoyable and successful week. The Yugoslavs were pleased with their efforts as they were not very used to international events especially in a small provincial town.

I had considered my job with Father Bell finished except for continuing to pray for him. We arrived home on the Friday night a week later, but on Saturday I was taken over by a strong desire to go back to Bart's to see him. We visited Kelly as usual, and found that he had heard all the details of Father Bell's accident through Keith. He also knew that Canon Denning had been saying Mass at 8.00pm each evening for Father Bell's recovery, and the church had been full each time. We told Kelly of our involvement. We realised that if he now considered himself a Catholic, Father Bell was one of his parish priests. Kelly had already felt this and said he was praying for him all the time. It was exciting to experience Kelly's wonderful conversion. His spirit was bright, and he was very optimistic, almost elated.

We went on to St. Bartholomew's Hospital, and found W.G. Grace Ward where Canon Denning had told us Father Bell now was. This was the neurological ward. He was lying motionless behind the large plate glass window, in front of the Sister's desk. The Sisters then at St. Bartholomew's wore a blue dress and a very pretty tall lace hat. We asked Sister if we could go in and see Father Bell. She replied in the affirmative telling us that he was now stable, and asked us if we would please shave him. She explained that they were busy and that no one had yet had time, adding that he would look so much better with a shave; she told a nurse to bring the things necessary. We went to his bed, his head was swathed in bandages, he was quite unconscious, and was naked to the waist. I was really nervous to even touch his hand. I was aware that we only knew him from praying for him. The personal side of his life was completely unknown to us. I stood beside him with Peter by me, and we prayed quietly under our breath, using the prayer gift we had been given.

Eventually the nurse brought a razor, soap and a bowl, there was no brush. I was terrified; I had never shaved anyone in my life, certainly not someone completely unconscious. Peter was less nervous and took charge. We tried to work up a lather with our finger tips, until we felt it was safe to use the razor. We did it between us, Peter shaving and me, rinsing Father Bell's face and drying it, praying all the time that it would be alright. The sister came in and was very approving, she had been concerned that although he was clean and well tended, he looked so rough. As we finished, a man from his former parish which was not too far away came in. We spoke to him for a little while, and then we slipped away. I found myself praying for Father Bell and thanking God for the tremendous improvement in Kelly Tighe. How extraordinary life had become. The very next day I felt an overwhelming inner desire to go back to W.G.Grace Ward. It is difficult to explain this feeling but it overruled everything else. Peter understood and said he would drive me. So started my daily visits.

I was at this time still teaching at St. Andrew's School. Five afternoons had been replaced by two days. Our prayer group was already growing in both size and maturity. We had been joined by several other people, two of them already very committed Christians. They had taken up both the causes of Kelly Tighe and Father Bell in prayer, in the group as well as individually. The prayer group at Wimbledon was also praying, and the crowds who came to days of renewal, both in Southwark and in Westminster diocese.

My life started to change. I would get up early, take a quiet time, do the jobs that were necessary. Then I would communicate with Clare about the shopping and the dinner. She was very happy to practise her quite considerable cooking skills and have work to do and she did it very well. Christopher was studying in Cambridge, and was only home for the holidays, Paul was the only one to be looked after. At the end of September he would celebrate his fifteenth birthday. Clare was already nearly nineteen, and had always had a very good relationship with Paul. Each day I felt a very strong move within me to go to the hospital, it was inexplicable. Fortunately my immediate family seemed to understand, especially Peter. The days that I was not working I went on the train as soon as I was ready. I would stand or sit by Father Bell's bed. Even though he was still totally unconscious, he had stabilised sufficiently to be moved into the next room on his own with a glass panel in the door. I found my courage to take his hand while I prayed, and would sometimes talk to him as if he could hear. I read passages from the bible, and even if he was not there for any reason, I would sit in the room and pray.

It was the most beautiful time for me. I felt the presence of God in a very real way. If Father Bell was not there I just waited. I never asked where he was or spoke to anyone. If the doctors came on their rounds, there were always four of them, I slipped outside. If the nurses came to attend to him I went outside and waited. I did not mind. I felt no impatience or need to know anything. If visitors came, I slipped out and went in to the Chapel of St. Bartholomew the Great which was just down the road. On Thursdays this was all day until about 3.00 pm. The housekeepers from our presbytery in Purley, Emily and Margaret, went every Thursday which was their day off. They said the rosary aloud between them. They never saw me because they would be there when I arrived and I could see them through the glass panel. I would go back about the time I knew they left. I always felt it was important not to intrude on other people. Sometimes people begged me to stay with them although they did not know who I was.

When visitors arrived I found a great peace in walking down to St. Bartholomew's chapel, I got to know every detail of parts of it.

The times I spent in the chapel were precious and blessed. I would go right to the far end of the church, through the large wrought iron doors to the 'Lady Chapel.' There was rarely anyone there, and I would sit and pray and cry. The tears were not in any way connected with Father Bell. Although I was sorry that he had been so brain damaged, I was fairly detached from his situation. The tears were a deep healing taking place in me; I knew instinctively that this was good. I always felt ready for anything when I had been there. It became a wonderful sanctuary. Peter would drive home from work in the evenings via the hospital about 5.45 pm and we would go home after a time of praying together with Father Bell, who remained totally unconscious. Paul would usually have been home from school about an hour. He was at Wimbledon College and had quite a long train journey. Clare would have the meal ready. She also seemed to understand what was going on.

On the days I was teaching I finished at 3.20 pm. My classes seemed to sense without my telling them that I needed to go quickly. They were speedy with their work and cleaning up was done with no fuss. Until this time, I had always stayed about an hour after school, planning and doing accounts, making lists and plans. This would now get done with less fuss and more speed. I would do this if necessary on the train going to London Bridge. I parked my car each day at school in a space at the entrance to the school playing field, facing the road, and was on my way home by 3.35pm. The train I caught to London Bridge left Purley Station at 4.13pm (the timetable has changed since then.) It was a double train coming from two directions, Tattenham Corner and Caterham, and had to be connected. I was always there waiting for it. No matter how little time I had I was never late. It was as if time stood still. Rather than have to go down to the pedestrian crossing as I walked from home to the station, it was as if the road cleared when I was ready to cross. I was never in a hurry and never felt hassled. I always washed and changed and had a sandwich and a chat to Clare before I left home, even though there was less than half an hour to get the train. It was an extraordinary time. On those two evenings Peter would sometimes come straight home and leave me at the hospital for the evening, and sometimes he would come and join me.

Right from the first day I had said "Father Bell, I know you can't see me, but this is Paulette." I never started reading or talking to him without saying "Hello," and saying my name, and Peter's as well if he was there. I asked Father Richard what music Father Ken liked to listen to, as Canon Denning had told me he loved listening to music. I found out that Wagner and Mahler were his favourite composers, and most of all the last movement of Mahler's 5th Symphony. We had a small cassette player; we bought two tapes, Mahler's 5th and a selection from Wagner's operas, and asked the Sister in charge if we could play them to Father Bell in his room. She was delighted and organised the nurses to turn the tape when it reached the end so that it was playing much of the time.

One day quite early on, I was chatting to Father Bell, just as if he was conscious. I asked him what he would like for lunch if he could choose. I said that I had no idea what he liked. Would he prefer steak and kidney pie, or fish and chips? I had got into the habit of holding his hand when I prayed or talked with him, and I felt his fingers tighten their grip. I was quite amazed at this as he was deeply unconscious. It made me think perhaps something was registering. Although I could not do anything about other people's activities, I felt it was really important not to discuss him in the room, particularly if it was about negative things. I really felt that he could hear. I did get to know one or two people quite well who asked me to stay while they were visiting. Sometimes people were afraid of the silence, and did not know what to say. They would say to me "I think it's hopeless don't you? It would be better if he died." I found that if I spoke to Father about music and asked him if he liked Wagner he would squeeze my hand quite hard, yet to all intents and purposes he was in a very deep coma. Clare came with me to the hospital sometimes, and she also could feel his reaction when she held his hand. I knew that somewhere he could hear something, however deeply, in his subconscious.

It was as if my life had changed and I was called to be at the hospital. It was never difficult, and always uplifting, whereas I realised that for other people it was very difficult. Partly it was because I did not know this man and was not involved in his life, but it was also because I was being drawn into a new kind of relationship with God and Jesus; a relationship of love and friendship, nothing really to do with a man lying unconscious, but to do with what was going on within me spiritually. It was exciting.

After one month there was medically absolutely no sign of improvement in Father Bell. There was pressure on the brain and hydrocephalus was setting in. It was decided to do another operation. The surgeons had evidently performed a very large one on the day of the accident, although I knew little about it. This time, they shaved his whole head, and removed part of the brain on the right side of his head; they fitted a Spitz Holzer shunt to drain the fluid. After this Father Bell floated between life and death and the prognosis was that he would most probably not become conscious, but there was a very faint chance. If he did, his mother was told that he would always be brain damaged. The words 'vegetative state' were used. We had at this stage met and spoken to Mrs Bell, and John, Father Bell's brother, who was eleven years younger than him. At this time Father Bell was fifty one years old, he had worked for Cubitts before joining the priesthood with a late vocation. At first Mrs Bell seemed very friendly and talkative, with very strong ideas. She definitely knew that being a priest's mother put her in a category above others. She knew that Peter and I were parishioners of his new parish, but she did not know then that I was visiting every day. It was obvious that she had a control over most of the visitors.

One day, a priest I had met briefly and who had given a talk at one of our Days of Renewal, sought me out and asked me about Father Bell. He wanted to know if he had been anointed recently since his operation, I said I didn't know, as I really had nothing to do with him except that I felt that each day it was very important to me that I was there. I could make no explanation, but he already knew this, and understood. I was able to share my thoughts easily with this priest, Father Jim, a holy man. I explained to him how I came to visit Father Bell in the beginning, and that my life seemed to have been changed to go in this direction. I told him that I was living day by day, and that a great deal was still changing within me. He asked if he could come with me one day to visit and to see if he could anoint Father Bell, and pray with him. I still keep in contact with Father Jim, who was for a time a missionary in Guayaquil,

Ecuador. We made the arrangement to coincide with Father Jim's day off. It so happened that when we arrived in W.G. Grace Ward, Mrs Bell was there, which was unusual in the afternoon. She was with some of the people who had offered to act as chauffeur to her as she was over eighty with a weak heart. I said to Father Jim that I would prefer to wait in the waiting room. I genuinely felt that I had no place with the friends and relatives, as I really did not know this man. It was only through my prayer that I had got to know him, and I felt there were few people who would really understand all that had happened even if I could tell them. I had a strange silence put upon me. Some people like our prayer group and Father Jim, I could talk to easily, with others I was made dumb.

However, Father Jim insisted that I went with him. He knew from my association with the 'Days of Renewal' and the prayer group that I would help him. He asked permission of Mrs Bell to anoint her son. She was unsure if he had been anointed. Father Jim assured her that it would not matter repeating an anointing, even if had taken place recently. Anyway, she didn't know, so he went ahead. We had a lovely little ceremony of prayer and singing, and everyone present was invited to join in. This kind of prayer was alien to them I could see. To have a priest and a lay woman praying for a priest and singing, 'Spirit of the living God fall afresh on him,' was a new experience, especially as Father Jim was expecting me to help, asking me to hold Father Bell's hands while he anointed them. We had of course learnt in our prayer group and at our regular days of renewal, to pray with each other, and singing was very much part of our way of praising God and thanking him for his love and for what he was doing for us, very often unseen. Although this was all absolutely Catholic, Mrs Bell had obviously not experienced anyone praying for so long or singing while they were anointing the sick. She asked Father Jim afterwards in the waiting room, who he was and why this was so different from the usual quick anointing that she was used to. He told her that we were part of what was known as Charismatic Renewal and that the whole church was charismatic since the time of the apostles, but that because of many changes and laws the church had lost its original way, which was the way Jesus was, with the apostles and their disciples after his resurrection, aware that the Holy Spirit was alive and active in a very real way. A new Pentecost.

From that day Mrs Bell refused to speak to Peter and myself. I don't think she saw Father Jim again. She spoke to Canon Denning about us, and told everyone that we were a different religion. All the people who came with Mrs Bell were forbidden to speak to us and she did everything she could to stop us visiting. Sometimes, John, with whom we had made friends, would come ahead of her entourage and warn us that she was on her way. The Sister or nurses would hurry us into the kitchen and hide us so that we could slip out quietly. It was like a charade. If by any chance we met, Mrs Bell would ignore us, and her power and hold over people was so strong that they would not dare to speak to us if she was there. We were always polite to her and said goodbye if we saw her, but she would not answer. At this time we came to know the man from Walworth Parish whom we had met on our first visit after our return from Yugoslavia. He visited quite regularly and he also had been told by Mrs Bell not to come any more. Strangely all this did not upset me at all. I felt secure in what I was doing. It was as if something was going on, on the sidelines, quite apart from me. I sought regular direction and advice from a spiritually wise priest, and was perfectly at peace. I was very careful not to intrude on anyone else's visiting time, and was as content to be in the chapel as by Father Bell's bedside. There were so many things that happened during this time it is impossible to recount them. Even though Father Bell was deeply unconscious, as he started to physically recover from the operation, they sat him out in a chair. He was a sorry sight with his head slumped forward and to one side and the feeding tube in his nose. His left eye was very damaged and turned upwards and because it was so unsightly it was usually kept covered. His right eye was tightly shut. His mouth hung open to the left side but his teeth were usually clenched. A stream of viscous fluid flowed from his bottom lip, and it was difficult for the nurses to know how to deal with this. His head had been shaved, and he was getting very thin. There were many long periods during the week when he had no visitors at all, so I would be quietly alone with him.

I felt a strong movement within me to pray for him to open his eyes. I would say to him "Father, I am praying that you will be able to open your eyes. I am praying to Jesus and to our mother Mary asking her to pray for you to Jesus as well, if you can hear me, just keep trying to open your eyes." I didn't indicate that only one eye seemed normal. This went on for several days, and I felt so strongly within me that I asked our group to pray and also Tim and Mimi in Wimbledon who had a time of prayer every morning with their family at 6.15am. We also prayed a lot with love for Mrs Bell that she would find peace. I was very at peace and all was going very smoothly both at school and at home. I was not able to explain anything but I felt the Lord was asking me to keep going to the hospital every day. Peter was very supportive and seemed to know and understand exactly what was going on. In fact every-one was very supportive and it all seemed so important even though we were experiencing such opposition, and I really could not understand why.

After a while when I had been praying and encouraging Father Ken for a long time to open his eyes, I could perceive that his right eyelid was flickering a little. I would encourage him with words saying that I knew he was trying to open his eyes. Imagine the delight when one day after a long time of prayer and encouragement, his right eye popped open. I praised him for trying so hard and could see from the look of his eye that it was quite 'unseeing'. I could hardly wait for Peter to come to try and repeat the process, but Father Ken had slipped back into a deep comatose sleep and could not be roused. I think at first even Peter didn't believe me, but as the days went by it happened again, until his eye would open after a much shorter time.

One day when Peter came in to collect me, I had been with Father very little as there had been several visitors. The Sister had been given a large crucifix for Father which she had placed on his legs in front of him. We decided not to stay but we said a prayer out loud, finishing with 'In the name of the Father and of the Son and of the Holy Spirit.' Father moved his hand and made the sign of the cross. As he seemed so unconscious, lying in bed with his uncovered eye tightly shut, I wondered if I had imagined it. Was it all wishful thinking? When we had said goodbye to him as we always did, and went outside, Peter was as amazed as I was. This was the first big sign we had that he could really hear and understand. To all intents and purposes he was completely unconscious. When we told the people who were visiting him these facts, they did not believe us. Even people who knew him very well were convinced that he would never become conscious, and told me quite frankly that they thought I was wasting my time. I could not make any reply to this because I felt involved with something, not of my own choosing, and that the results were out of my hands. I was convinced I was doing only what I had to do. This crucifix now hangs in our bedroom.

Canon Denning, speaking to the congregation at Mass one Sunday said that he thought it was unlikely after so long that Father Bell would ever become conscious. Peter and I plus all our praying groups continued to pray. We did not argue with anyone. On Sunday I would go to the hospital in the morning and then we would do something as a family in the afternoon and on Saturday we would continue to visit Kelly in St. Olave's, which was always a tremendous privilege and pleasure. We would share all the news with him, and hear all the wonderful things that were going on with him. Then we would go straight on to Barts afterwards. Kelly was getting better all the time, in a most amazing way, and against all expectation his spine recovered so much that on the 14th December he was allowed home. This was wonderful for him, he was able to walk, albeit very badly, but he was given a few months of freedom. When he left St. Olave's I felt my time with him had really finished. In some way, to visit him at home seemed an intrusion. My job, whatever it had been, I felt was done, and he was very content to be home, and attend to his beloved stamp collection. There were several occasions when he managed to walk from his house to the church for morning Mass, and on one of these I offered him a lift home which he was pleased to accept and invited me in for a coffee. We shared and talked about many things that day. We were on our own as his wife was at work. He again told me how sorry he was for all that he had done in the past which was so impregnated with bad temper. He could recall every occasion with me and my family and wanted us to be sure that he was truly sorry. He knew that Jesus had forgiven him and that everything was now alright. This was a very blessed time and I felt very privileged to have known him, and to have shared with him the finding of Jesus as a real living person. He was only a little man but as he saw me off, outside the house, he gave me a great big hug. This was the last time I saw him. I think we both knew that some sort of task had been completed. After a few months at home Kelly was taken into a London Hospital, with a recurrence of the cancer, and died a very peaceful death. It was after this that I spoke to his wife for the first time, and I met her on several arranged occasions afterwards, until she moved away. We actually attended a seminar together about St. Mark's gospel given over breakfast at the local Baptist Church.

My visits continued daily to Bart's Hospital. I continued to help Father to get his eye open, the other one remained very distorted, turned upwards and open all the time. Each day I prayed with him or talked with him about some of the gospel stories, sometimes about St. Paul, even though he was totally unconscious to all intents and purposes. As time went on he was moved into a ward with four beds. It was usually impossible there to play his cassettes, although there was a time when only one other patient was there; he was an old man who loved a little chat and was very happy for the music to go on. We had bought more Wagner tapes but they were all rather well worn by now. During the day when I was sitting with Father the nurses would sometimes ask me to try and get him to take some food, a little chocolate mousse, or custard. Once they even ask me to make a scrambled egg, and try and feed it to him. It was a hopeless task. Sometimes his teeth were tightly clenched, and even if they weren't his mouth hung so wide open that the tiny amount of food we could get in would not stay. He had no sensation of anything happening, and he was still in a very deep coma. One morning John came in to visit and asked me to stay. We tried together to feed Father Ken but to no avail. He continued to be fed through his nose tube, but because he was only getting thin liquid food his weight had dropped to six stone, and the nurses were getting concerned. He was often either in the physiotherapy department when I arrived, or was taken there later. I would either wait in his room or walk down the road to the chapel. There was a little café nearby where I would go and have a bowl of soup and a roll. I got to know the owner quite well.

It was in November after his physio sessions that Father seemed sometimes not to be in such a deep coma. I could get him to open his eyes more easily. One thing that I was sure of, when he was roused from the depth he could understand even if he could not move anything to make a sign. Still no one else believed me, and people would just stand by his bed talking about anything. I had by now made friends with more of the people who came, but there were some who would refuse to speak to me. I still only stayed if I was invited. At this time there were new developments. Father started to move his lips as if trying to speak when I was there. He would be lying on his side, as they were then having difficulty in healing his bedsores. I would put my face near to his and say that I knew he was trying to say something and that when I could understand what it was I would repeat it to him. He would go on and on moving his lips, and I would say that I was sorry but I couldn't understand. Then one day, when he was sitting in his chair, (I used to tie a scarf round his head and round the back of the chair to hold his head up,) I said "Goodbye," and "I'll see you soon," etc, and "Bye-bye," and his lips moved together but with no sound to say "Bye-bye." I was so excited and ran back to reassure him that I had understood. At this time I don't think his eyes could see, but I knew without a shadow of doubt, that inside this sad misshapen head there was a brain that was not totally dead. No one would believe me, with the exception of my family, and my praying friends. With each new revelation the prayers seemed to get stronger if that were possible to judge. The nursing staff could see that he was sometimes in a lighter comatose state, but could get no breakthrough.

It was about this time in November that the Sister on W.G. Grace Ward asked me if Mrs Bell had told me not to come. We had in fact had a rather nasty meeting with her, quite by chance, as John was not with her, and she had arrived unannounced. She told us to take our musical 'thing' with us as it was not needed any more, and not to come back again because 'Father' would not be there any more. We had already gathered our coats, so we removed the cassette player and although she obviously did not wish to speak to us, we went over to just say good night to her. She ignored us, and the man who had brought her to the hospital and had previously been very chatty with us, refused to shake our hands across the bed when we held them out. This man, sadly, has since died, although he was comparatively young.

The Ward Sister again reassured me, and told me to take no notice. She said that Mrs Bell was trying to get her son moved to a geriatric hospital nearer her home at Clapham, and that the St Bartholomew's authorities were fighting a battle with her. I asked nothing more and said that I really knew nothing of what was going on. I don't know how she knew that Mrs Bell had spoken to us. The next time I saw John, he was very apologetic for his mother, and we could assure him that we understood that it was difficult for him. I assured him that in no way did we wish to upset her. He told us that she was very possessive and jealous, and that 'Ken' was the favourite. She was not at all well and visiting three or four times a week was as much as she could manage, and that even this was too much for her. Canon Denning had been very kind to Mrs Bell and had found her charming, as we had previously found she could be. He advised us to go on as we felt guided and to continue to try to keep the peace, which is what we wanted to do. I wondered then, would this be the end of what the Lord had asked me to do, I just had to go on in trust. My journeys were still so easy and everything was going well at my school. Home plans were working out very smoothly and Paul was working well and seemed happy. Sometimes he went to stay with friends, and sometimes they came to us.

It was at this time that we started calling Father Bell, Father Ken, although there was no way that we could say that we knew him. It was a one way relationship but we had really come to care very much what happened to him and I believed strongly that he would become conscious although medically this was not the prognosis. We heard a report from the physiotherapist through John, who said that Father Ken had become rigid and immobile, and that it was getting more and more difficult to exercise his joints and his muscles. His left leg was set firm in a bent position and there was little that they could do, only to continue to do the best they could. However his hands at this time started to be more mobile, although his fingers were tightly coiled. The rest of his body was completely motionless. He was conscious of his nose tube which protruded for about four inches. He would sometimes grasp it and try to pull it. The nurses found it easier to clean inside his mouth, it was as if he sometimes co-operated, by unclenching his teeth. They used a little brush and a kind of suction pump, but he was still apparently totally unconscious. About the middle of December we heard that he was going to be transferred to the Eastern Hospital at Homerton near Hackney after Christmas on the 5th January. There was no way that we would be able to visit more than once a week. The journey would take at least one and a half hours each way. It was only afterwards that we heard that it was literally a do or die attempt by St. Bart's. The prognosis was very poor for his recovery and they were very worried about his continual weight loss. He was now only five and a half stone and had several sore places.

During the autumn I had often talked to Clare about getting a job, or furthering her education, and the subject had come up again over dinner. It was two weeks before Christmas. She was always adamant that she was waiting to hear from Dr. Barnardo's but I was convinced that if they had wanted her they would not have waited three months. That night after we had washed up and tidied the kitchen, Peter and I were going to the eight o'clock Mass which Canon Denning was still celebrating on some nights in the week for Father Ken. Clare came to the door with us and I said to her, "Clare, if you have not got a job to go to by Christmas I will find you one myself." I remember feeling very angry and actually slamming the door quite hard. When I got to church I thought a lot about my behaviour, and why I had felt so angry, I wondered if I felt guilty. However I needn't have worried about apologising that night because when Clare saw the car as we returned, she ran to the door and opened it. "Mummy, Daddy, guess who has phoned?" It was obviously not bad news. We thought of everyone we knew, she held us at the door refusing to let us move, making us guess and guess, in the end, she was forced to tell us. It was Mrs Kennerley, the lady from Dr Barnardo's who had written to her. She wanted Clare to go for the day on the 15th January, to see if she thought she would like the work, and get on with the girls, who were known then as delinquent. Then, if she did like the job, and they liked her, she could start immediately as a volunteer for four months, when they would decide if she could continue on the permanent staff and receive training. As a volunteer she would have her keep, pocket money and fares. Clare knew that it was what she wanted to do. It was only afterwards, looking back, that I realised how neatly everything had fallen into place. Just like a lace d'oyley that is being made, always growing and changing. Clare had been at home to help, just at the time when we had needed her, and now she was moving, leaving home for the first time. It was obvious to those of us who believe, that the Lord was truly in charge. My life as I thought then would be returning to normal. We had just visited Kelly Tighe in St. Olave's for the last time before he went home, and Father Ken was moving on and possibly going out of our life for ever. I was always saying to the Lord, "Please help me to do your will," and realising more and more how seemingly difficult this was.

I felt at the beginning there had been no problem, because every-thing seemed so clear, now it was not so clear cut. I prayed that I would have patience to wait and see what was to happen. I was very repentant about my behaviour with Clare, and told her that I was really sorry. She just laughed and gave me a hug, she was so pleased to have her way made clear. She knew in her heart that it was right. I visited Father Ken every single day, and sometimes when there was time, two and occasionally three times a day at weekends, from September until he left St Bartholomew's on the 5th January with the exception of Christmas day. When I went to see him on Christmas Eve in the morning, I was his only visitor and I was offered a glass of sherry. Father Ken was also given one, and the nurses tried hard to get him to have a taste but he was completely unconscious, and unaware. They thought if he could smell it, it might stimulate him. I could make no contact with him in any way, and neither could they, but they assured me that they knew that he was sometimes quite aware, and that they thought he could sometimes see, but they were not sure.

I suppose the nursing staff were less busy at Christmas, they had moved quite a lot of people out of W.G.Grace ward and only had comparatively few to look after. They were very relaxed and gave Father Ken lots of attention beyond the usual care, which for a totally unconscious person is a tremendous amount. They all said that he would be better off now at Hackney because the staff were trained for rehabilitation, which they were not, and also they would have more time for him apart from the absolute care necessary. By this time fewer and fewer people were visiting, there were just a few faithfuls who went each week, apart from those who accompanied Mrs Bell. I had no further meeting with Mrs Bell in

Bart's. The Ward Sister had told me of her usual visiting times, and I was careful to keep out of the way. I really believe that she thought I had stopped visiting. It was just before Father Ken moved to Homerton, in fact the last time that I saw him in St Bartholomew's, he was lying in bed and suddenly seemed very distressed. I watched his lips and he was obviously calling "Nurse," but with no sound, I quickly called the nurses and they were able to help him. It was very exciting. At this time I was not even sure I would ever see him again and I felt rather sad, but really believed that if I was meant to see him again I would. I chatted to him about his move and told him that I would only ever be able to come on a Saturday. I told him how much better I thought he was, without knowing of course, what he could really understand. If it was nothing, it didn't matter, but if it was something, then it was all important. We shall never know.

Chapter Eleven

The Eastern Hospital

It so happened that we were not able to go to the Eastern Hospital at Hackney on the first Saturday Father Ken was there, consequently when we saw him he had already been there well over a week. I was both pleased and distressed when I saw him. He was sitting in a wheelchair with a table attached to the front of it on which was a plastic mug of water, even though he could not pick it up. His nose tube had been removed and he was swathed in an over wrap to try and catch the mixture that was running from his gaping mouth. His seemingly lifeless head was resting heavily on his chest, as it had been before unless I had tied it up around his forehead holding it against the back of his chair. Here there was nowhere to tie it. The chair had a low back and he was slumped in it.

He was based in a large long ward with approximately twenty five beds, with a locker and chair beside each bed. Many people were in wheelchairs, some were watching the television which seemed very loud. They were all in varying stages of brain damage. There were apparently no other visitors although I had telephoned and was told that it was alright to come before lunch which was at twelve midday. We greeted Father Ken warmly as always, saying who we were and asking him did he remember us? He showed no sign of recognition although his good eye was open. He had a black eye patch over the other damaged eye. Nothing moved. I felt a great desire to clean him up and help him in some way, but realised now that I must just allow myself to let go all my hopes and all the little things I had done. I felt we had been removed from his immediate situation and this was rather painful. I realised that he had moved into another stage of recovery about which I knew nothing. We sat with him chatting about the hospital and the changes that had happened. I asked him if he would like a drink of water, and I thought his right eye flickered a sign of something. I picked up the plastic mug and put it to his mouth. He could not drink it because his mouth hung so open that the water just poured down his front. It was almost lunchtime when we arrived and wheelchairs were being pushed to the long centre table which was laid with cutlery and glasses.

A nurse of Asian origin came over to Father Ken, who was not taken to the table, and took off the dirty cloth which was round him. She put a plastic apron over his head and tied it round him, threading the tapes through the neck loop so that it pulled up tight under his chin. She then fixed the plastic bowl she had brought onto his lap against the arm of the chair. She said hello to us while she was working and asked us if we were relatives. We told her that we weren't but that we had been visiting Father Ken in Bart's. She then disappeared through the door at the end from which lunch for the others was appearing. She returned almost immediately with a large plate of fine mince and mashed potato and a dessert spoon. She took a little on the spoon and tested it on the back of her hand for heat and then, taking a full spoonful from round the edge of the plate, she proceeded to push large spoonfuls of the mince and potato into Father Ken's mouth, quite a lot of which ran out and was caught in the basin. She went on putting in spoonfuls until he almost choked and at that point she stopped.

She explained to us that the only way he was going to learn to eat was by forcing him to swallow. She said feeding him with a teaspoon would be no good because it would not make his muscles work. They had removed the feeding tube immediately he had been admitted, and he was only being fed by mouth. He moved his mouth up and down struggling to get his breath, swallowing some food and losing some. When it had all gone, she started the process again, and it was obvious that he was actually swallowing quite a lot as he almost had no option, once the food was in his mouth and pushed back into his throat he had to swallow, it was an involuntary act. She repeated this three times, showing me how important it was to push the dessert spoon right into his mouth. I could see that Father Ken was aware of what was going on, but could say or do nothing to stop it. Occasionally he moved his right hand, but the nurse held it down. I wanted to clean him up between the bouts of feeding, but the nurse said it was better to leave it to the end and that keeping him clean while feeding him was not important, it was better that he ate. She chatted to him all the time, in a friendly encouraging way, persuading him, and telling him how well he was doing. She then asked me if I would like to try. I was terrified. This was something different, and I had had no experience. My timid efforts in Bart's with a tiny bit of scrambled egg on a teaspoon were far removed from this. At first I was not able to do it, but then she held my hand and forced the spoon right into his mouth. "It's no good unless you get it to the back of his throat. He will at least swallow some then." I begged her not to leave us because I was afraid he would choke, but she assured me that even if he choked he would survive. It had to be done if he was to eat properly again. She explained that with four months of feeding through the nose tube, it was going to take time to get his muscles working again. "Don't worry" she assured us, "he will eat." She spoke with such conviction that my spirits were slightly lifted again because it all seemed so hopeless. Where was my unshakable faith of his recovery to some sort of consciousness which I had experienced previously? I continued until the plate was empty. The nurse then appeared with a dish of rice pudding. "He is doing marvellously." she said, "Last week we could hardly get anything down him. You're doing great aren't you my darling?" she said addressing Father Ken. Peter sat by me all the time until the plate was empty and then we started to clean up. I took the basin to the sluice which was on the opposite side of the ward, where a nurse told me to leave it, and gave me a clean one. I asked for a cloth and having asked what it was for she gave me a clean one, and I put some warm water in the bowl. Peter helped me and we did our best to clean up the mess, it was really impossible because the flow of saliva and food continued from Father Ken's mouth. 'Our' nurse returned and was really pleased with our efforts. She took his toothbrush and gave his mouth a little brush using the mug of water. It didn't make a lot of difference. She brought a clean mug of water and tried to get him to put his hand round it and pick it up. I noticed for the first time that his hand was very misshapen, his third and little fingers were locked onto the palm of his hand and his first and second fingers and his thumbs were bent and rigid. This I realised was the spasticisation that we had heard about. I had not noticed before, because his hand had always been in the naturally closed position. If I had held it, it was either by putting my hand on his, or by slipping my fingers under his. I had not realised what this meant until that moment. She stretched his hand out as far as it would go and put it round the plastic glass as well as she could and lifted it to his mouth with her hand helping his. He seemed to make some effort with his arm. I thought he could see what was happening. Although it was all so messy I could see the methods involved were not a chance trial but had most probably saved his life. There was a long way to go.

At 2.30pm. we saw through the window that Mrs Bell had arrived. We quickly gathered our things and said our goodbyes. Father Ken tried to move his head a little and it was quite difficult to leave him. He was such a very sorry sight. We thought that he was showing that he did not want us to go. We promised to come the following Saturday. Mrs Bell did not see us as we left by a side door.

Each time we visited there was an improvement of some kind. Father Ken became more aware although still staring and unseeing, after three weeks he was consciously swallowing and was able to eat crustless sandwiches, and to my surprise, they gave him peeled seedless grapes among other things. He was not apparently more aware but the fact that he was eating better was a very positive sign. Each week I brought a large bath towel with me that I could pack round him, and pour water at least into his mouth and let it run through so that a little stayed. I felt he was thirsty but was unable to drink because of the state of his mouth. He enjoyed having water poured into his mouth and indicated he would like me to do it again, or so we thought. I had to remember that I only came on Saturday, so the rest of the week whatever was done had to be sufficient. The nurse told us they gave him the grapes to help quench his thirst. They didn't mind whatever we did to help; they were always very busy and obviously expected the visitors to do something if they could.

We continued to go to the hospital every week and towards the end of February something very exciting happened. When we arrived Father was in bed and we could see that he had visitors, people that we had not seen before, with a little boy who was then seven. They were chatting to him and trying to get him to eat something. We watched for a little while, unseen, and then decided to go and have some lunch and come back later. When we returned the visitors were still there and we went in just intending to say hello, and then go home. We realised always that we had no place there when there were people who knew Father well, and strangely we could absolutely accept this. We asked them if they would mind if we just said hello to Father Ken and before we could say any more they asked us if by any chance we were Paulette and Peter. They said that Father Ken had been asking them if we were there. They had not visited before so they did not realise that we had not actually heard him speak. He was actually making sounds through the movements on his lips, and with patience and listening, you could sometimes decipher a word or two with difficulty. This was indeed a wonderful breakthrough. When I took hold of his hand and said "This is Paulette" and "this is Peter," he squeezed my hand, and I knew that he was going to be alright. The tears rolled down my cheeks. It was an incredible moment. Had he really known it was Saturday, and was he actually expecting us? We shall never really know because each day is sufficient for itself and there was no way that it mattered at that time. The fact was that in all the time that we had been visiting, he had heard our names. He must have realised what was going on. I always said to him "Father, this is Paulette," and if Peter was with me, "and this is Peter." We introduced ourselves to his visitors and they said they were friends from his last but one parish which was Sevenoaks. They evidently had not seen him in Bart's because of the long journey. Today they had brought a picnic so that they could stay. They had come early and were just leaving anyway. We went outside while they said goodbye to Father Ken and then we went in. Sadly these people must have moved and they lost touch with both ourselves and Father Ken although we did at one stage go to visit them at their house in Sevenoaks.

We noticed about this time that things were changing around Father Ken's bed. There were a whole lot of children's pictures pinned up, there was a box of tissues on the locker, and altogether Father looked cleaner and more cared for. We knew that his mother was not able to do much for him, particularly at the distance that she was from him. We wondered who it was helping him because it had made such a difference. We found out that he was in bed because he was getting sores from sitting in his chair. He was so thin and there was no flesh on his bones. We tried to extract from him who else was visiting for it was more obvious than ever that someone was taking a lot of care and interest. He made an effort to say something but try as we might we could not understand. We then decided to ask the ward Sister who we had not really spoken to before. She told us that a religious Sister, who had previously visited the ward from time to time, had been coming in every day, and was looking after Father Ken; more than that she didn't know. She told us that the Sister was usually there early on Saturday morning, and that she was gone by 11 o'clock. We decided to come early the next week to meet her. It was such a comfort to know that someone local was taking an interest.

The next week we arrived to find Sister Patricia. We had an immediate rapport with her. The first thing she asked was did we know Mrs Bell. Mrs Bell had evidently found Sister Patricia sorting out and removing his washing and had told her to leave him alone. It appeared that Sister Pat had been making her usual visit to the ward, and had come across this sad-looking emaciated man, very in need of personal care of every kind over and above the nursing. She asked if she could see his name, who he was and where he came from, only to find out of course that he was a priest from the Southwark Diocese. She immediately made an appointment with Bishop Guazzelli, her own bishop, to ask if she could have permission to bring him communion. Bishop Guazzelli commissioned her straight away. From that day she had taken Father Ken under her wing. How good the Lord is. Patricia had already devised a method of keeping at least his front clean...er. A stream of viscous fluid flowed continuously. She had machined round the edges of oblong pieces of terry towelling and sewn large press studs on the corners, so that there were six layers. These were fixed on a bottom layer which pinned on his shirt. As the top layer of towelling became dirty it could be peeled off to expose the clean layer, and because it was absorbent, it helped to mop up. Pat had made several sets of these to allow for washing. This was a tremendous improvement. She had a little plastic bag handy to collect the dirty squares which she took each evening to wash. She came in early each morning to bring communion and help him in whatever way she could, before she went to school.

She was a teacher in the local Catholic school, hence the children's pictures. In the evening she returned to take Father Ken's dirty washing, and to say goodnight. She knew nothing of his background, and although we also knew little, we could tell her of the events since September. This was obviously the reason for his great step forward. We met Patricia from then on every Saturday morning and exchanged news.

It was on the 18th March 1978 when Patricia had gone and we had decided that it would be good to go out for a little walk. It was cold so we wrapped Father Ken up well with jacket and blankets and hat. He was back in the wheelchair, his sores temporarily better. While we were walking I was chatting to him and trying to understand what he was saying. It was still very difficult; we stopped at a seat for a little while, and he said "It is the feast of St Joseph tomorrow. Pat has given me communion." Whether he was just speaking more clearly, or whether I had got used to translating the noises, I don't know. From that day it became easier to understand him, insofar as he could try and speak. Sometimes it was of course impossible. Meeting Patricia had been such a blessing. Her influence had undoubtedly helped him greatly. She was so sensible and down to earth and was daunted by nothing. In the Sacred Heart Convent, where she lived, there were no facilities for her to do machine washing at night, so she did it all by hand, and hung it up where she could, to dry. She always had washing and ironing on the go and of course with her full time job, she had become very busy, but she coped with it very well.

It is interesting how St Joseph's feast day became an important day for me, just as Camillus of Lellis' did with no real known reason. It was only afterwards that I really 'heard' the words which appear in the 'Prayer of the Church' on St. Joseph's day from Chapter 11 of Hebrews about faith:-

"All these died in faith before receiving any of the things that were promised, but they saw them in the far distance, and welcomed them, realising that they were only strangers and nomads on earth. People who use such terms about themselves make it quite plain that they are in search of their real homeland."

The writer of Hebrews is speaking about people of faith from the Old Testament, but in reading this passage I could better understand how I was caught up in something that was inexplicable. It was to do with trust and faith in God in a way that made me do things now, which seemed to have no ending, in the sure faith that God loved me and wanted me to do it for some purpose that I didn't then understand. I didn't have an easy explanation for people who questioned me. Many thought I was stupid and unwise and possibly interfering and said so. There was no argument, perhaps I was, but a force carried me on that is impossible to explain. It was 'Good News' and not 'bad', but to the human and worldly eye it looked like bad news. I knew that God loved me and that he wanted the very best for me, and whatever that meant, I was willing to go along with it. There were so many arguments against it. To me they were quite irrelevant. Peace reigned within Peter and myself, and all was well. One of the intercessory prayers on the same feast day is:-

"Father, give us that faith which gives substance to our hopes, and make us certain of realities we do not see."

We came to know the nurses who were regularly on duty, and most of them were very kind and caring. I think we knew them well too, because of Patricia. When they saw our relationship with her, they trusted us more. They also came to know Father Ken very well, as he was beginning to respond they talked and teased him all the time. He was always pleased when we arrived although we were not sure whether he recognised us by sight or only by the sound of our voices. At this time Father Ken was being taken to the physiotherapy unit each day, except Saturday and Sunday, and because he was a little more responsive they could do a little more with him. The unit was open five days a week, and everyone else in his ward went to some sort of therapy all day on those five days. Because of his comatose state Father Ken had been left in the ward and had received some therapy there, but as he was gradually becoming more conscious they found it fruitful for him to actually be in the physio unit all the time. At least there was more mental stimulation there than on his own in the ward all the week. We only came to know this through Sister Pat who took on the role of carer. Father Ken was becoming able to show his emotions, he was usually very distressed, and cried a lot, and was sometimes very angry. Patricia occasionally helped to put him to bed in the evening and she said it was quite a big job. On Sunday night particularly they were usually short staffed, and she helped to lift him out of the chair and onto the bed before they got him undressed. He would cry with fear because he felt so insecure. She told us that he was often very angry. Patricia had started reading evening prayer to him before he tucked down for the night, which he obviously liked very much. We had found praying with him more difficult as he had become more conscious, because there was so much more to do, and also that he wanted to try and talk more. I found I was praying silently for him, and we would always say a prayer aloud with him before we left the hospital. We heard from Sister Pat all the every day stories about the happenings in the ward, and about the other people. There was Sid who was very pleasant and very willing, but sometimes forgot who he was and where he was. He sometimes got lost and disappeared into other parts of the hospital. They had to keep an identification tag on him. It was impossible to watch him all the time. He was very mobile, and took it upon himself to push Father Ken's wheelchair from the ward up to the physiotherapy department which was quite a long way and involved walking outside. This was okay until one day Sid got a bit exuberant and tipped Father Ken into the bushes by accident. Another time there was an Italian man in the next bed to Father Ken who could speak very little English. His relatives also could only speak a little English. They gave Ken a little rosary when they knew he was a priest, and he said, "The only Italian I know is.... 'La tua manina gelida." (Your tiny hand is frozen, from Verdi's opera.) This became a huge joke with everyone. It was the beginning of understanding Ken's great knowledge of music and opera. It was an intellectual knowledge both of the lives of composers and their music. It did not take us long to find out his great likes and his extremely strong dislikes. Even at this stage he could be scathing about the music that he did not like. He had never played an instrument, so his knowledge was not practical. Sometimes Ken would try and read 'The Times.' It was obvious that his sight was improving and already his left eye was returning to normal, even though it had been said he might never be able to see with it. He would also use words in an extraordinary way. I can remember him saying, "This paper is devoid of any news," with great anger and disgust. I guess it was because he was unable to read it.

Because of his inability to move and because of his thinness, the sores on his bottom and back had never properly healed and because he did not get 'nursed' in the physio unit in the same way as in the ward, they became very much worse. We arrived one Saturday at the beginning of April to find him not only in bed, but on a water bed with the doctor visiting every hour. He was crying and in great pain. Everyone thought he was going to die.

They had previously removed his catheter as he was able to be more in control, but now it had been replaced. He was unable to eat and they were loath to put him back on artificial feeding. He was only five and a half stone. It was a sad and worrying time. The sores were evidently very bad. Patricia had actually seen them. How they ever treated them I don't know. The water bed helped, and they turned him every twenty minutes, from one side to the other. They tried to lie him on his front, but his body was so immobile he couldn't breathe properly. After one week when we saw him again he was slightly better and was able to eat. By the second week he was greatly recovered and took on a new lease of life.

It was during this period that Mrs Bell arrived at a different time from usual, with her nephew Christopher who was visiting from Australia. (We have during the intervening years entertained Father Ken's cousins and second cousins from Australia, and I write to them regularly. One second cousin Peter is a priest, who we have come to know well). Mrs Bell saw us immediately as we were sitting in the waiting area, while the nurses were caring for Father. She said, "So you're here are you? I thought I wouldn't see any more of you." She did not introduce us to her nephew, and obviously did not know that we had been visiting each week. When she went to see the Sister in charge, he spoke to us and said his name was Christopher, and that he had just arrived from Australia and was over here for a year, working. We said hello to him, introduced ourselves, and just said we were parishioners from Father's new parish. We went home as it seemed pointless to antagonise Mrs Bell by being there.

As Father recovered from the bed sores and became more interested in food and what was going on, it was decided to remove his catheter again. This was a major step forward and at first he was very anxious because he could not manage on his own. This time, although he was over-anxious it worked well, and gave him a sense that he was making progress, or rather perhaps gave us the sense that he was making progress. He was very low and distressed most of the time. By now he was just able to move his wheelchair by walking his feet. They had taught him to do this in the physio department according to Patricia. He would slip down in the chair, so that his feet were flat on the ground, and walk forward. It was very much hit and miss to start with because he could not steer, but in an amazingly short space of time he understood how to turn it to the left and the right. Reversing was more difficult because he could not move his head, and his chin was still locked down on his chest. As he made more progress his distress seemed to get worse. I think that perhaps he was more aware of his disability. It wasn't any good to reassure him that he was doing well, because he couldn't manage and he knew it. Pat would phone us sometimes during the week to keep us in touch and tell us the news. She had also fallen foul of Mrs Bell again who said she was interfering, but Pat also used to avoid her visiting times which were now getting fewer owing to the longer distance and the difficulty of finding people to bring her; also the fact that Father was in the physiotherapy unit all the week until 5.00pm. There were still one or two very faithful people, who regularly were willing to act as chauffeur for Mrs Bell when they were not working.

Father Ken was unable to move any part of himself on his own, except his arms a little, and now his feet. It took two nurses to lift him all the time and dress him. Eating had improved quite considerably, but it was still very difficult for him, and he could not feed himself. A nurse would put a spoon in his hand and hold her hand round it, then take a spoonful of food and bend his arm round to get the spoon to his mouth. It was still a tedious and messy process, but he was getting more food, and swallowing had become much easier. The following week when we visited, we found him sitting in his chair in a different area. I think they had put him where he could see the television (which he obviously hated), so that he had something to do. It was very noisy and dominated everything. He was crying and moaning. We asked him what was the matter and he tried to tell us. We found it very difficult to understand what he was trying to say but eventually we could get it together. He said, "God helps those who help themselves, and I can't help myself, so how is God going to help me?" We were really moved by his distress. Peter and I both strongly disagree with this idea that God only looks after you if you can look after yourself; to us this was a very worldly saying. I, for the first time, was able to put my arms round Father Ken and hold him. He really cried and it was as if he was in the depths of despair. We comforted him and told him that God loved him just as he was, and that he was already being helped by God. This day was a big breakthrough in many ways. Pat, from the beginning, had addressed Father as Ken, but for us it was more difficult as we had first known him as Father Bell, not even as Father Ken and this was very distancing, although I had not let this aspect worry me. Now, I asked him if we could call him Ken, and he nodded and answered, "It's my name." I also felt on this day I was free to touch him, or put my arms round him, when he needed it. Previously I had felt shy and unsure, and a little afraid in some way of Mrs Bell, although she did not know.

In the Sacred Heart Convent at Blackheath, which was a sister community of Pat's, there was a young Sister named Angela. She was unable to walk and had a little car for her own use. She had a wheelchair and was very independent. It was decided between them, that if they had help either end, and if Angela left her own wheelchair at home, putting his wheelchair in the car, they could take Ken to tea at Blackheath so that he could meet the sisters and have a change of view. Pat was sure they could manage it.

A great deal of planning went into it so that Angela would arrive on time and help be available to lift Ken out of the wheelchair and into the car, then the reverse procedure for the return. Pat usually went everywhere by bicycle. She had a padlock and would chain her bike up wherever she happened to be. The trip to Blackheath was a very daring expedition. They fixed it for a Saturday afternoon and all went very well. Peter and I were there to help at the Homerton end, and we saw them off on their fairly long journey which took them through the Blackwall tunnel. The sisters at Blackheath were delighted to have him, and they made a great fuss of him. Whether he enjoyed it was another matter, and was difficult to estimate, but Pat thought anything that moved things on must be good. She had endless energy and great enthusiasm. The second time that Angela and Pat took Ken we were invited as well, and we met them at the convent at Blackheath. The sisters were very welcoming, and they were delighted with the improvement in Ken even in those few weeks.

Ken was becoming more conscious, all the time. He had 'made up' names for the nurses, given and remembered, I think, with Pat's help. One I remember well was Princess, she had told him that in her own country she was a princess, and the name had stuck. Ken however was very angry much of the time. His voice was loud and uncontrolled. His fear made him nervous and altogether he was a sorry sight. One day we knew that he could really see detail, at least with his right eye, (his left eye was turning down in the right direction daily and was looking more normal). It was ten past twelve by the large clock just above and in front of Ken, on the wall. He walked his wheelchair to the centre table and when one of the nurses came in, still with no sign of food, he shouted at her, "Where is the lunch? It is supposed to be here by twelve o'clock." She said to him with great good humour, "Why dear, are you hungry?" "No I'm not," he shouted aggressively, "the hospital rules say lunch is at twelve and they should be kept, you are paid to do your job properly." We began to see more and more that we were getting to know someone who was a man of the rule, and a hard taskmaster, but already the Lord had put love in my heart for him. I cared a great deal what happened to him even though I was now only seeing him once a week.

We had several adventures on our visits to Homerton. One day we overshot the entrance to the hospital. It was a comparatively narrow drive leading in to the car park and you had to watch carefully for it as you came near. We drove past it and turned into the fire station which was next to the hospital; as we drove up the concrete to the red doors which were closed, intending to turn round, our car stopped and refused to move. We tried everything to start the car, but to no avail. Suddenly the fire engine appeared behind us, waiting to get in off the main road. The driver hooted gently and then realised that we could not move. Several of the firemen came and tried their luck at starting the car unsuccessfully. The engine was causing quite an obstruction on the main road, and we did not know what to do. We were well aware that we should not have been there in the first place. Eventually six of the firemen got hold of the car, and lifted it off their 'runway.' We were really embarrassed. It was all done with great humour. We then spent all day, waiting until it was dark, for the AA to come. We had to take it in turns to visit Ken because we couldn't leave the car. The day finished with a fish and chip meal wrapped in paper and eaten with our fingers in the back of the van, which towed us back to Purley.

It was about this time that we heard through one of the ward maids that Ken was moving. She knew no more than that. I went through the process again in my prayers, that maybe the time had come to let go of Ken and Pat and everything that I was doing. We didn't officially ask anything. I still recognised that we had no official capacity. I thought that if we waited we would hear from Pat, when we saw her the following week. In my heart I knew that it was right not to ask questions or to strive unduly, the Lord knew that I was here, and it was within his power to show me something else if he so wanted, if I waited patiently and kept a low profile, but Pat knew no more than us. She also kept a low profile and asked nothing. She had heard that Ken was moving to London, and that was all. I think we all guessed that Mrs Bell had eventually got her own way and that he would be going out of our reach. I felt very sad as we were just making contact with him as a 'real' human being, and saw his anger and his fear and his sadness. He was always dour and miserable, and needed a lot of help and encouragement.

Every weekday morning Peter went to early Mass at Southwark Cathedral, where he had made friends with some Sisters of Mercy who indeed I had also met in other circumstances, at the 'Southwark Days of Renewal'. They had all been praying for Ken at our request. One day soon after this, Sister Elizabeth greeted Peter, and said how interesting it was that Father Bell was going to be coming to the nursing home near the Cathedral, which belonged to their order. (It has since been sold and has become a private clinic). Peter showed great surprise and interest. Sister Elizabeth thought that it was for some weekends only. It was all done with great secrecy, not even Pat knew until the last moment. It was to me as if the Lord really wanted us to know where Father Ken was going. We actually visited the Eastern Hospital at Homerton early the next Saturday as usual to find that Ken had already gone.

Pat had been so rushed getting his things organised when she had arrived in the morning that she had not had time to telephone us and when she did we had left home already. The Sister in charge told us that he was going to Southwark every other weekend. Mrs

Bell thought it would be a change for him and that it would be easier for her to visit, but she had wanted it kept quiet. Patricia, whilst accepting what had happened, was obviously upset at the way it had all been handled. I think she felt if she had known before, she could have prepared him for the change. She waited at the hospital until we arrived and we had a long chat with her, seeing again how we could help each other to help Ken in a way that would enable him to develop and grow within the limits of his brain damage. We also prayed together that we would be guided by the Lord and not try to go our own way. We all wanted to do what the Lord wanted. This is sometimes a very difficult discernment when one feels there is lots of opposition. We prayed for Mrs Bell that the Lord would bring her peace in what was a sad and very difficult time for her, and that we would have love and patience when she confronted us. We weren't sure whether we would be able to visit Father Ken in the Nursing Home in Kennington or whether we might be intruding. On Sunday we were out in the north of London and, as we came home through the centre of London, Peter suggested that we popped in to the nursing home quickly just to see how things were. We were not even sure that Ken would still be there. We knew exactly where we were going and when we arrived we were immediately shown into a room with four beds, but only one of them occupied. Father Ken was sitting by a bed with a fixed table in front of him eating his supper on his own. Food was all round his face and he had in front of him a glass dish with the remains of a fruit salad in it, which he was eating with his hands. There was fruit salad all over the table and he was in a real mess. As soon as he saw us he started crying, saying he could not manage. It was very sad to see him. I found a spoon and cleaned him up and helped him to feed himself with the spoon. He was very unhappy and was not able to communicate with anyone. I think they could not understand him. He was still very dependent for absolutely everything and, although he was now free of the catheter, he needed total help in the toilet because he was unable to use his hands properly. His fingers were locked into his palms and they were stiff. He was more aware of his helplessness than before. We reassured him as much as we could.

As we left the nursing home and were just getting into the car, a man approached us in a very distressed state. At first we had a difficulty in understanding what he wanted. His mother had died in a hospital in London and he was trying to get there to find out the details. It was only when we offered him a lift we understood the real tragedy that surrounded him. He was unable to get in a car, or indeed onto a bus because he had previously been in a terrible road accident in which his wife had been killed. His legs were set straight and wide apart and he could only walk by moving them wide apart with great difficulty. As we listened to his story, we felt great compassion. He had walked all the way from a residential home in Sussex where they were looking after him. He said he could do a little work on the farm and that was all. He was hoping to have more operations on his legs so that he could walk more normally. He had been through a terrible trauma and really wanted to find out the details of his mother's death. I guess that no one was able to help him get to London because he could not travel in a car or a mini-bus, and he had taken the matter into his own hands. He wanted to know the way to the hospital where she had died. He told us that he had left the residential home without them knowing, as he had been told he could not go to London. We decided that it was best if we took him on the underground, and we walked with him very slowly to the nearest underground station, which was Lambeth North. He thought he might possibly be able to get on an underground train as it would not be crowded at that time of night. It was really difficult for him since everybody had to keep out of his way as walking took up so much room. It was especially difficult on the escalator which he could manage better than the stairs. Once we reached the hospital he said he would be alright. He was sure they would in some way help him to get back. Peter gave him some money which he did not really want to take. He took our address and promised to keep in touch but he never did. I often think of him and have prayed for him, but with all we were involved with in our own lives at that time we had to let it pass. I think the Lord has been trying to teach me that I cannot take on the whole world (except in prayer), and that I must listen to Him and do what He wants and not what I want.

We continued to visit the Eastern Hospital at Homerton on Saturdays when Ken was there, and we went to Southwark on Sundays, when he was at the nursing home. We asked the Sisters if anyone had thought of taking him to Mass at the Cathedral, it was about ten minutes walk. No one had, so we arranged that if they had him ready we would come on Sunday morning and push him to Mass in the wheelchair. We left armed with his toilet bottle, hidden under a rug. He could not move without it. Since the catheter had been removed this was a source of great worry to him, he was not actually incontinent but was never sure of himself. We arrived at the Cathedral and took him down to the front where we were all hidden from the main congregation by a large pillar. The Cathedral has been reordered since, but this place was ideal for us, then. The first time we went, Father Joe Collins was saying Mass and Ken knew him and remembered him. At communion Ken was given a whole host before we thought to say a half, please. He could not swallow it, and as always the stream of viscous fluid was flowing freely. Peter went to the sacristy, a long walk on the other side of the Cathedral to find some water. There was no ordinary glass and he came back with water in a pint beer mug. I meanwhile had been scooping up pieces of soggy host, and popping them back in Ken's mouth as well as I could, feeling quite sure that the Lord understood. Ken was crying and was very upset all through the Mass. He was aware that he was not able to manage anything. He was very depressed, yet he wanted to be there.

The second time we took him he was even more upset. There had been a terrible event in the nursing home. All the patients had been given Christmas pudding for supper the night before, even though of course it was not Christmas. Whatever had been the matter with it I don't know, but all the staff felt sure this was the cause of the disaster. Everyone had an upset stomach and as almost everyone was immobile, it was very difficult for the staff to cope. When we arrived they were still very busy changing beds and dealing with the laundry. They had found it difficult to get breakfast to everyone. Ken was still crying. He was humiliated and embarrassed. He was eventually able to tell us how terrible it was for him. He found his inability to move devastating and he could not be comforted. He held on to me all the time and kept on saying "Don't leave me, don't leave me." Father Tony Charlton was saying a Mass for the children. We armed ourselves with the glass of water beforehand and set ourselves up behind the pillar. Ken was distressed all through Mass. When Father Tony sang "The banner over me is love," with actions for the children, in a way that the children loved, and so did we, Ken became angry, and tried to tell us through his tears and distress, that this was not the correct way to say Mass. I was beginning to see that he had very definite ideas of his own, and sick though he was, he was able to express his dislikes very strongly.

We found out that an arrangement was being made to take Ken to Lourdes for a week. Patricia was asked by the hospital if she would get his clothes ready, and when the time arrived we met at the Southwark nursing home to see him off. Mrs Bell was very annoyed with both Patricia and myself as well as Peter. She did not like it that we were there. We realised perhaps for the first time that she had no idea of the help that Ken was getting. It was for me very difficult to see him shouting and crying, so insecure, and so unsure of what would happen. All the helpers were busy with the organisation. Patricia and I put our hands on him to try and comfort and soothe him, but Mrs Bell told us to leave him alone, that he didn't like being treated like that because he was a priest. His own attitude showed her that was not the truth, but she did not wish to know. He was very unhappy inside and needed comforting just like a little child. I know that it is said you are never too ill or too weak to go to Lourdes but I was aware of Ken's distress because he could not do anything for himself, and also because no one could understand him. He was also afraid of going with complete strangers, although of course we knew they would look after him. He had one person who was detailed to look after him alone for the whole week. Ken found it a very difficult experience and his body was quite bruised afterwards by the manhandling on and off the mini-bus each day, as they evidently had no wheelchair lift. When he returned they had to keep him in bed at Southwark for the whole week as he was so tired and ill and bruised. Far worse than when he went, physically anyway. He had been looked after by his carer and by the group with a lot of love, and they said certainly in some ways it had done him good, but the whole expedition was too much for him. He was put off going to Lourdes again for a long time.

By now we were into June and he had a very big disappointment. I am sure it came about by misunderstanding. It was very difficult to make any definite arrangement directly with Ken because it was impossible to know if he understood or not. It was evidently arranged, or so the Ward Sister had thought and so had Patricia, that someone from his seminary class would come and collect Ken on the 8th June. It was the day that his class always have a celebration to commemorate their ordination. Mrs Bell had sent his black suit to the hospital and Patricia had come in earlier in the morning to help dress him. Peter and I did not know about all this until afterwards. No one came.

Ken thought they were going to take him to Mass and then to lunch as was their usual celebration. He, of course, had no idea of the difficulty that there was in looking after him for the day, especially for someone who was not used to him. Whatever had happened in the talking about it no one knows. We guessed that someone had come to see him, had told him of the reunion and said they would leave it until another year without realising Ken's limited understanding. We shall never know. The result of this was that he insisted on keeping his suit on all day, which was about five sizes too big, and even in the evening he did not want to take it off in case they came for him. This incident upset him very much, and after this everyone including the Ward Sister was very careful to make a note of everything that anyone said that was not in the hospital routine so that she would know what actually had been arranged. The staff were on the whole, very caring and compassionate. Ken was still upset about it when we saw him at the weekend. He felt he had been abandoned, although in actual fact we are sure that he had misunderstood, and whichever of his classmates had visited him had been quite unaware. It showed us something very important though, and that was that Ken had a great desire to be associated with his past. It was impossible to know how much he actually remembered. His distress was so great that one could not find out his exact thoughts.

After this I discussed with Peter the possibility of bringing Ken home for a weekend to see if we could bring some joy into his terrible depression. Our youngest son Paul had already accompanied us to the hospital at Homerton so he knew the situation. It would mean a total concentration on what had to be done for Ken. The next week we went to Homerton expecting to find him, but it had been arranged suddenly that he went to Southwark. I was able to have a talk with the ward Sister, who by this time knew Ken well. She knew all about his anger and shouting, and his frustrations as well as his deep depression. I asked her if there was any treatment that he was having that we could not give him if we took him home for a week-end. She said that what he needed more than anything, was love. We could manage his tablets, and she knew that we could handle him physically because she had seen us lifting him and helping him. She didn't ask us who we were, but she obviously had noticed that we were regular visitors. She was most encouraging and said she would do everything she could to help.

We phoned the nursing home when we returned home and arranged to collect Ken in time for Mass the following morning. They were very happy to have him ready, and thought it was very beneficial that he went out. We arranged on these Sundays to have an evening dinner at home. Paul liked this as it gave him a freedom for the day; he was always very sociable and had lots of things to do. He was often away with the Venture Scouts, he and Clare had been members for quite a long time. Now of course she was living away from home and was only with us on her days off duty. She had already been accepted on to the permanent staff and had started training with Dr Barnardo's and was very happy.

We took Ken to Mass and afterwards we asked him if he would like an ice cream. He was able to hold it for himself, with some help; I always carried large cloths and handkerchiefs with me in case we needed them. We went into the park near the Cathedral, and stopped by a seat. I asked Ken if he would let me look after him if we took him home for the weekend. He burst into tears, and said "Yes." I explained to him that it would mean a long journey in the car on Friday night, and again on Sunday, and that we would have to learn how to manage, but that I was sure that we could. He wept and wept and said "Yes, yes, yes please." At this time Ken could not even sit up on his own, he was like a little baby. When he was lifted out of his wheelchair, he either had to be put in another secure chair, or if he was put on the bed he had to be laid down. We knew all these things including his toilet needs, but it did not seem too difficult. We spoke to Patricia and asked her if she would like to come down for the day on the Saturday and help us. She thought it was a marvellous idea and said she would and she agreed the sooner the better. She arranged with the Sister that we would come and collect him on Saturday morning and return him on Sunday night. We had wanted to say from Friday night, but felt for the first time it was better to start simply. I was rather concerned about Mrs Bell and I think that the Sister phoned her to say he was going away. The Sister said he is a grown man and well able to answer for himself what he liked and what he didn't.

I prepared everything during the week so that I could make the weekend easy. I did the shopping and cooked and prepared food for all of us. We brought the bed from the spare room down to the dining room and placed it under the window. It was the bed that had been Alan's, with the same two blankets. I had already purchased a waterproof mattress cover. On Saturday morning we were up early, and when we arrived Patricia was waiting with everything ready. It was decided she would come with us in the car and return in the evening on the train. I lifted Ken from the wheelchair into the front seat of the car in the same way as I had seen the nurses do it and there was no problem, he was not heavy at all. He had gained a little weight but it went on very slowly. He was very apprehensive, but also cooperative. And we managed the journey with no problem. We fortunately could manage to get the wheelchair into the downstairs cloakroom with ease. It had been the one thing that I had been slightly concerned about. Patricia and I had both been helping Ken in the toilet so this was not a problem for any of us. Ken settled down extremely well until the afternoon when we tucked him up on the bed for a rest. We went in another room and left him. I crept back after a few minutes to see if he was alright. At first I could not understand what the matter was. He was not able to express his exact feelings in any way but I could see he was looking afraid. I asked him a lot of questions and eventually reached the point that I could begin to understand that he was really afraid of being left on his own. I suddenly realised that he had never, since his accident, been left alone. He was used to sleeping in a ward of people with a nurse present, and during the day was always with somebody. We all moved back into the dining room and I sat beside him until he became peaceful and went to sleep.

Between us we managed everything very well, the biggest job as always was not the physical 'looking after', although that was time consuming, but keeping Ken's spirits up. He was extremely depressed. He was on a variety of drugs that were given him to keep his brain balanced and to avoid epileptic fits taking place. Every now and again for whatever reason he did have a 'petit mal' which lasted a few minutes and made him feel ill. Speech became much worse than usual at this time and it upset him a great deal. He made it clear to us that he did not like it in the hospital. It was obvious that he felt no trust in the doctors. It was mainly a lady doctor who looked after his psychological welfare and this did not please him either even though she was actually very interested and caring. We later came to know clearly that he had no trust in, and no liking for doctors, solicitors or bank managers. Pat helped me to put Ken to bed about the same time as he went to bed at the hospital. He still found drinking very very difficult, not only actually keeping the liquid in his mouth, but also swallowing was difficult. It took a long time to help him drink even a half a cupful, and we got a little bit later than we had intended. However, Pat knew the times of her trains and she was not worried. She had chained up her bike at the station near the convent and assured us that she would be okay. She left at 9.00 pm. and the journey took her one and a half hours. That night we put a mattress by Ken's bed and I slept beside him. There was no way that he could go to sleep alone downstairs, he was terrified. As soon as he knew someone was going to be there he began to settle down. He had already had many phases of not knowing where he was in the hospital, for long periods of time. We knew this, and it was obvious that his mind played tricks but once settled, he went to sleep, and slept quite well. In the morning we got him washed and dressed and pushed him to Mass in the wheelchair. We took him to the front and lifted him onto the pew, with some difficulty, sitting him on a cushion. He cried a lot of the time. It was impossible to know why and he did not know himself. This is the result of terrible trauma. There were several people at Mass who had spoken to him when he was first in Purley, and they were very pleased to say hello to him, others felt unable, or more than likely had no idea who he was. His appearance had changed tremendously. The day went well and Patricia was waiting at the hospital after our long journey to help us put Ken to bed. This was the first time of his spending every weekend with us. The next weekend we managed on our own, without Patricia. She was quite pleased to have some extra time to plan her school work.

The week of the 4th July was nothing short of a miracle, as I look back, but at the time we just took it in our stride. It was our twenty fifth wedding anniversary. We had already invited eighty people for lunch on the Saturday, as well as our own family, and the 'Over Sixties' club were invited to tea. For several years four of us had been running the club together. As well as this, all my family including my sisters and their families were invited to stay for a chilli con carne supper. This had all been planned beforehand and we certainly had not foreseen the way things would go. Patricia said she would come and help, if only to completely look after Ken so that I was free. We were sure that whatever happened it would be better for him to be at home rather than at the hospital, and he wanted it like that. They had already seen an improvement at the hospital. He was beginning to take a bit more notice of things about him. Peter went over to collect Ken and Patricia on the Friday evening, and I stayed to finish off the preparations. I had planned a cold buffet for lunch, and planned to have four food points in the house so that there would not be too much queuing. We had borrowed tables and chairs from the church hall and there was a lot of furniture moving to do. I had lots of willing hands from my own family staying in the house and everyone worked very hard. I prepared things during the week to get everything possible done that could be done. Clare had time off and helped me, and all was well. I also had two ladies to help serve and wash up. Ken's bed remained permanently in the dining room. We had covered it with a fitted bed cover, and people could use it for extra seating.

We had invited everyone to a celebration Mass at midday, with Canon Denning and Father Geoffrey Burke concelebrating. Father Geoffrey (now Canon) had married us way back in 1953, on July 4th. Ken was not able to take any active part in the Mass, although he really knew what was going on. He sat on the sanctuary by us; we had dressed him in an alb and stole and had a clean set of terry towelling squares tied round his neck to catch his perpetual stream of viscous dribble. His head was still locked solidly on his chest. He was really pleased to be able to do something as a priest, although he was very tearful and anxious. He could understand everything that was going on but his eyes still looked vacant.

After the Mass we arranged, with his consent, that he would give a blessing to anyone who wanted to come forward. People were invited to kneel in front of his wheelchair, which we placed in the opening at the centre of the altar rails which have since been removed. In this way he could just reach to place his hands on each head. Many people came and almost everyone was in tears but almost certainly he was not aware of this. We had given an open invitation to the Mass, so the church was full. The presbytery housekeepers were there and they were so pleased to see Father Ken back in the church. I had talked to them many times, and they had known that I was visiting St. Bartholomew's. I explained to them that I had seen them there but did not intrude on their visit. They were very caring, and were upset that they had not been able to visit Father Ken in the hospital at Homerton. Without a car the journey was too difficult and most probably too expensive for them. Our day went wonderfully well, and we saw many old friends as well as all our family. Ken said hello to those who went to him, and then in the afternoon he had a rest on the bed when most people had gone after lunch. Patricia did nothing all day but look after him and she had lots of willing help. At this stage he was just beginning to hold a spoon and fork on his own to eat. He found it very difficult to both reach his mouth and to get the food to stay in, but there had been a tremendous improvement. We served tea to the 'Over Sixties Club' in the afternoon, and again there was lots of help. They were all transported by car, by the usual helpers, and everyone who helped stayed for tea as well. In the evening we served the buffet meal in the dining room, and all the people still in the house then left the dining room so that we could prepare Ken for bed who by then was very tired. Everyone helped to clear the table, so that we could pull the louvered doors across, and Ken could sleep without any further disturbance. He was not at all worried by people walking around while we were undressing him, he was so used to it at the hospital that he took no notice; it was as if it was all that he knew and this was, at the time, a great blessing. It was only a few years previously that we had made a major change in the downstairs arrangements of our house. We had found that as the older boys in the family had grown large they could not fit round the fixed seat in the kitchen which Peter had built when we moved into the house, nearly twenty years previously. We had decided not only to remove the seat but almost the whole wall between the kitchen and the dining room and a lintel was put in place to take the weight. The door from the hall to the dining room was bricked off, and a wide door opened between the lounge and the dining room. We then fitted louvered folding doors. We could have them wide open giving a large through room from kitchen to dining room, or they could be closed. We could not have known how useful this was going to be in looking after Ken. The original idea had been born because everyone always wanted to be in the kitchen where the action was. We thought by opening out the house we could all be together all the time, with more room. It was a very successful idea which transformed the house with the overwhelming approval of the whole family. This had been done in 1973, the year before Gerard went to University. He was doing some extra A levels at college as he had had a late change of mind. He decided to read French and Spanish instead of French and Archaeology, which seemed a good move. I remember it because it was the year before we had a freezer, and he had a holiday job at St George's Hospital as a night porter before it moved to Tooting. During this time there was a garden party at Buckingham Palace, and in the evening much of the remaining food was taken to the hospital for the patients and for the staff. The patients were not allowed to have it for reasons of hygiene so it was therefore distributed amongst the night staff. There was a great deal of very beautifully prepared food, most of which would go stale quickly. Gerard was given two large brown paper sacks full. We had never seen such wonderful cakes, even a large perfect Sacher Torte, sandwiches and tiny scotch pancakes, attractively served and garnished. Because we could not eat it all we served it to the workmen in the house with their morning coffee lunch and tea, much to their pleasure and amusement.

In the weeks to come this open plan proved invaluable. I could get on with the food preparation while Ken was in bed or sitting in his wheelchair, and if he called or was very distressed as often happened I could hear and see him and be with him instantly, he was never out of sight. Sometimes he would sit and cry for hours, moaning and asking what was going to happen to him. One could only hold him, and comfort him and pray. He was very depressed. When I collected him from the hospital at Homerton, which I very often did on my own as I could be there by four o'clock and bring him home for the evening meal, he would start crying and would cry all the way home. He said it was because he was so pleased to leave the hospital. In fact he sometimes continued to cry on and off for a long time. We would take him out in the car or for a walk in the wheelchair, but as soon as we got back from church on Sunday morning he would start to cry again because he didn't want to go back to the hospital. His tears were uncontrollable and we felt that there must surely be a healing purpose. Although we did try to cheer him up, it was impossible as he could see no future.

In the summer Peter and I went to Rome with a group, staying at Palazzola, the summer residence of the English College. This is a beautiful old monastery which has gradually been restored and since 1978 improved even more. It lies about three miles from the village of Rocca di Papa on the shores of Lake Albano opposite the Pope's summer palace, Castelgandolfo. There is a beautiful garden and an Olympic size outdoor swimming pool. During the two weeks that we were away, Patricia took Father Ken to stay in the Sacred Heart Convent at Herne Bay where she had often stayed before. He could sit in the garden and get the sea air, and it was a change for both of them. He was very secure with Patricia, and she looked after him well and with love. He needed one person all the time, without constant changes, his emotions were very troubled and he was still totally dependent. We had wanted to take him to Rome with us but realised that it would be too much for him. When we returned to England, Ken was once again very pleased to be collected on Friday afternoon and brought home for the weekend. Sometimes he would have visitors from his former parish, who knew him well, and sometimes other friends would come. He always perked up for a little while when visitors came, but he could not keep it up for long, so he was soon back in the doldrums. He liked to listen to music, particularly Mahler and Wagner, and Richard Strauss, but even this made him sad and low. We would take him out in the car to local beauty spots and try to get him to hold his head up to look at the trees, particularly in the autumn when the colours were changing, but he showed no interest.

We had started teaching him to read again, although his sight was not very good. We were advised not to have his eyes tested as his sight was continually changing as he recovered and continued to

become more conscious. Father Martin Lee came in each night that
Ken was with us at 5.45 to read evening prayer with him. Father
Martin was the priest who had replaced Ken as assistant priest in
Purley. He was a very stabilising influence, and Ken looked
forward to his visits. He became a good friend. We also made
several attempts to get Ken to learn to say Mass again. We started
by just getting him to hold an empty chalice which Canon Denning
had given us. For a long time Ken not only found this too difficult
physically, but he could not manage it emotionally. His hands could
not go round the chalice as the fingers were so locked down. He
had learned to use his hands with the fingers locked in to move
himself from his wheelchair onto a dining room chair. The arm of
the wheelchair was removed and by pressing on his closed fists he
could lift and shuffle his body over. This was a great move forward.
The physiotherapy was certainly beginning to show results. Miss
Ashcroft was in charge of the physio unit at the Eastern Hospital,
and she was very interested in Ken. The prognosis for his recovery
had been poor, but she could see that he was making progress if
rather slowly. He was talking better, beginning to read and she
could tell that his intellectual side was functioning. This of course
helped him with everything else, although he was not 100%
cooperative. They worked hard with his whole body to try and
get the muscles to work, and we were given helpful advice. For
instance, to play throwing and catching a tennis ball, which made
Ken stretch out his hands. I used to massage them each day with
cream and physically pull the fingers back until they hurt.
Gradually his hands became more open and he could pick up
larger objects with more ease. We continued to take him to Mass
on Sunday. As he became a little more in control of his emotions
and felt more secure, we would dress him in an alb and lift the

wheelchair up beside the main altar before Mass. Peter would stay beside him. He didn't exactly concelebrate, but it gave him the feeling of being part of everything, without having any demand made on him. Emotionally he could not cope, as well as of course physically. It was a step forward but in many ways he was extremely demanding. He knew what was going on, wanted it right and knew how it should be, but he could get frustrated and angry very quickly. He had no understanding of anyone else's feelings or abilities. He just demanded. It was very like looking after a small child. In the family, as he became better, the continual crying changed to demands and anger. He had to be disciplined to learn to wait his turn. Sometimes he would shout and demand and we had to be very firm. It was sad because on the other hand he would suddenly become very aware of his disability in a new way. I remember the first day that he realised his hands were deformed. This was an enormous lesson for me, I had thought that he realised his difficulties and deficiencies to a certain extent but he didn't. I knew then that he was not aware of his dribbling, or of his facial deformity. Inside he felt the same as he always did. He only wanted to get on with his life, and felt determined that he would just get completely better, and that it was everyone else's fault that he was not getting on as quickly as he thought he could. He held up his hands and examined them, as if seeing them deformed for the first time. "How am I going to live with hands like this?" he cried, and they were real tears. "How am I going to manage?"

We had long since seen that his hands were the least of his problems, but he had to go through the discovery for himself, which was to be a long painful process. He was for instance quite unaware that his speech was damaged. He became really annoyed if people could not understand him. We found we were torn between helping Ken and protecting those who spoke to him. Many people would ask questions of us, like "How is Father feeling now?" when he would be sitting there in his wheelchair. We would suggest that they asked him themselves but sometimes this was a risky business because he would answer in a way they could not understand and sometimes his humour was very caustic. Few people had the courage to pursue this as he was often difficult or seemingly rude. Inside he was the little lost child who was scared and frightened, very insecure, and wavering between demands and real tears. He needed constant reassuring, yet we had to let him be exactly how he was with everyone. We could not protect him against himself. Of course as we had not known him before his accident we had not known what he was really like. This proved to be an enormous blessing. Peter and I just accepted day by day what happened, keeping things on an even keel as far as it was possible. I was aware that the Lord had given me a tremendous love for this difficult priest and that He was sustaining me with everything that I needed. There were many problems, not the least that sometimes after Ken had been asleep, he would have no idea who he was or where he was. This became more obvious as he recovered because he could explain more clearly what was going on. Sometimes for three hours he would believe he was in China, or in France, and he could really see things which seemed to confirm this. I would try to bring to his notice the things around him that were familiar, but in this state he could not see them. This was always worse in the morning after a long sleep. I began to understand why he had been so afraid to be left alone, particularly at night. While his fear continued in the day, the nights were better. He had accepted that he could go to sleep and that I would come the moment he needed anything. We fixed up a bell for him, but on the whole his nights were peaceful, it was the mornings that caused him problems for a long time.

During this time that Ken was coming at weekends we did not know too much about Mrs Bell. We knew that she saw Ken during the week. We had heard reports both from Patricia and from the Sister and the Princess, that Mrs Bell and Ken had had some shouting matches. No one knew exactly what they were about. We guessed that she couldn't cope with the great change in Ken who she had always relied on. I think she found it more difficult now that he was becoming much more conscious than when he was completely 'out'. She was either all over him and loving or very dissatisfied. She was well over eighty and not in good health herself. Canon Denning had seen her once or twice and he asked me if I would invite her to tea. Ken stayed with us longer if there was a Bank Holiday or half term holiday, especially if the physiotherapy unit had closed down. We were quite happy to invite her. Canon Denning arranged that Father Martin would collect Mrs Bell from her home in Clapham and stay with us for tea. Clare also was to be with us but Peter was working on the chosen day. I prayed to be loving towards Mrs Bell, as I really wanted to be, and in fact had always been. Canon Denning almost guaranteed her behaviour. I had no idea how she had accepted Ken's regular visits to us and also Patricia's involvement. Patricia had seen her sometimes on her visits to the hospital, but she was always very uncommunicative, and would not speak to Patricia.

We had a nice little tea party and, in fairness, Mrs Bell was very pleasant to me and polite, if rather restrained. It was sad of course that she was too old and not strong enough to look after Ken on her own, she would have liked to do this I am sure. I found it also sad that she had taken the attitude she had, because we could have been such good friends and helped each other but that was not how she wanted it. Father Martin was very diplomatic, and Clare also helped the afternoon along. It was a blessed time, and we were able to thank the Canon for suggesting it.

As the Christmas of 1978 drew nearer we were invited by Miss Ashcroft to come and see her. Ken went every week to another local hospital where she also worked, for aqua-therapy, which he hated. She wanted to talk to us about an operation that had been proposed by some of the doctors.

Miss Ashcroft was very interested in Ken. She was able to perceive that his progress had been remarkable, considering the seriousness and extent of the damage to his brain, both from the accident, and from the further operation. Even though his prognosis medically was poor, she felt that he was making excellent progress and should be given every chance.

As things were it seemed impossible that he would ever walk or even stand again. His left leg was immobilised in such a way that it would not straighten and this prevented him from standing. His back muscles had so improved with exercise that he could now sit up on his own without falling backwards. This not only gave him a greater sense of security, but made looking after him so much easier.

Miss Ashcroft was convinced that if he had an operation on his leg to straighten it, there was a big chance that he would be able to stand and possibly walk. Some of the doctors opposed this idea, they said that his physical condition was not strong enough to withstand the trauma of a major operation, and mentally that the anaesthetic would have a detrimental effect on his already damaged and confused brain.

It was impossible for us to make any comment, as our knowledge was insufficient, but Miss Ashcroft just wanted to know our reaction. A senior surgeon at the London Hospital, where Ken had been taken for brain scans and who knew all about him, despite everything, was willing to take the risk. There was to be a meeting in order to come to some conclusion. They had already consulted Ken, but knew that he also was not able to make any decision. I believe he said he was willing to go through with it if they really thought it would be an advantage. I do not know who else was consulted. It had become fairly urgent to make a final decision because there was already talk of discharging Ken from the Eastern Hospital. I think that it was Miss Ashcroft's enthusiasm that carried the meeting. It was arranged that the operation would be carried out at the beginning of February. It was a major operation and involved two long incisions down the back of his leg, the cutting of the muscles and tendons, splitting them in two length-ways and then stitching them together and replacing them, stretching the leg by force and placing it in plaster for seven weeks from the toes to the groin.

At the mention of discharge Ken became really worried. He knew that he needed complete care and was naturally concerned what would happen to him. He had heard his mother mention a geriatric home. Peter and I were able to reassure him that we would not abandon him. We felt quite secure within ourselves that we would with the Lord's help be able to look after him. It was as if the decision was already made. The Archbishop agreed, and our family were in favour as long as they felt we could manage. I felt in no doubt of this at all. I realised that I would not only have to give up my job at St Andrew's School, but also the other organisations to which I belonged. I was very happy in my job, and had not thought of leaving it before. We had built a beautiful new school in the early years of my time there and I had taken the position of part-time Home Economics teacher there in 1960.

The headmaster had encouraged me to develop a course with the fourth year boys and girls, which included relationships leading to marriage, and the conception, growth and birth of a baby. This then included the care, bathing and feeding and caring for the baby clothes. I was allowed money to set up a corner with the equipment and books needed. Without actually teaching about abortion, by the time the pupils had finished the course they so believed in the humanness of the foetus after conception and before birth, that in open sharing of their thoughts they usually came to the conclusion that abortion must be murder. During this year the course included the study of food in third world countries and the need to under-stand basic nutrition for adults and babies. The special needs of education and help in local food growing and production were studied, with a brief look at the difficulties. Another part of this course was the feeding of the sick and elderly and the more straightforward groups practised cookery skills and home craft. The pupils worked on a rota basis in groups of three and had great freedom to research their current projects.

In the year that I left, the original headmaster was already an inspector, the next had died, and the third, who was also very kind to me, changed the whole structure of the school timetable, and during the following year half the time for the subjects I had been teaching was given over to teaching German and Latin. The standard of the school had gradually been rising and it was considered that languages were more important then than some of the subjects that had been in our syllabus. The discipline had always been good on the whole, and it was a very amenable school to work in. My room was pleasant with enormous windows overlooking a grass quadrangle and the main entrance. I loved the children but yet I felt quite strongly that I was doing the right thing in leaving. I explained the situation to my headmaster and said that I did not know exactly when I would need to give up my job, but that it would be at some time in the New Year.

Everything worked out well because my colleague Jeane Spriggs who shared the full-time job with me was willing to take over my part of the work. I was concerned about the disruption in the work as I took the senior exam classes, but I felt I just had to trust. In view of the circumstances of the change-over my headmaster explained that I would not need to give the normal lengthy notice before leaving, and that as long as it was mutually acceptable I could go whenever the time came. The exam results in 1979 were as good if not better than ever before.

At Christmas it was arranged that Ken would come to stay for two weeks, just to make sure that he understood what it would be like living with us permanently. It was necessary for a social worker to come to the house to see if we could manage on that basis. She spoke about bathing him and explained the equipment that I could have when and if Ken could get upstairs. This seemed like a dream at this time if not an impossibility. I explained to her that I gave him a full blanket bath, and that would have to suffice. We had devised a system for washing his hair by using the brim of a large hat with the crown removed. I needed someone to help me, but I could just about wash his hair without getting the shampoo and water in his eyes. His left eye had healed wonderfully well, and had turned down again in an amazing way, although it was still very delicate. He could see with it even though it did not blink or close, so it was important to protect it from anything that would sting. When he came at weekends, Ken usually had been bathed and had a hair wash on the Friday afternoon just before I arrived. They lifted him with a hoist, and he hated the whole procedure. I think he must have been frightened by water as a child for he never learnt to swim.

We planned a family Christmas. The whole family as usual were coming to stay. Peter had decided that it would be a good thing to invite Mrs Bell over the Christmas period. We wrote her a warm letter inviting her for either Christmas Day and/or Boxing Day, also saying that Peter would come and collect her and take her home. She accepted for Boxing Day and was very pleased to be with us, pleasant and gracious; even so, by the evening she and Ken had a terrific argument and disagreement. She found it difficult to accept that he could not remember things or muddled them up. She wanted to pretend that nothing was the matter with him except his appearance and difficulty with eating. She found it too much to accept that his brain was damaged, so instead of encouraging and being optimistic, she picked on him and corrected him all the time, which annoyed him. We knew that she did not approve of his coming to live with us. We had heard that from various sources, but she did not mention it and neither did we. On the whole we had a pleasant day, we exchanged some small gifts, and she was charming with all the family. We really felt some progress had been made. I made her an early supper and Peter took her home afterwards.

At that stage Ken was completely unaware of any problem with our relationship with his mother, which was good. She was obviously very worried about the operation he was to have. She disapproved, and felt strongly that it was better to leave him as he was than to risk something unknown. The weather was so bad in January that I had to take unpaid leave for another two weeks, in order to look after Ken. As the snow was so deep we decided with the hospital's permission that it would be better to keep him at home than risk being unable to bring him back for the weekend. My colleague Jeane was willing to take my classes as we always had done for each other during illnesses.

During the short time between the long Christmas holiday and the operation on Ken's leg, Mrs Bell arranged to have Ken home to her flat for a Saturday and Sunday. Transport was arranged for him, and she asked the caretaker of her block of flats, (an Irishman named Paddy), to dress and undress him and put him to bed and get him up. John Bell was with them during the day and physically looked after Ken, and Mrs Bell prepared the food.

This proved to be a blessing as less than two months later, two weeks before Ken was due to move into our house, Mrs Bell was discovered by her priest quite dead, sitting in her chair, having had the first course of her midday meal. She must have died just before eating her pudding. The priest told John that she had a smile on her face. He had evidently been paying a routine visit but when he could get no reply, he got the key from a neighbour. I praise God for Mrs Bell and for his love for her.

Sister Patricia had prepared Ken's things for the journey to the London Hospital in February, and I arranged with her that we would both visit each day to see him through the worst part of any trauma. It was going to be very difficult for him to manage with his leg in plaster; it was believed he would be at the London Hospital for a minimum of two weeks, or possibly three, depending on his progress. It was estimated that if all went well he would be completely discharged from the Eastern Hospital in April. On this information I decided to leave school at half-term. This would give me time to get everything in the house in really good order, so that I would be free to look after Ken. There were several jobs that needed attention, relining the lounge curtains was one, and of course spring cleaning the whole house. I knew that would give me a good start.

The operation, although it went according to plan, was a traumatic experience for Ken for many reasons. The anaesthetic caused him tremendous regression and for several days he was completely non-compos. The medical staff had been concerned about the reaction of his brain to the anaesthetic after a lengthy operation, but no one could foresee exactly how it would be. It was several days before they could begin to move him out of bed.

On my last day at school a presentation was made to me at assembly, and many of the children brought a little present for me. This was all a lovely surprise as I had intended to just slip away. I was very moved. The weather was terrible. Snow had fallen heavily overnight and there was a complete 'white-out' over Croydon, which was to get worse and there were radio warnings of black ice. The headmaster made the unusual decision to let the school home very early. There was an added complication. A strike of hospital workers meant that there were no hot meals and all that was being served was sandwiches. These were being made by one of the hospital charities. Pat and I arranged on the phone to take some other food that would be more suitable for Ken. We also felt that it was important for his recovery that he was stimulated. We were not sure at this stage who else would be visiting him; in fact he had very few visitors while he was there.

The journey took me three hours by car. When I told them in the staff room that I was driving to London, everyone thought that I was crazy or at least very unwise. I knew, as did Patricia, that this was the most crucial time of Ken's recovery. I set off in a blizzard and prayed for protection all the way. I felt very at peace. Neither Pat nor I was very sure the other would be able to manage the journey with the weather so bad. Patricia found the ice and snow very treacherous when she was on her bicycle, even on the main roads which had been cleared of snow, and she didn't get far before she had to abandon her bike and chain it to a church railing, making an exact note of where it was. She had tried unsuccessfully to push the bike, and keep it with her as she had quite a heavy basket to carry which easily strapped onto her bike. There was very little transport running and she walked miles in order to bring the food she had prepared. Strangely we both arrived at the same time to find Ken in a terrible state. He did not know if it was morning or night.

Having sandwiches for every meal confused him more; also the nursing care had inevitably deteriorated as the nursing staff had so much more to do. Ken's brain was barely functioning. We could not persuade him that he was in hospital. He thought he had been transported to a London railway station. It was impossible to convince him of anything else and this delusion lasted almost all the time he was in the London Hospital. We had real fears for his return even to the mental state that he had attained before the operation. That evening Patricia and I prayed together before we left the hospital for Ken, for our own journey and for our families. I had asked Peter not to worry if I was late home for he knew that I would go to the hospital even if the weather was bad. He had arranged to make sure that Paul was alright; he had left London early and was home when Paul arrived home from school. Both had tales to tell of their travelling experiences.

Patricia, however, would not let me take her to find her bicycle. Amazingly, we were in very high spirits and we were sure we would both be alright. We laughed a lot about our situation when we had settled Ken for the night and had moved away from him. Pat did not have to make an early start the next day and she was warmly wrapped up. My journey home again took me three hours. This was mostly due to the slow speed caused by black ice even though there was almost no traffic on the road. I really felt the protection of the Lord all the way, and I was very pleased that we had gone to Ken. Patricia and I felt enormous strength not only from God but from each other. Ken had eaten a hot meal and a dessert and we managed to convince him that it was night time. We felt that he was a little less confused and he did at least know who we were. We had left food for the next day which hopefully someone would heat up at lunchtime. We did not dare to predict when we would visit again, but the bad weather started to break the next day which made things easier.

It took just over two weeks for Ken to be well enough to go back to the Eastern Hospital or perhaps it was because they needed his place in the London Hospital. He was still very insecure and this was not helped by the fact that the ambulance drivers were 'going slow'. They were not sure how they would transport Ken to Homerton, and this caused him great worry although he could do nothing about it. We found all the argument about it between the people arranging his journey (which sometimes went on in his presence) was not helpful to his progress. Not many people on the periphery realised that he was also suffering acute brain damage and was not able to cope with all the questions he was asked. He cried a lot, and although he did not complain about his leg being in plaster, he was low and depressed, and could not see how in the end there was a possibility that he could be better than before. Everything was black for him. In the end the problem was solved by a nurse travelling with Ken in an old-fashioned taxi, the only other kind of vehicle that he could be lifted into. Patricia was there to meet him in his ward at the Eastern Hospital. As soon as he was back in the familiar place in his ward in the hospital he began to recover a little mentally. Compared to the London Hospital he looked on the Eastern almost like home. The nurses gave him a big welcome back.

The doctors would not even let us try to bring him home for a weekend for the next two weeks because they needed to monitor his progress. After this they said he could come for the weekends until he had had the plaster removed and this took seven weeks altogether. The time finally came for us to bring Ken home for the weekend while the plaster was still on. We removed the front seat from the car, and with a great deal of lifting, pushing and shoving, we managed to get him onto the back seat with his plastered leg stretched out where the front seat would have been. He was so pleased to be coming home he would put up with everything, or so he said; in actual fact it was not quite like that.

He was still rather tearful and very depressed. Nothing seemed to brighten him. He was an out-and-out pessimist, always looking on the black side and expecting the worst. We got him home without incident, and managed to push and pull him out of the car and into the wheelchair, which of course had an extended part to support his left leg. Fortunately we could manage the wheelchair in the house, with his leg fully outstretched, and by going forwards and backwards like a three-point turn we could just get the wheelchair into the downstairs toilet. Once there I could manage well. Lifting Ken had not been any problem from the beginning when I had learnt by watching the nurses, and he still weighed only seven stones. It was a little more difficult with the plaster on, but he did not resist with the practical things, and would try to do what I said as far as he could understand and was able.

It was mentally that he was difficult or obstinate, and he would quickly go from tears to being very angry and aggressive. We managed everything well between us considering all the complications. We had altered several pairs of trousers so that the left leg was cut open lengthwise and could be tied round his plaster. He collected a large number of signatures on his plaster, but nothing really amused him; he remained serious and insecure. When the day came for his plaster to be removed, Peter and I arranged to keep him with us an extra two days instead of returning him to the hospital on the Sunday night. We took him to the London Hospital and met the surgeon who had performed the operation. The nurse who removed the plaster was named Pearl; I remember her well, a rather beautiful black woman. We were allowed to stay with Ken all the time as he was very nervous, especially when the electric plaster saw appeared.

The surgeon was pleased with the operation and with the straightness of Ken's leg. After the removal of the plaster and all the examinations we took him back to the Eastern Hospital where Miss Ashcroft was ready to put him through some intensive physiotherapy. We were still allowed to bring him home at week-ends, and the date was decided for his final discharge at the end of April. Arrangements were made for him to continue physiotherapy at a Croydon Hospital.

It was just at this time that Ken had to be told of his mother's death and the Archbishop came to the hospital to tell him as soon as he heard the news. We felt this was a kind gesture as we were all rather nervous of the effect that this might have on Ken. However, whatever went on inside him he showed very little sign of grief, and we had no way of estimating his sadness or suffering. We later tried to talk to him about his mother but he found he could not remember.

Mrs Bell whose name was Agnes, was given a beautiful funeral at Clapham and all the people who had previously felt so restricted in speaking to us were set free. Peter and I wanted to stay at the back of the church, but John Bell insisted that we came to the front to look after Ken. We saw many people there that we knew, including many of Ken's former parishioners and friends of Mrs Bell. Afterwards we went back to her flat where friends had prepared a buffet meal and it proved to be a time of great healing and reconciliation.

The Bell family itself is very small but we met Ken's cousin Leslie for the first time; he also regularly visited Ken and we became good friends with him. During these months we became steadily more friendly with Ken's brother John who had always been pleasant and understanding, without asking or wanting to know who we were or what we were doing. He sensed that we only had a good purpose and came over to our house to see Ken from time to time though he hardly knew him as a brother. By the time he was old enough to remember Ken had joined the Army, and after the end of the war when he returned home to take up his former job John was so much younger that they evidently had little in common. John told us that it was as late as 1955 when Ken entered the seminary, the first year of which took place in part of the presbytery building at Walworth, more than seventeen years before he returned to the same parish as assistant priest. John sometimes brought his daughters with him to see Ken, although I think they found the visits quite stressful. They had been used to their uncle Ken as a very busy super-efficient and evidently lively priest, wanting everything to time and in order. The change in him must have been very difficult to accept. Inside, Ken was crying out to be in order, but no longer could achieve any of these things.

The battle continued within him and without. He had visits from people who had been friends with him in his former parishes, and for a very short time he could put on an 'alter persona', which always amazed Peter and me, in fact all our family too. He struggled to be 'Hail fellow, well met,' but as soon as they had gone he collapsed in a heap of misery and self-pity and anger. Some of his friends knew him as a very lively friendly sociable person, and some found him more difficult. He was evidently a man of many parts. It was only those who knew him really well who asked me how I coped with his anger. We learned a great deal about Ken from his close friends.

In spite of all the apparent difficulties in looking after Ken and the family when they were all home, I found tremendous peace within. I began to realise that my time of visiting in St Bartholomew's Hospital and the hours spent weeping in St Bartholomew's the Great, had been a time of great inner healing, in which the Lord healed many of my own childhood hurts and showed me his love. I found a great love not only for Ken but for others. Even people that I had previously found quite difficult seemed more lovable. It did not matter what actually was going on with Ken inside, for the most part I was at peace, and could just accept his unreasonable behaviour. There were times when this was stretched to the limits when he was going through a new growing or learning process. His anger was tremendous, although he could not recognise it himself, and his memory was very poor. If you tried to talk to him about his anger he would deny it and say, 'But I'm not angry.'

There were many times when we felt we had to teach him just like a young child in the family, and it was during this part of his recovery he started to call me Mummy.

At first I thought it was because he heard my own children, and that may have been part of it, but I now think he had a strong desire to be loved and accepted like a little child. Indeed this is how he was loved. I would put my arms round him and hold him, rather than scold him. The Lord put a flowing channel of love in me for Ken that rarely seemed to run out. Even when he was totally exasperating as often happened and we had to discipline him, this love was still there; I could go to him and explain to him the reasons for what had happened. It was always difficult to know as with a child, how much he understood, and also what was brain damage and what was the inner child hurting. Clare and the boys would sit with him and talk with him trying gently to help him. Certainly he did need loving and eventually learnt how to accept love in many ways, but this was a slow process.

Ken blamed everyone for his shortcomings, and could not begin to accept what had happened to him. In the mornings he still was a very long time becoming conscious, worse than ever before. He would lie in bed in our dining room and would be quite sure he was in another country. It was often China or France. No amount of pointing out the familiar objects and furnishings in the room would help him. Sometimes I would not be sure if he recognized me. He was sometimes quite afraid of things unseen by me. In this mood I was not able to get him up and dressed, he would not be able to respond. At these times I prayed with him but it was seemingly of no help. Then gradually everything would become better and clearer and he would not remember what had been happening, asking why it had got so late when he realised the time. We tried everything we could think of to help him over several months.

Finally Peter decided to try another way. He came down to have his breakfast very early as he still went to Mass at the Cathedral in the morning before work. (He travelled by car and found the journey much easier at 6.30am). Instead of creeping about so as not to disturb Ken, he would wake him up, very deliberately, and tell him that he was Peter. When he seemed quite awake, he would lay his hands on Ken's head and pray for quite a long time. Gradually this seemed to ease the situation. Ken became more conscious more quickly in the morning with less distress.

From the time that Ken came to live with us, he spent one day a week at the Waylands centre for the physically and mentally disadvantaged. This was arranged by the doctors from the Eastern Hospital and by our own family doctor who at that time was Dr. Lees. They all insisted that Ken was to go out of the house for care for two days a week. We suggested that it was perhaps wiser to wean him gradually from one day to two days, as he was so insecure and change of any kind was upsetting for him. I think that it was presumed that he would be glad to be at the day centre, as there was company and activities, but he hated it from the beginning. It was difficult to explain to him that it was necessary for us and good for him because he could not understand either concept. He would keep saying to me 'You're trying to get rid of me,' and he would cry and throw a tantrum. To strike a balance between showing love and the discipline of what had to be done was very difficult. He would say to me, 'If you loved me you would not let me go to Waylands at all.'

We had to be very firm because although he was handicapped he was very dominating, and did not mind who he hurt. Even at that stage of his recovery he could be very manipulative. Because he needed the attention and could do nothing for himself, I felt I could ignore all these things which made him so unlovely and love him like a needy baby. I prayed to Jesus a lot that he would continue to give me his love for Ken. Without it I could not manage. With it, it seemed as if I could do almost anything for this difficult priest. It was to be many years before he began to see even slightly that there was another way.

During these first months living with us, Ken had many things to learn about family life, most of which he did not want to learn and did not like. They were to do with sharing. Because of his great needs and inability to do anything for himself he had my first attention and it was always there for him in his need. My relationship with Peter was fortunately very secure most of the time, although I am sure sometimes the family were under stress. Paul recounted later how jealous he had felt of my attention to Ken. We were able to talk about it and now that he is adult and mature and has been through some difficult times himself, we are sure that these experiences have helped us all to grow in love and patience.

Ken had always shown tremendous jealousy of my care for the rest of the family. There seemed to be no way to break through it and speaking to him about it made no difference. I think his lack of trust was so great that he thought even giving the slightest room to finding another way might deprive him of his care. He wanted his own way all the time on every occasion like a baby crying for his needs to be met, and in some way we all felt that he had reverted to babyhood. The only way that I could see to deal with it was to love him and reassure him, and try to ignore the fact that he was actually a grown man. As this went on he lived two lives, the one he pretended when he chose and the real suffering needy child.

There were times when I did not know how to deal with the situation. If Peter was present, he would act as 'back stop' and speak to Ken very firmly. Usually this worked. If Peter was at work there was usually someone who could help. One of the main problems was over music. Ken's likes and dislikes were not just normally strong. He would be abusive and derogatory to everyone who liked something that he did not care for. If we explained to him that some of us did not like all the music that he listened to he would be very sharp and caustic and say that was too bad and that we needed to get ourselves educated. We bought some earphones which solved the problem most of the time, because he liked his music very loud. We were living in close quarters; he had a comfortable chair in the corner of the dining room with all his personal things by him on a table, and we sat on the other side of the double louvre doors which we kept open in the lounge.

The most difficult times were meal times when Ken said he had always been used to listening to music. Christopher liked Handel, Vivaldi and Bach and so did Peter, but these composers with Chopin were Ken's pet aversions. Christopher would put on a cassette, and if it was one of those composers that Ken hated the most, he would scream and shout and say he would not listen to it. No amount of telling him that we had all listened to Wagner the night before helped him to understand. We had literally to remove him from the table and put him in the lounge with his dinner on a special table which fitted in front of the wheelchair. We felt it was very important for him to learn that he could not always have his own way, and that he did not get it either screaming and shouting or being dominating. Having said that, he did not learn for a very long time. He did not like eating on his own and I had problems sometimes when I was alone with him. He would be dominating and demanding. Although at this stage he could eat with a knife and fork it was a slow and difficult process. I found that if I started my lunch at the same time as him, I was finished long before him. It was no use using this time for talking because he couldn't manage to eat and talk, anyway he always had his own choice of music at lunchtime. I didn't mind and found it easier to cope. I would sometimes give him his lunch and then get on with the washing up and tidying up. Even then I would finish before him. He liked me to sit with him and he would shout, 'Sit down and eat your lunch, sit and eat it. Sit down.' I was very firm with him on these occasions, and I would say, 'Ken you will not dominate me, if you insist on shouting at me, I will put my lunch on a tray and take it upstairs to eat it.' At this he would calm down. This was only ever a threat because I could never actually leave him since quite often he choked and would need some help. The left side of his throat was paralysed and swallowing was still quite difficult.

Afterwards I would put my arms round him and say to him how silly he was to make so many unnecessary demands when he was loved so much. I would tell him how much God loved him, but his image of God was the God who punished if you didn't do everything you should, and as he couldn't do what he felt he should, he didn't feel loved by God. I tried to explain to him that he would get everything he needed, and it could be done in peace and love rather than in anger. But I always felt that I might as well have saved my breath; it was always just until the next time. I would put my arms round him and hold him, and it was obvious that he felt so unloved. Only gradually did this enormous barrier begin to break down many years later. He trusted no one.

At this time Ken started to go to Waylands for a second day in the week. He shouted and said he would not go, but at the time there was no alternative. The Croydon coach came to collect him in the morning and would bring him home in the afternoon. It had a lift for the wheelchair at the back and then the chair was clamped to the floor. He complained of the length of time it took to pick everyone up and deposit them back. He complained about the stupid things they tried to get him to make, and he complained about the physiotherapy he had each day.

Although the operation on his leg had been a success and he could now rest it on the ground it had no strength or power in it. We were told it would need a great deal of exercise. It was not only that though, Ken was very nervous and frightened. He was already doing exercises lying on the floor every morning, stretching his legs and crossing one over the other with some help, reaching as far as he could go. He thought it was all useless and had no confidence that he would ever walk. The more optimistic I was the more cross and pessimistic he would get.

Father Martin continued to come in every evening to read evening prayer. When we tried to get Ken to read we realised that he could not see properly even if he could read. It also happened that we had some problems with the earphones that Ken was using. He kept saying that they were not working, yet when we listened we could hear the music. It took us a little time to realise that Ken was quite deaf in one ear. Although he allowed me to make an appointment through the doctor, to have his eyes tested, he refused point blank to have an ear test. He would not believe that he was completely deaf in one ear, and whatever we did to try to convince him, he would not listen. We decided to leave it and eventually he realised that there might be a little truth in what we were saying, and condescended rather unwillingly for me to make an appointment at the hospital to have an ear test. We were thinking that anything that could be done to help restore him would be beneficial.

He was fitted with spectacles which helped him enormously, and when after the ear test it was found that he was stone deaf in his left ear, he shouted at everyone and told them it wasn't true. From this time on there was a tremendous improvement in his understanding, and I realised that quite a lot of the time he just had not heard what was being said. If you sat on his left side and talked to him he could hear nothing. I realised that in his damaged mind, by trying to deny there was something wrong with his ears he would be able to preserve his ability to listen to music that he knew so well and liked. His fear was tremendous.

Lessons in reading began to take on a different meaning, and although progress was slow, we started again to teach him to say

Mass, literally for about five minutes at a time. He was continuing to have physiotherapy on his hands and I took every opportunity when I was sitting talking to him to pull back his fingers and get him to exercise them. He could just about manage to lift the chalice. Gradually he improved enough that Father Martin thought that it would be psychologically good for Ken to practise the Mass in the side chapel at church on a Saturday afternoon. Ken was willing and I believe he really wanted to re-learn how to say Mass. We set him up with a little table in front of his wheelchair and each week he would practise for about half an hour.

It was painful for Ken because he understood sufficient to know that he should be able to do it all without help, and yet he found it so difficult. Peter and Father Martin were patient with him and his progress was good over the weeks. He still dribbled a great deal, which he continued not to notice. He was on the whole fairly oblivious to his physical state except for his inability to walk. At this stage he had no idea that his speech was difficult for most people to understand, and that combined with his dribbling frightened many people away. To a certain extent his left leg was much better and he could certainly take some steps with someone on his left side and a tripod stick in his right. His balance was hopeless and you could not leave him standing alone, he fell immediately.

By the autumn the visits to Croydon General Hospital became a nightmare because the ambulance which did a round tour collecting people would sometimes be two hours late. Ken could not take this in his stride. He would sit and watch the clock while getting more and more angry. He refused to listen to music to pass the time, which he most probably would have done if he had not been waiting. Also we usually put the chair in the car and went out somewhere if we had time in the day, so it did seem to him like a waste of time. I tried to keep him calm explaining that there were a lot of other people with similar needs to his own and they all had to be collected. I tried hard to find out why this service could not be better timed, but no one had an answer. In the end I decided that it would be easier for me to take him myself and wait for him.

This was indeed a big revelation, because the hospital was finding it impossible to deal with him. He would arrive angry and shout and tell them what to do, particularly if he was kept waiting yet again, as there were always six or seven people in the room having treatment, sometimes more. There were two or three physiotherapists, one would start to exercise his arms and his body, and he would shout that it was his legs that needed help not his arms. He could not understand that in order to walk his whole body needed to be exercised.

Eventually he was able to walk with a little more ease still holding the tripod and with his arm held on the other side, but he could do nothing on his own. In the end the head of the department asked me if I would stop taking him as they could do no more for him because of his attitude, and the fact that he was upsetting the other patients. In all this he had one stalwart supporter, a spastic handicapped lady, with a lot of difficulties in being understood. She was totally sympathetic and understanding of Ken. She saw him each week at Waylands as well as at the hospital. She still keeps in touch with me through letters written by a carer and signed by her. She has never forgotten Ken.

In a strange way when Ken misbehaved, I felt detached from personal responsibility for his behaviour. We tried several times to get help for him from psychiatrists and priests who we knew could help him if he would let them. The result was always the same, he would be over-polite, pleasant, and put on a show, so that no one could get near to what was going on within him or sometimes he would just shout and be really objectionable so that the doctors became more concerned for my welfare, which made Ken furious.

I would take him for a walk each day with the tripod, holding his left arm, and gradually we could go further and further as long as I could hold onto him tightly, eventually reaching the end of the road and back, about two hundred yards. This in itself seemed like a miracle to me. I would praise him and say how wonderful it was, but he would be full of doom and gloom because he could do so little.

There was another difficulty which I could see held back his progress. When we were out walking or sitting in the car, his head would be locked down on his chest. The only way he could see when I suggested he looked at the beautiful trees, or the colour of the sky, was to lift his eyes and look up, but he was never sufficiently interested to make any great effort, or so it seemed. But this did not stop my enthusiasm for getting him to do as much as he was able. During the day I was alone with him so he had my full attention. This worried me a little as he was not only demanding, but he became very possessive. I had to trust that as he recovered this would diminish.

In August 1979 Peter and I returned to Palazzola. After making

many enquiries and ascertaining that we could have accommodation on the ground floor near an accessible toilet we asked Ken
if he would like to come with us. He said 'Yes' straight away, but
went into fantasy thoughts about going to the opera in Rome.
He had told us many times that he had spent much of his free time
at the opera as well as at concerts. He was unable to relate his
present situation to the difficulties. We didn't say that it would be
too difficult, but that maybe the opera season would not be on.
At this time Ken needed a great deal of rest and if he did not get
it he became almost unmanageable. It was always a risk travelling
with him, partly because of his moods and partly in case of delays.
However, as we prayed to the Lord for help and guidance we felt
very at peace.

We were going to Rome with a group of Catholics and Anglicans
mostly from Deptford, a hundred of us altogether. We already knew
that we could manage Ken in the beautiful garden either in his
wheelchair or practising walking with his tripod, and there were
many helping hands. The journey went well. Some of the group
were very caring and really loved him. They would sit with him or
hold him while he walked.

We were allotted the Rector's suite, which was large and had an
adjoining room for Peter and myself, and a private bathroom. It
was all rather primitive as it was a stone-built monastery which
had not had more than basic renovation, but to us it was luxury to
be self contained with lots of room to move about. Also it was very
cool which was sometimes a great blessing in the heat of the day.
People were very kind and it gave Peter and me some time to swim
in the lovely pool, or completely relax.

We made one trip into Rome by coach which was hired for the day. We made several stops at places of interest, but it became really difficult getting the wheelchair out each time and lifting Ken off the coach. We decided it would be better if we let them go on without us if the coach could pick us up in the afternoon when we were going to drive along the Appian Way and visit the catacomb of Saint Callixtus where Saint Cecilia, the patron saint of music, was buried.

We were dropped off by the Piazza Navona where there was shade and somewhere to sit for our picnic lunch. We had a walk and looked at the fountains which always have a wonderful cooling effect. We saw the palaces and churches around the square and watched the artists who paint and sell their work in the Piazza. We sat and enjoyed watching the people while we had a cool drink, but Ken found it hard to enjoy any of it. He was consumed with his own inability to do anything. As he was interested in music he said he would like to see St Cecilia's tomb and he already knew where it was. His memory was erratic and in many ways he was full of surprises. I so wanted him to enjoy something, but of course each one of us has to find our own way in our own time.

Ken had definitely wanted to come to Palazzola and had opted to go to Rome on the coach. We were not sure how possible it might be to get him down into the catacombs where Mass was to be celebrated. We had been in the catacombs on previous visits to Rome and knew the difficulties. We had three priests with us as well as Ken, and a chapel had been booked. Four strong men including Peter found no problem at all in lifting the wheelchair between them and carrying it down the steep narrow stone steps to the bowels of the earth. This was after a preliminary lesson on how to pick up the chair. It had removable arms and legs which pulled off very easily. At their first attempt Ken became very nervous and thought he would be dropped but we were able to settle him with the prospect of concelebrating Mass. People's enthusiasm to help with the wheelchair always caused the same problem: they would take hold of it and lift before we could explain exactly where it was safe to hold.

Nor was it easy to push the wheelchair over the rough ground and through the winding passages, and Ken was not particularly impressed with the crypt of St Cecilia. When it came for the time for Mass, there were so many other tourists crowded in with us that we nearly all fainted. We decided that it was most probably better that we did not attempt the trip to the Vatican which was made the following week. Ken seemed much more content in the garden sitting quietly. We decided there would be other opportunities later, which indeed there were. There was, however, a chance to go to Castelgandolfo and actually hear the Pope speak. We learned the best time and place from the Swiss Guards who regularly used our swimming pool. Ken was more interested on this occasion, although we could only take transport to the bottom of the hill, and the cobblestones up the hill were very heavy going with the wheelchair. As soon as we were seen we were ushered into a place of honour inside the courtyard. Ken was able both to see and hear the Holy Father when he came out on the balcony. Apart from this he stayed at Palazzola. Several people went on a day trip to Assisi and arrived back very late, but he realised by then that this was more than he could have managed. Every day Mass was concelebrated and the other priests were very good at including

Ken as far as he was able. Altogether it was a good experience for all of us.

Once back home again Ken continued to make gradual progress during the year in spite of all his difficulties. Reading became a little easier, although his concentration time was very short, and reading aloud was still very tedious and inaccurate. He could begin to do those things for himself that he wanted to do, like switching his radio on and off and putting on his earphones. He could manage the toilet partly on his own, at least when we were at home, and he could propel his wheelchair fairly accurately around the downstairs of the house with his feet. He was never able to use his hands for this because they were so misshapen. Eating was getting a little easier, but drinking was still slow and difficult. He was also very tearful, and was still angry, intolerant and rude. We put this down to frustration and grieving for his lost abilities. I was not spared any of this although he liked me to look after him and did not like it if I was out of sight. He demanded my attention. Canon Denning continued to bring him communion at 11 o'clock every day.

We had two prayer groups running at this time, the original on Tuesday evenings which was now meeting in the convent owing to its large size, and one on Thursday mornings which met in our house in the lounge; we later moved it upstairs. On Thursday mornings I would get Ken dressed and he would have his breakfast. I was very often only just in time to welcome the members of the prayer group who arrived after 10.00 am Mass. Everyone would go into the dining room and say 'Hello' to Ken, and he came to know them all very well. They were all very kind to him and tried to brighten him up because he was so depressive and pessimistic. Mary, one of the Thursday group used to make him fresh scones for his tea, and she was always a favourite. Ken's choice of favourites was always based on what people did for him or what music they liked. Those who knew him well trod carefully in the field of music. His wrath and caustic tongue could scare the most hardy if they happened to let slip that they liked Purcell or Chopin but Mary had a soft spot for Ken and was full of compassion. Her brother had died of alcoholism, and she was most caring.

One Thursday Ken had a very bad morning and was more than usually angry while I was washing him and helping him shave. He shouted so much he went out of control. He would always blame me for everything, which perhaps helped him, I was never sure. This day I was on my own and could not pacify him. He was still in his pyjamas, sitting in his wheelchair, screaming and shouting. His arms were flailing and he was foaming at the mouth. I tried to understand what was the matter, but couldn't get through to him. There was no way that I could get him dressed. It was about 10.20 am and I had reached the stage of praying for our safety and protection. I said all the prayers that I could against the devil and his power, in the name of Jesus, quietly and aloud, and sprinkled holy water round the room. Previously I had had little experience of situations like this and it was really frightening. I decided it would be best if I left Ken alone as I seemed to be making him worse. I couldn't go further than the room next door in case he fell out of his chair in his frenzy. I was distraught to see him like this which did not often happen when I was on my own. I was standing in the kitchen wondering if I should phone someone for help, when the door bell rang. It was Mary, full of apologies that she was so early. She had come from Coulsdon and a bus had arrived very promptly which was unusual. I pulled her in saying 'Thank God you're here.' She could hear the shouting and raving. I said 'Mary, it is Ken. I can't manage him, would you go in and get him dressed?' She said, 'My God, it sounds like the devil,' and ran into him with arms outstretched. 'Hello Father dear,' she said,'how are you then, I've made you some lovely scones, come on then,' and she put her arms round him. He was so astonished that I would let someone in from the prayer group that he was silenced. If anyone ever offered to look after him he would be very rude and say 'no' and say he had all the help he needed. Mary managed to persuade him to let her dress him. I went upstairs to recover and thanked God for sending Mary just in time. It was a great help to me to have the prayer group in the house. I received such a lot of support both personally and from all the prayer. All my friends were so willing to accept Ken just as he was. At various times they all heard him in full flood and his greeting to everyone was always harsh, cutting and rude. They just embraced him.

We had many occasions like this but rarely when I was on my own. I could hardly believe it that by the time Canon Denning arrived Ken was sitting quietly and, as always with the Canon, beautifully behaved. He would have been really surprised on the days that he was slightly delayed to see Ken's angry face and hear his disapproval as 11.00 o'clock came and went. No explaining that the Canon had other things to do ever sufficed. Yet Ken would receive communion from him very quietly and sit in silence without a word of criticism.

We had tried to take Ken to the Tuesday evening prayer group, but found that he preached a long sermon to everyone which was impossible to understand. It became difficult to have a time of praise and worship. He didn't like the repetitive singing of songs and I think he felt, because he was a priest, he should be controlling everything. Peter and I decided it was better to go back to what we had been doing and that was to take turns to stay and look after Ken. He was inclined to get worked up and angry about our kind of free prayer and the openness to the Spirit.

As leaders we joined in prayer with our district leaders, and with all our groups together we were quite a strong team. We prayed for a whole year for guidance as to whether we should lead 'Life in the Spirit Seminars' in our area. It was a matter of finding a suitable hall, and a sympathetic parish priest. Canon Denning had never objected to the prayer groups, in fact he was the one who gave me a book about starting a group. However he was always very reticent to show enthusiasm when we shared with him some of the wonderful answers to prayer and maybe this was quite right. Discernment is learned through knowledge, practice and faith. I think he was afraid of becoming involved. He always used to say he didn't want miracles in his parish because it caused too much fuss; there had been a story of everlasting cut flowers in a church in the north of England which he always quoted disapprovingly. Anyway, through persistent prayer a decision was made unanimously by quite a large group of us from the area to ask Canon Denning if we could use our parish hall for this purpose with his support. Peter was detailed to ask him.

We both felt very nervous about it as we were not sure of the Canon's reaction to having 'Life in the Spirit Seminars' in the parish; our plan was also to invite Bishop Langton Fox, then Bishop of Menevia, to speak in the church to whoever would come to hear him as an introduction to the Seminars. Before Peter had a chance to make an appointment with the Canon, he had made a social call on us, mainly to see how Ken was getting on. After we had all chatted for a while, Peter broached the subject and opened out our idea of inviting Bishop Langton Fox. Canon Denning was delighted; he said he knew the Bishop well and had taught him in earlier years. He said to tell him that he was invited to dinner and could stay the night in the presbytery. After this we felt sure in what we were doing. The seminars were planned for the autumn and the Bishop proved very popular. He said Mass and spoke about the meaning of the seminars. He explained that they were aimed at a personal renewal of our life as Christians and to help us to open ourselves to the action of the Holy Spirit. The church was packed and about a hundred people, many of whom were visitors to the parish, signed up. They included members of the local Methodist Church the United Reformed Church and the Anglican Church.

The introduction on the first evening was given by the retired head of Ramsgate Benedictine priory, Abbot Parry. He gave a wonderful witness of his second experience of the Holy Spirit at the age of seventy, and how he wished it had taken place earlier in his life. We have this talk recorded.

We brought Ken to the Seminars, not because he wanted to come, although he did not object, but because we both needed to be involved and we thought it might be helpful to him. We had a different speaker for each of the seven talks which were spread over seven weeks. Ken was quiet during the talks and I had him in my group for the sharing time after the talk. It wasn't easy as he mumbled a great deal and no one could understand him properly, but he kept talking about what he chose to talk about which always reverted to why wasn't Our Lady mentioned more. A Dominican Sister tried to explain to him that the talks followed a theme, the first about God's love for us, the second about salvation, the third about repentance and so on. Ken became very disruptive and annoyed and we thought it best to ask him if he would rather not be in the group. He agreed that it would be better as he was very cross at having to listen to people talking a lot of rubbish. He understood that it was necessary for me to be there, so in the end he sat on his own with his breviary which he was trying to learn to read again, and peace was restored to the group. He maintained this stance all along and talking about God was a very dangerous area for a long time.

Ken's God who he now knows loves him, he believed was still the God to be feared if you didn't absolutely come up to standard. Anything I ever said about what I believed, and how I saw God and my relationship with Jesus as a loving and caring one, and that God was interested in every detail of our lives, brought shouts of 'Rubbish.' Ken was convinced that we all had to earn God's love. He could not get his head round the New Testament account that Jesus had died on the cross to pay for all our sins, or indeed that he was a sacrifice for our sins, and that his blood was shed as the animals of sacrifice were slaughtered in the Old Testament; that all we had to do was to repent and believe this, that God had sent his beloved son because he loved us so much, and Jesus had already reconciled us to God; as we came to repentance for our sins, we were already forgiven, that we didn't have to struggle and be worried and miserable; Jesus wanted us to look to him for the help we needed and be at peace, the peace that the world cannot give; that even with illness or difficulties we could still have inner joy and peace if we looked to him and allowed him to run our lives, and that is why the gospels were called the 'Good News.'

It was hopeless. To talk to Ken of these things caused him to shout and become abusive. He knew he was right, he had learnt it all in the seminary. (1957-1963). We decided it was best to leave this area well alone for the time being, and to try to exercise the love of God in practice, whatever he was like, and however difficult. We tried to see the good in him which was not easy. Because of my great love for him, which I did not understand, I was most probably over-protective. We were at this stage not sure how much was due to his brain damage and how much belonged to the Ken of pre-accident days, who of course we did not know. He continued to be sometimes the tiny child needing nothing but love, and the unbearably aggressive adult whose ideas were the only correct ones. Love and care had to become our watchword.

Chapter Twelve

Clare

At Christmas 1979 a young lad whose family we knew came to live with us. We will call him James. James was adopted not long before his brother was born and found this out by chance when he was about ten years old. James always seemed to be in trouble when he was young and as a teenager it became serious. He was in trouble with the police as well as not being able to manage his life. He found himself without a home after his parents put him out of the house. Fortunately he got on well with Ken and was very kind to him. James had a lot of problems but praise God, all worked out well and he is now married and father of two teenage children. It was during the Christmas of 1979, when James came to live with us that Clare started feeling ill and tired. She didn't complain much or make a fuss but visited the doctor at her work who examined her and said he could find nothing wrong. Clare was still working at Wokingham with Doctor Barnardo's and was very happy. She had a pleasant room which she had made look pretty, and she had a lot of friends. She shared yet another room in a rented house with a friend. This meant when she had free time she was able to move out from her work without the long journey home. She went to the doctor several times, trying to make it a different doctor in the practice each time. The result was always the same, nothing was the matter. Clare became quite disinclined to speak about how ill she felt, because the doctors gave the impression to her that she just wanted time off, and this went on throughout the year. I found out later that she had felt so ill one night when she was working that they had sent for the duty doctor. He had examined her and indicated that there was absolutely nothing wrong. It seemed that perhaps she was having a nervous breakdown. At her place of work they were beginning to think that it was psychosomatic. At the Sealed Knot weekends, an organisation to which she belonged, she would evidently sometimes be too tired to take part and would just lie down in the grass and go to sleep. I did not hear all this until later as Clare was very unsure herself as to what was going on and did not want to worry us. When she came home she was bright and did not want to talk about herself. On the day Prince Charles married Diana, the 20th July, she had a meal at home with us and a friend Paul who she had met when he rented a room at the house, and then later joined Clare to work at Doctor Barnardo's. Paul eventually became a good friend of the whole family, studying at college with Paul to do a four year teacher training course. Clare seemed much better that night and they went off to watch the firework display at Crystal Palace, although I heard afterwards that she had actually felt quite ill. She had become very skilled at pretending as no doctor would believe her. She spoke very little about it at home, and we did not see a way forward to help her. We did not know, at that time, about her numerous visits to the doctor. The following week she came home for her days off, and said she felt ill and tired, and that if she could have a week off to rest she would be better. I persuaded her to go to one of the doctors at our practice. She saw a woman doctor that I did not at that time know and she told Clare that there was nothing wrong with her and that if she had three days off anyway she could rest at that time. She refused point blank to give her a certificate for the week. I wanted to intervene to explain to the doctor that Clare seemed tired and ill, but Clare wanted no fuss and would not let me interfere. She went back to work after three days and was looking forward to her two weeks annual leave in August which was almost upon us. Peter and I had booked up to take Ken on holiday to Rome to stay at Palazzola during August for two weeks. During her holiday Clare wanted to live at home and look after the plants for me. We had invited her to come on holiday with us, but she had declined as she wanted to spend some time with her old friends which she saw little of. We didn't actually see her before we left but on the phone she said she was much better, and I believed her. She had no apparent symptoms of anything, and I really thought she needed a good rest, there seemed no other explanation. We went off to Rome, knowing that she would be home in a few days. I left everything ready for her so that she could have an easy time. Christopher had gone abroad, Paul was on holiday with Steve and it was arranged that James would live at the priest's house while we were away. Our parish priest and the housekeeper were quite happy to keep an eye on him.

The holiday in Palazzola went off quite well. We had the same rooms which were very convenient for looking after Ken. As he became better there were different difficulties but we all managed quite well. One day we visited Rome while some of the friends we had made the previous year looked after Ken, then another day Peter and I walked the three miles up to Rocca di Pappa, the nearest village. Ken seemed quite okay although we could only persuade him to go in the pool once with us holding him, and that was with great difficulty and protestation. We enjoyed the swimming as Ken was beginning to be able to sit on his own trying to read a little although his concentration was still very poor. There were always offers to hold him while he walked with his tripod, and he was very peaceful. It was as we were preparing to leave Palazzola a message came through to say there would be a flight delay of about 4 hours. I settled Ken for a rest on his bed, which had actually been made up for the new arrivals. I undid his belt and loosened the top of his trousers to make him comfortable; it was always essential that he started travelling in a relaxed state of mind. He dozed off, so I was reluctant to wake him until the last minute when we settled him in his wheelchair and all was well. Peter lifted him up and helped him on to the coach to take us to the airport as I went up the steps ahead to guide him to a seat. There was a sudden yell from Ken, "Mummy... my trousers have fallen down." I quickly turned back and he was standing on the bottom step in his pants, with his trousers round his feet, laughing, and of course we all then laughed. Very often it was his humour that saved the day; he was fortunately unconcerned about what people would think, and I was grateful as it was my fault for having forgotten I had undone his belt.

We were pleased to get on the way home and I was already wondering how Clare would be after a rest. We arrived home about seven o'clock in the evening after a good journey, but the moment we entered the house I knew something was wrong. At first it was difficult to know what it was. There was a musty smell as if the house had been shut up, then I saw the plants were wilting. Usually whoever has been at home, whatever was not done during the rest of the time, there was a mad cleaning and polishing session however brief, before our arrival, to give the house a smell of having been cared for, and this had not been done. There was a dusty stillness everywhere. Nothing had been disturbed. I looked in the bread bin and there was a thick green mould over the few pieces of bread left there. There was no sign of Clare and no note from her. We became really worried and were just about to phone around when we heard a key in the door. It was Clare, her friend Mavis who shared her room in Wokingham and Mavis' fiancé, Charlie. Clare went straight upstairs and Mavis told us that Clare was not well, had fallen off her moped and had cut her knee badly. When Clare came down she burst into tears, and said "Mummy, I am so sorry I haven't done anything in the house, I haven't been well and I went back to Wokingham." I felt terrible that I had not been there for her. She would not let me look at her knee and said it was nothing, but it was obviously painful. Mavis and Charlie said they had brought her back in the car. Mavis shrugged her shoulders as if to say she did not know what more to do. They had some coffee and slipped off home very quietly, indicating that Clare needed help but would not receive it. Clare would not talk about how she felt, and when I suggested calling the doctor, she became cross and said she would absolutely not see another doctor. She had not been eating while we were away and had lost a great deal of weight. She went to bed and I felt that the next day we would have to sort something out. I was extremely worried.

In the morning Clare allowed me to take her a cup of tea, I sat on her bed and suggested again going with her to see the doctor. She refused point blank and told me of the times she had been to various doctors who had examined her thoroughly and found nothing wrong. She looked very ill with dark rings round her eyes. Her long dark hair which had never been cut short lay smoothly in two plaits either side of her shoulders. She had plaited her hair to keep it out of the way. I wondered again whether she was having a nervous breakdown. She said she would get up and have a bath, and then come downstairs. It was a very hot day, and she was a very long time. A friend called in to see me, but I excused myself to see what was happening to Clare. I found her at the top of the stairs, barely able to stand or breathe, with a summer dress on showing exactly how much weight she had lost. I took her in to her room and helped her onto the bed, and said I was going to call Doctor Lees. She pulled away from me and I could see in her face real fear, she told me that if I did she would not speak to him. I called the surgery and explained the urgency. I asked my friend to leave, which she did, as soon as she understood the situation, and I made Clare comfortable on several pillows so that she could get her breath more easily. Doctor Lees arrived before lunchtime, and Clare made no protest. He examined her fully and could find nothing wrong. Her blood pressure was normal, she had no temperature, and he started questioning her about her job and the tensions and stresses. It was then I found out that she had just given in her notice at Doctor Barnardo's. She had told them she felt too tired and ill to do her job. It was the only way she could see how to cope with feeling ill and having nothing wrong! I realised all this time she had been trying to protect us from worry but nevertheless had been terribly worried herself. When later we pieced together everyone's evidence many things became clear. I think that day we all presumed that the difficulty in breathing was a recurrence of Clare's childhood asthma. She was furious that Doctor Lees thought she had a psychological illness, and I did not know what to think. Whatever it was I knew it was serious. It was only after they had been talking for a long time that Clare told the doctor of her night sweats about which I knew nothing, and how she felt her head was burning as if she had tight burning curlers in it. This had evidently just started during the last week. Doctor Lees gave her an antibiotic, which he thought might help, and told me to call him if she was no better. He said the antibiotics needed at least three days to start to show an improvement. Clare could not eat and she became more breathless and weaker. I was up at night changing her nightdress and her sheets which were wringing wet, making her cool drinks, and trying to help the pain in her head. I would sit beside her with my hand gently touching her, praying to Jesus for help. By morning she was cool, the pain had gone and she would just lie quietly in bed, sitting up against five pillows to breathe more easily, looking about twelve years old. Clare was always pleased to see Peter when he came in from work, but she just wanted everything to be very quiet. Towards the end of the first week I called Doctor Lees, explaining that Clare was worse, and describing her night symptoms in detail. He came immediately and examined her again and said she had all the symptoms of viral pneumonia except he could not understand why he could hear nothing abnormal in her chest. Although I had described to him in detail the nights we were having, it was hard to believe, because in the day Clare looked so peaceful sitting in bed, cool, unruffled and clean, with her two neat plaits. However, she was so weak that she could hardly walk. Doctor Lees said he would treat it as viral pneumonia, and altered the antibiotic, with the same instructions as before. I was up each night with Clare, and as the days went on I knew that she was dying. She asked me to bring her little bible over and to read to her. I would sit in the room with her and pray, waiting for the medicine to take action. Her breathing became worse, not only were we using the ventolin prescribed by the doctor to help what seemed to be the return of asthma, aggravated by the pneumonia, or so we thought, but I fixed up a steam kettle. I did everything that I knew how. I was even nervous of lifting her out of bed and changing her nightie as she was in such a poor state.

We had not long had a change of assistant priest in the parish. Father Martin had gone, which was a great loss for Ken as he had been helped so much in saying his daily office, and indeed, so had I. He was replaced by Father Robin who had actually given the first talk in the 'Life in the Spirit Seminars' the year before. I asked Clare if she would like to see him, if he would come and be with her. She said that as she didn't know him she would be very shy, but she didn't refuse. That night was the second night of the Bishop's three-day parish visitation, and there was a parish meeting. I had come to excuse myself because of Clare. I did not know beforehand, but Father Robin had been detailed to stay with the Bishop and look after him. When I asked Father Robin if he would come and see Clare as she was seemingly dying with no one knowing what the matter was, he hesitated, and then said, that it was quite extraordinary because the Bishop had just given him the night off. Peter was at home with Clare and it was then decided that I should go to the meeting, and Father Robin go to Clare.

Robin stayed with Clare for two hours, and she witnesses that they were two of the most important hours in her life. When I returned she was very at peace, but still very ill. The following morning by 11.30 Clare was finding difficulty in drawing even the shortest breath. I picked up the phone and asked to speak to Dr. Lees. I said "Doctor, Clare is much worse; if you don't come and do something quickly she will die." He was with us in five minutes. He took one look at her and went to the phone. He spoke to the chest consultant at Mayday Hospital and asked if he would come immediately and examine Clare. The consultant replied that it would be much more effective if we ordered an ambulance and brought her to the hospital so that he could give her a thorough examination with X-rays. His clinic started at 2 pm and we arranged to be there. The consultant had Clare's chest X-rayed, and examined her without me being present. He then called me in and cross-questioned Clare about her work. By now her mind was not working properly and she was answering in a very simplified way. The consultant called me into another room and said to me, "Mrs Coldham, I can treat the physical, I hope, as there is a new drug out now which is marvellous, but the psychological I cannot, she will have to see a psychiatrist, she is in the last stages of tuberculosis. He showed me the X-ray and her lungs were almost solid white. He was definite and in no doubt. He arranged for her to be taken over to the isolation unit where he said she would remain. She was to have more tests and start treatment, she was very ill and could do very little for herself. Peter and I were allowed in to see her at any time, but we had to 'gown up' in clean white garments and wear masks. They started Clare immediately on a new treatment for tuberculosis. She had to take enormous orange capsules, which was very difficult for her. Eating was difficult, but she did drink some milk. They questioned her and did many tests, one of which was in order to grow a culture which was to take six weeks. She was still having the extremely distressing night sweats lying against six pillows which were covered with heavy plastic with just a thin cotton pillowcase over it. I asked permission on the second day to bring in cooler pillows. The sister said that I could, providing I was willing to leave them there, and of course I was. I went again to Allders, bought six pillows and put them into hospital pillowcases. This was a great improvement, and did help slightly to keep Clare cool.

Peter came in every evening and I stayed with Clare as much as I was able. She actually had a lot of visitors but was sometimes too tired even to talk. No one in or out of the hospital, including Dr. Lees, could understand how she could have caught tuberculosis. It had almost disappeared in England and there were very few cases, most of which were found in the early stages. As time went on there was absolutely no improvement in her condition, in fact we watched her failing and becoming worse. Some smaller tests they had done for tuberculosis had proved negative. Even the consultant himself began to doubt, though the evidence of the X-ray was there for all to see. Breathing had become almost impossible for Clare, and the slightest exertion was completely disabling. Many consultants and doctors came in to question her; they began to think it might be some rare Eastern fungal infection in the lungs which were apparently the only part of her that was affected. They asked her if she had been with anyone of Asian origin and of course she had, she had been living with and looking after several girls of African and Asian origin. By now her thinking power was so weak that she found this all too much. Everyone we knew was praying for her, but I think we all felt doubtful of what we were praying for. It was obvious to Peter and me that it was not tuberculosis. The culture had shown no sign of growing in the laboratory, but no one actually told us that it was not tuberculosis. Clare eventually was unable to keep the orange pills down and she was very sick. Not only was the medication causing distress but it was useless. Three weeks had passed since she was taken into the isolation unit, and although we were all still outwardly calmly praying and trusting in the Lord, asking him to help Clare and us and to show us what was wrong with her, we also wondered how he would help, because it all seemed hopeless. We were constantly reminded of the song we sing in the prayer group, "Nothing , nothing, absolutely nothing, nothing is impossible for God." Clare had whispered to me with the small amount of breath that she had, "Mummy, I think that I will die, and no one will know what is the matter." I said to her, "Clare, if you die, you will be the blessed one, and go straight to Jesus, it is we who shall be left without you, and will be devastated." I quickly turned our minds yet again from these thoughts to renewed prayer for courage and trust.

Just at this time a hospital consultant named Dr Livingstone returned from three weeks' leave. He was asked to examine Clare's case. He spoke to us and said that he was going to have a biopsy done on the gland in her neck. He said that he had a very good idea of what was wrong with her. We did not understand, but he seemed efficient and interested and we could only continue to pray and trust. He explained to Clare that the following morning she was to have nothing to eat or drink, and that she would be taken to theatre. It was at this time that only one theatre was operating in Mayday Hospital, as an enormous building programme was in progress and there was much disruption. It so happened that in addition to the normal list, a prisoner in one of the police cells had tried to kill himself by eating his bed springs, and had been in the operating theatre until 10 o'clock at night. An Egyptian surgeon came to apologise to Clare and said she would have to wait until the following day. We were all very upset. She had some milk to drink, and tried to sleep.

The following day we were with Clare all day, evening came, and she had still not been called to the theatre. By 9.00 pm I was really angry that she had been left again. She had been all day a second time with not even a drink because of the impending operation and I was really afraid for her life. She was extremely weak and listless. I went to the sister who obviously knew that Clare was still waiting because she was in the first room with a big plate glass window on to the corridor. Also there were very few people in the unit and Clare needed constant nursing. It appeared that this was the day that there had been a raid on a bank in Addiscombe, and one of the robbers had been shot in the stomach. He had been in the theatre for many hours having an emergency operation so the arranged list had yet again been delayed. As soon as I spoke to the sister, she phoned the theatre, and within five minutes Clare was on her way. The biopsy was done that night and she was left very weak and sore and bruised. We had to wait twenty four hours for the results of the biopsy. It was Friday when Peter and I were called urgently to the hospital for a meeting with Dr Livingstone. He told us that he had been almost sure before the biopsy, but that now it was confirmed. He had seen one similar case before but that it was most unusual. She had a rare type of Hodgkin's Disease, which is cancer of the lymph nodes with the complication that the nodes affected were only in her lungs. Usually the nodes were affected in other places as well which had made the diagnosis so difficult. He said they had blown up the X-ray as large as they could, which had shown clearly what the problem was, and that as he had experienced it before it enabled him to recognise it. Dr. Livingstone had made an appointment for Clare at the Royal Marsden at Sutton, which was to be with Dr. MacElwee at his Tuesday clinic. Peter and I were stunned and speechless. Dr Livingstone explained that Clare would need a long course of chemotherapy. As is usual with the diagnosis of a rare illness, we knew very little about it, only afterwards does one think of all the questions.

Paul had come to the hospital with me to see Clare and we had waited together for Peter to return early from London. I took Paul home while Peter went to Clare. I went straight to the priest's house and asked if they would please announce at all the Masses that Clare had a rare kind of Hodgkin's disease, was dying and to ask everyone to pray. I then went back to the hospital to see Clare and collect Peter. Clare had seen Dr Livingstone and had been told what her illness was. She seemed relieved to know that at least now someone understood. She was very calm and we were uncertain whether she understood the seriousness of the illness, and what chemotherapy would mean. The following day she had a visit from the original consultant who had wrongly diagnosed the tuberculosis. He apologised to her and asked her forgiveness. He also came over to see us as soon as he knew we were there. What could we do but forgive him; the poor man was very upset. The person who dealt with Clare from the path lab in Mayday had suggested that we should sue our doctor, and then when we got to the Marsden they suggested we should sue Mayday. All we wanted was for Clare to be better, we were not a bit interested in recriminations. Later that day Clare was moved into a small ward in the main hospital. This was a backwater where nothing happened; an area of waiting!

Christopher, on one of his visits had brought 'Emma' by Jane Austen for Clare to read, but she had been both unable to read the print easily or indeed to concentrate. However, someone else we knew, named Mary who worked in the linen room at Mayday Hospital, and kept an eye on all the Catholics who were admitted, brought Clare a book called "I dared to call him Father." It has a picture of a Muslim woman on the front and is the true story of the persecution of Christians in Pakistan and the conversion of one woman to Christianity. Clare could not put it down. She wanted time to read, and she cried and cried. Even at the end of visiting time she would be anxious for people to go so that she could turn back to the book which affected her deeply; it was exactly the right book for her. She was obviously praying and trusting God herself. During the three days of waiting we were very fortunate that she was in such a little backwater in the hospital, because although she was nursed as much as she needed, we were able to stay with her even when the whole family were there together, and we were quite a crowd. The boys came and stayed with her, and Paul's friend Stephen stayed with us. They talked about many important things, especially about how much love was shared even though the boys did not often mention this. We all had a good cry and later we even collected a 'take away' and shared it between us, Clare trying hard to take part. She wanted us to stay and keep her company; by now the book was finished.

On the Monday evening when we were making plans to go to the Royal Marsden the next morning, a place we did not know then, but were to come to know well in future years, I was upset by the staff nurse in charge. I wanted to know if we should go with Clare to the Marsden, meaning whether we should come to Mayday and travel with her in the ambulance or meet her there. The staff nurse completely misunderstood me and thought I was asking whether we really needed to be with Clare at all. She jumped down my throat and severely scolded me. She almost shouted at me that Clare was very seriously ill with a strong chance that she might not recover, and the least her parents could do would be to stay with her. I was desperately set off balance by her attitude and had a very difficult time in finding out what was to happen on the following day; I was very upset and felt rejected myself. Finally it was arranged that we would go to the Marsden and wait for the ambulance with Clare to arrive from Mayday. We were there very early and met the ambulance immediately it arrived. We took Clare into the hospital in a wheelchair; she was in her nightie and dressing gown, and as we went through the door, she saw that many people were without hair. Whether she had been thinking about hair loss or whether this was the first time of realisation, I do not know. As we did not know what kind of chemotherapy she would have, this subject had not been broached. We had not actually used the word cancer to her but we knew later that she had suspected for a long time she was dying of cancer, but hadn't dared say.

This day was a very difficult one for all of us. Clare went through many blood tests, examinations X-rays and scans, including an ultra sound. At the end of it all, we had a meeting with Dr MacElwee, or 'Big Mac' as he was known by everyone. He saw us all together with several students present after asking Clare if she

minded them being there and she said she didn't. This meeting took
place in Big Mac's office which was a room off the main lounge
known as Pinkham Ward. It has since been reordered. The lounge
was full of people in various stages of cancer with drips fitted into
them, which they carried on a movable stand. Peter and I found
this a rather frightening place on that first day, but we were to
change our minds as the experience became more familiar. Big Mac
asked us all whether we knew and understood exactly what was
the matter with Clare. We all said that we only had a vague idea.
He then explained in detail exactly what Hodgkin's disease was
and told us how Clare had a very rare type. It was very unusual
for it to be entirely centred on the lungs. He explained that the solid
nature of the cancer in the lymph nodes which was continuing to
spread had caused her lack of breath, and this was why there had
been no sound in her chest when she was examined and why
diagnosis had been so difficult. The illness affected the temperature
control of her body. It was as if the thermostat stopped working.
He then explained the treatment that Clare would receive. He
said that they would keep her in hospital for a little while to
establish the treatment, which would be chemotherapy given by
regular injections at the hospital, and large and small brown pills
taken in differing quantities through the week. This would last for
six months. He explained that she would most probably lose some
hair, maybe all of it, but was certain that it would grow again, and
that this was better than an illness which was killing her. He also
told us that she would experience sickness and feeling ill but he
also held out great hope that it was possible for the treatment to be
successful, but that the cancer was well established and it was
impossible to know exactly how it would respond. He explained
that every ten years there was an international symposium, and

that each time the treatment and results for Hodgkin's disease were greatly improved. He promised to do his very best for Clare. As Big Mac spoke about Clare's hair, I felt the tears run down my face. I was aware just how important her hair had always been to her. I could not help noticing that she herself was quite dry eyed about it.

We emerged from Big Mac's consultation room and sat in the adjoining lounge with all the people receiving treatment. There were vacant armchairs, and Clare of course was still in her wheelchair. We all three had a good cry and hugged each other. After a short time Clare wiped her eyes, waved her arms and shushed us to be quiet. She said she wanted to tell us something. She said "Listen, Mummy and Daddy, I want to tell you that I know I am going to be better, in fact I feel better already. I am going to be healed." I remember feeling my spirits rise as my tears left me. It was the beginning of a new era.

We had been told that when we were ready the Sister in charge of Pinkham Ward would show Clare where she was to settle. She was anxious to get on and do what she had to do. Sister showed her the corner bed in a room of four. The room was quite a long way from the bathrooms, and Clare had already made it clear that she was going to walk and not go in the wheelchair. Sister offered her a room nearer the toilet facilities but she was insistent that she would manage. Clare came down in the lift to see us off and insisted she would be okay going back in the lift on her own. Knowing what was the matter was such a relief to her, and the fact that she could now start doing something about getting better had given her new energy. Big Mac was always a great support and encouragement to her. The lady in the bed opposite Clare, was very ill and seemed as if she had not long to live. I was seeing things that I had never seen before. Another person in the room was Bridget who has since died, but helped Clare to get through many things with her sense of humour and laughter. She was about forty-five and had a grown up family and was in the advanced stages of her illness. She had lost her hair several times with the treatment she had received. She told Clare many stories during the next week, one of which was about the time that she was out riding in Derbyshire with her wig on, the horse went under a tree and her wig caught on a twig and was whisked off her head. Clare laughed and laughed with her every day, and I am sure this was a release from trauma in the same way as tears are. When Clare had to be measured for a wig she was ready to face it and took it in her stride.

We found the nursing staff very supportive, and there were several times when this was put to the test by me. It was not an easy week, and there were many hurdles to be overcome. Clare went from strength to strength. The very first part of the treatment which took place the first day was for her to receive four pints of blood. The difference in her was phenomenal. We realised that lack of blood caused by the cancer was the reason for her mental state. She became very mentally active and was a great force for good in Pinkham. She not only ate her own meals, but encouraged others and helped them. She made friends with a nineteen year old boy, who had cancer of the testicles which was already spreading, he also sadly has died. She lifted his spirits and chatted with his mother and father. I found the experiences during this time very demanding, and when I went out to the car I would sit for a while to be quiet, and make my transition from the world in the Marsden to the world outside. I did not know that Clare watched me from her room which overlooked the front of the hospital and the car park and guessed correctly the reason for my delay in going. I must say that I often had a good weep for all I saw, and prayed to the Lord for all that I could not understand. During this time of Clare's illness when Peter and I were out of the house together, Ken was looked after by friends who came to the house to 'baby sit'. I had many good friends who would love him and be kind to him, whatever he was like, and however difficult he was. When Patricia could be free she would come over and be with him. Preparing meals was no problem, especially with the freezer. It was actually giving time to Ken, which was what he needed. He literally could not be left alone unless he was asleep; he would be upset and very insecure. He tried rather unsuccessfully to understand Clare's illness but he was consumed with jealousy, and often accused me of putting him second. I was aware that this was most probably something in him that had been there before his accident, a kind of paranoia. The only way we knew to deal with it was to love him and be firm and understanding, whatever the cause.

After a week in the Marsden, Clare was settled into the treatment and was home. Having got over the first injection, she was 'apparently' well, and took some interest in cooking and doing some of the jobs in the house. The transformation was amazing. She was invited to a wedding, and we were amazed that she wanted to go. I had gradually been cutting her hair shorter and shorter as it became thinner. She had been recommended not to wash it more than was necessary. As we washed it so it came out in handfuls. By this time she was wearing a little scarf tied round behind her ears. I was concerned that she would be taken ill away from home, but she was seemingly well and very determined. She always went to lie down when she could not manage. She was convinced that she would be quite better and we were all praying that she would be. She went to the wedding and enjoyed it and we tried hard afterwards to live a normal life. She became very involved with a group of young Christian people. She lost all her hair and for a little while, until her hair started to grow, wore her wig regularly. She accompanied Father Robin to some of his school visits with her guitar. At first she felt too shy, so he asked her to make tapes of the spiritual songs he wanted to play. Eventually as she gained confidence, she helped quite often with day and weekend retreats. She continued to attend the Royal Marsden regularly and had many tests and scans as well as a bone marrow test, which was very painful. She was always pleased that she did not have to stay in and have a drip for her chemotherapy.

Having left home originally to work at Doctor Barnardo's she moved right back into the family circle, where she could be loved and looked after, as well as being able to help when she was feeling well. The chemotherapy continued for six months, and Clare grew to love and trust Big Mac and all the doctors who worked with him. The Marsden became a place of hope for all of us. As the treatment progressed the queasiness and sickness increased but Clare never made any fuss. She would just quietly lie on her bed for a few days until she felt better. She turned to Father Robin for her spiritual help and her faith became very strong. When the chemotherapy was finished, Clare was told that the cancer seemed to have cleared but she would have to attend for X-rays and blood tests every two months. She wanted to get a job so that she would get back to normality. It was not an easy decision as the work she knew was very demanding. The chemotherapy had taken a toll of her energy and she was not feeling strong enough to do a full-time job. After a while of convalescence she took some irregular short term jobs. She continued her work with the young people, and was waiting to get her full strength back. Her hair grew back beautifully. At first it was very curly as it was when she was a small child, and then as it grew longer it became more gently curled.

It was Christmas eighteen months later when the cancer returned. By now Clare had her own car, and she insisted on driving home early after a party on Boxing Day at Gerard and Celia's house in Woking, because she didn't feel too well. I had noticed that she was rather short of breath. She didn't mention this, and I think we were all afraid of what it was. The next day I spoke to her of my fears, and she said she would wait until her regular appointment at the beginning of January. She also felt sure it was a recurrence of the cancer in the lymph nodes of her lungs, but at that time she did not say so. I decided it was best to leave her to her own decision without trying to persuade her to return immediately. The visit to the Royal Marsden confirmed our worst fears, but Big Mac was very reassuring. He said they would step up the injections of Vin Cristine and the large brown pills. Whatever Clare was feeling inside, she put on a brave face and wanted her life to carry on as usual, or any way as much as she could manage. On her second visit Big Mac arranged with her to carry out a big examination to find out if the lymph nodes in other parts of her body were affected. This entailed putting a blue injection into her feet and X-raying her in stages. Her appointment was on a Friday and I was with Clare in the hospital all day. They were expecting her to stay for the night in case there were any after effects. At this time her hair was quite long in curls down her neck. That weekend Clare was leading a group at a Christian youth weekend at St. Mary's School in West Croydon. She explained to the nursing staff that there was no way she could stay the night, and of course they could not force her. She went off that Friday night with her friends. It was only those who knew her very well who were aware of her new situation.

The next day, Saturday morning at 8.30 am, when our phone rang it was Clare, requesting that I go quickly to St. Mary's with her wig, hairbrush and mirror. She said all her hair had 'come off'. She told me where to find her and said she would be waiting for me at the main entrance of the school in fifteen minutes. It was only afterwards that I heard the full story. She had tried to comb her hair, and the whole lot was loose on her head. She and her friend Helen had locked themselves in a staff cloakroom and had had a good cry. She had then borrowed a kind of tam o'shanter from one of the boys, and came out to phone me. Afterwards, they went back to the staff cloakroom and locked the door. They lifted Clare's hair off her head, almost in one piece; she brushed her wig, put back the hat and rejoined the group. No one but Helen knew what had happened to Clare. She continued to wear the tam o'shanter for the rest of the morning. The weekend was very successful, and continued without a hitch. I remember that morning well. It was freezing cold and snowing. On the way home as I was coming slowly round a large bend in Pampisford Road, my car skidded and gently hit a van coming in the opposite direction. Without knowing what I had just been doing, everyone was very understanding, especially the driver of the van. None of the damage was very bad, and it was all covered by insurance. This was a very sad day, and I was aware that the only way through this time of trial for Clare was to renew my trust in what God was doing. It was impossible to understand anything.

At this time Clare and her friends were organising a Youth Mass in the parish every Sunday evening. A small group would come together in the week to pray, read the scriptures for the following Sunday, and then plan the music etc. This Mass proved to be very popular not only with our own parish but with the youth of the deanery churches and a large crowd always attended. The piano would be brought through from the hall, and the instrumentalists varied from guitarists to flautists and sometimes percussion. They would meet early to practise and the enthusiasm was tremendous. This spell of chemotherapy was very much more intensive than the first course, and Clare suffered much more. She felt more ill and had to rest more. Many people were already praying for her and indeed for us all, and their prayers intensified when they heard the news of the recurrence of the cancer. It was during this time that Clare was told that it was unlikely that she would be able to conceive, even if her regular monthly cycle did return. This was a very big blow to her as she had always looked forward to having children. Peter and I were very sad for her, and it brought to reality the seriousness of all that she had been through. The day she heard the news her friend Helen was with us all as well as Father Robin, who had been the channel for the Lord's strength and prayer behind both Clare's conversion and the Youth Masses. I asked Clare if I could tell him her sad news, so that we could pray with her together. With Father Robin leading the prayer we laid hands on Clare and prayed that the Lord would send his healing love through every part of her body, mind, and spirit so that she could be used in whatever way he wanted. Clare continued to go regularly to the Royal Marsden Hospital until her course of treatment was finished. Amazingly she managed to carry on with her interests most of the time but with some difficulty. After this she was required to go the Marsden every two months, and eventually every six months.

It was with great joy that Clare announced to us that her body and her whole system had returned to normal against all the hopes of the team of doctors attending her. As she began to feel better and her hair started to grow again she felt that it would be good for her if she tried to do some regular work which was not too demanding. She explored the job market, and applied for part-time work in the bakery of the newly opened local Sainsbury's supermarket. She served on the counter most of the time. She started at 8.30 am and finished at 1.00 pm five days a week. It was a wonderful opportunity to regain confidence and learn regular time-keeping again and she enjoyed being with people. Many people in the church would go to her and ask her to put things by for them and she had many friends. We continued to praise and thank God for all he had done for her. Her witness is that this illness was one of the best things that ever happened to her. It completely changed her view of life and what she actually believed.

After this part-time work experience Clare was able to return to work with children again until in 1985 she fulfilled her long term ambition of going to college to train as a social worker. She went on to train as a probation officer and to work with prisoners about to be released from prison. She is now married to Jonathan, also a Catholic Christian, and they have three lovely children.

Chapter Thirteen

Ken

In 1980 there was a wonderful breakthrough. We had never stopped trying to get Ken more help. Although his doctor was also our doctor, and interested and sympathetic, it was difficult to find the help that was needed. At this time a new doctor temporarily joined the practice. His special interest was brain damage. This happened to be the same man who had come to me in the night after Clare had started her chemotherapy when I had been taken ill with an apparent heart attack. When he examined me he was quite cross and said there was nothing wrong with me. However when he eventually heard the full story from Clare of all that was going on in our house with Ken, James and Clare, he was very apologetic. He had heard about Clare as they had had a meeting of all the doctors in the practice about her illness, so that similar diagnostic mistakes would not be made. He said I was suffering from what he called 'a broken heart'. He prescribed two weeks bed rest which was a wonderful healing. After the bad start we had experienced with him, this doctor proved to be very interested and helpful during the fairly short time he was in Purley, particularly with Ken. He made many enquiries to try to find a rehabilitation unit where Ken could stay for a few weeks to experience concentrated physiotherapy and general help. It appeared that there were only a few places of this nature, and the only one that could consider taking him was in north London. We needed somewhere nearer so that we could visit him daily. However, after much searching and patience, a place was found at Headley Court, a magnificent establishment basically for personnel from any of the services. Its situation is about ten minutes drive from Epsom racecourse, and is easily accessible from Purley. During the war it was used for the rehabilitation of wounded airmen. After a preliminary interview with Ken and ourselves, the doctors in charge agreed to take Ken for a period of five weeks. At this stage we were still using the wheelchair, although he could walk short distances with the tripod and someone holding him; they were able to find a place for him within two weeks. The first thing that was said to us was that we could take the wheelchair and the tripod home, Ken would not need them any more. Their intention was to get him walking on his own. He would have one-to-one physiotherapy, and would be cared for in every way that he needed. At this stage Ken was still totally dependent and very, very upset to have to go away from home. He cried a lot and was unhappy all the time for the first few weeks. I drove over to see him each evening to settle him down and help him choose his menu for the following day. Each patient was stretched to the utmost; it was part of the therapy. A Scottish man named Jock was Ken's personal physiotherapist for most things. Ken also spent some time doing craft work which he found extremely difficult. He made two lovely stools while he was there, but he had to keep asking for help as he could not under-stand what he was doing. This made him angry, as his fairly undamaged intellect told him that a grown man should be able to understand a simple thing. The instructors were persistent, caring and patient, and he did eventually improve.

Ken's non-understanding of his own disability was his greatest handicap and he learned early on to put on a good show with some people so that they were easily misled. He felt some kind of shame at not coming up to his own standard in some areas, whereas in others he was quite unaware. Although after several years he was able to wash his face and hands and shave with an electric razor, and dress himself reasonably well with some help, he could never organise his clothes or recognise clean from dirty. Everything he learned to do was not from understanding but from teaching and constant repetition. The difficulty with this was that if some area of routine needed changing, his whole being was upset. The five weeks in Headley Court proved to be enormously beneficial. He could walk reasonably well on his own in the security of the surroundings that he came to know. He was not allowed to lean on walls or hold on to railings, but was taught how to keep his balance, and towards the end, the transformation was amazing. Jock explained to Peter and me that when he came home he would find it a little more difficult, as he would have to get used to walking in new surroundings. He walked very badly at home, almost tottering sometimes but mostly managing not to fall. His balance was very unsteady and I found it difficult to let him go and not hold him. To begin with I accompanied him all the time while he was walking, sometimes just lightly holding the back of his coat so that he was unaware. As he became more sure I became a little more trusting when he was on his feet, but temperamentally and emotionally he was insecure like a little child. First we let him practise on the terrace in the garden, and then we walked down the road. When walking, Ken veered to the right because it was his left side that was weak, and I was afraid he would fall into the road and go under a car. It was after my own fear was healed that we were eventually able to let him go on his own on the pavement, to begin with for about ten yards and then about twenty. As our confidence grew this distance lengthened, but we were always nearby watching every move.

The day came when Ken wanted to go down the road on his own. If he fell he seemed to fall softly like a baby, but of course we were hoping he would learn not to fall. Peter was more able than I was at first to let him go, I could not bear to watch. Gradually over a period of months we could let Ken walk round to the shop, about a hundred yards away. For a long time he could not cross the road, which was a blessing, because he could not keep his balance going up or down a step. Peter would see him over the road, then watch for him returning and bring him back. Ken could never ever manage more than one step up or down without a banister or rail to hold on to. Occasionally on his little walks he fell and people would pick him up and help him. I pinned his name and address on his coat when he was still unable to remember his address and phone number and often people would walk with him up the road even though he had not gone far. Ken became very persistent in wanting to walk and practised every day. The other difficulty that he had was not being able to recognise either people or places, except those that he knew very well. When he could physically manage to walk at a later stage he was not allowed to go further than the shop because he could not remember where he was. With repetition over months and with the constant slow improvement that there was anyway in his brain, this gradually became better and over the years he became more daring. By 1993 he could walk across the pedestrian crossing, often asking someone to help him, and very occasionally walk into Purley, but he was always very tired afterwards. People who did not know him often thought he was drunk, and sometimes said so. Strangely this did not seem to worry Ken. He was, though, always worried about his lack of balance which seemed to vary from day to day, and caused him much distress.

During 1981 Father Robin was very good to Ken and arranged to collect him on a Monday and Wednesday from Waylands and bring him home. This helped Ken a great deal as he felt he had a friend. Father Robin also took him to a charismatic conference for a week at Hopwood Hall in the north of England. Although Ken was pleased to go he found the programme tedious as he still had very set ideas of what he believed and how everything should be done. I think both of them found it hard work. It was also quite demanding for Father Robin as Ken needed constant care and could still not manage in the toilet on his own because of his deformed hands, and of course he needed a great deal of help with dressing at that time.

When Ken had been living with us for about three years he had a kind of breakdown. At this stage of his recovery he had never been left alone except when he was asleep. His bed was still in the dining room and he needed constant supervision and help. His moods changed all the time and his spirits needed lifting in one way or another. He was very angry, and very jealous. He was quite unaware of his behaviour however we pleaded with him. He would always say that attack is the best method of defence. He was very paranoid and felt everyone was really against him, especially if they were not actively involved with him at that moment, and yet he was still like a little child needing constant reassurance.

He was sometimes quite illogical, demanding, and merciless, but then he could suddenly change and be the helpless crying child full of self pity. His moods changed quickly and he had a very rasping tongue, whatever you said to him he was right. Sometimes I would pray with him, sometimes he needed listening to, sometimes he needed to hear how to cope with the daily difficulties and frustrations and sometimes he needed straight-forward discipline. I always put my arms round him to reassure him and comfort him, which he recognised and he could then usually find some peace for a little while. However, at this time his behaviour became more and more unmanageable and irrational in a way we had not seen before. Gradually he came to the point when he was so frightened he wanted to literally hold on to me and not let me move. He was at the same time quite rude and abusive to our visitors, and insisted on them going in to the dining room and greeting him through the wide doors which we kept open. If they didn't he would come out and shout at them. When we reprimanded him he would become abusive, and his behaviour became worse and worse. One day we recorded his abuse, but it was so terrible we could not play it back to him and we burnt the tape.

Peter and I prayed together about it all and this helped us to keep our peace, but it did not deal with what was going on. We had taken Ken to many professional people where he had been given very specific help as well as prayer, but he was usually rude and scathing and impatient, and consequently unable to receive. He had seen a psychiatrist in Harley Street who only listened to him and did not want to hear what we had to say. He did not understand that Ken was spinning him a yarn of unimportant things. It was as if he could not receive help because he was unaware of his real need. Ken told this consultant that his main problem was that he kept crying for no reason. At the end of the session which Peter and I had attended, we had been asked nothing, and were not allowed to say a word; the psychiatrist prescribed some pills which he said would help Ken to stop crying. Crying was a very minor part of all his problems, but this psychiatrist failed to discern his real needs. On the second day of taking the tablets, Ken could not stand up and was falling everywhere. Peter and I had difficulty in moving him or getting him to the toilet. I telephoned Doctor Lees, who looked up the side effects of the tablets to find they were also muscle relaxants, the very last thing that Ken needed. I stopped them immediately on Dr Lees' advice. When we returned for the second appointment with the psychiatrist and explained what had happened he said there was nothing else that he could do.

One day when Peter was at work in London, Ken started shouting at me and being abusive, threatening me and raving uncontrollably. I telephoned Peter in London and he said he would leave immediately to come home. He suggested I phoned the doctor. I immediately telephoned the surgery and asked to speak directly to Doctor Lees, who although he knew Ken quite well, had only seen him in his polite controlled mode. He could hear Ken shouting at me, because he had followed me into the hall and was trying to grab the phone from my hand. I was not physically afraid of Ken because he was so unsteady on his feet, but his shouting and abuse were frightening because there was no stopping him, he was foaming at the mouth and totally out of control. Doctor Lees said there was no way he could come to the house until surgery had finished. He suggested that I telephoned our parish priest, I did this and Father Salmon came immediately. It was the only time in fifteen years that he came to see Ken. He read the riot act in a very loud voice and Ken became quiet and sat down. I guess perhaps he prayed some silent prayers as well but nothing aloud. He told him to stay sitting down and behave himself. Ken, I could see, became frightened, then Father Salmon left without another word. It was not long before Peter arrived. Ken would usually take notice of Peter as he had a great respect for him. When everything had settled down Peter and I talked about what we would do. Peter spoke on the phone to the then Vicar General of the diocese, Canon Joe Cullinane. He invited Peter to have tea with him the next day to talk through all the possibilities that there were to help Ken. I did not want him to be taken from us for good as I knew we had already been through so much that we would find a new way to help him, but it was obvious to all of us that Ken had to learn something, or at least be brought under control. Perhaps we also had something to learn, or maybe we just needed a rest. How was it that I had such a love for this difficult priest? Only the Lord could have put this love in my heart.

During this tea party after a great deal of discussion, Canon Joe suddenly had the idea to telephone Canon Pierce, who at that time was the parish priest at West Croydon. He was known for his kindness and willingness to have people stay in his presbytery and within minutes it was all settled. Canon Pierce would take him for two or even three weeks. He had two parish nuns who would help, two assistant priests, one of whom Ken knew well as they had been together in the seminary, a housekeeper, and various other parishioners who would be willing to help. The idea of going away from home even for a short time filled Ken with horror. Peter and I had discussed all this before we spoke to him, and decided to try to harden our hearts against his pleas. When I left him in the bed sitting room which was provided for him, I felt terrible as I knew that he was unable to look after anything for himself. We made sure he knew his way to the cloakroom across the hall which he was to use for washing and the toilet, and Canon Pierce then insisted we left him to be looked after by his team. It was a difficult time for me as Ken had come to look on me as his Mummy. He was just like a little child in need having started calling me Mummy very early on, he did not want to be left out. He so needed to be loved and recognised as someone important yet we knew he required other help as well. Canon Pierce suggested that I should not see him for two weeks, but said I could phone him at any time. The three priests and two nuns between them had a difficult time, and were glad of the help from two ladies in the parish who came to sit with Ken and help him. Although we went to see Ken after two weeks it was decided he should stay another week as he was still proving to be quite difficult. He would then return on condition he behaved himself. Quite how much of this advice Ken could understand we did not know.

After three weeks I was really glad to have him home and indeed he was overjoyed to be back in his own bed in the dining room. He seemed more settled. It was a long slow job teaching Ken and trying to get him to be amenable to everyone. If he had visitors he put on a very good show for them, but was not able to keep it up for very long, but with the family he could still be rude and hurtful, and extremely jealous. The family grew to understand his ways and on the whole either took no notice or tried to show him another way.

We knew that he must have been very frustrated, but living with him all the time required a certain amount of cooperation from him. Most of the time I could go to him and put my arms round him and change his angry mood but occasionally Peter and I had to take firm action. It was still often at dinner that there would be trouble and several times we would threaten to remove him from the table. If he would not be quiet Peter would take one arm and I the other and we forcibly with great protests from him, would sit him in a deep armchair that he could not get out of in the lounge until we had finished eating. I then warmed his meal and he ate it on his own. He did not like eating alone. It took a long time for him to learn that he could not always have his own way and that when he had sweets or chocolate it was pleasant to share them with others. Gradually over the years he became more amenable. Because I looked after him he gradually became more generous in spirit to me personally, but I guess there was a certain amount of manipulation going on in his mind but all that did not bother me. I saw my role in looking after him as a privilege which had been given to me. I knew the great love and care that I had for Ken through all the difficulties came from God. It was not natural. I cared deeply how he was and felt as if he was my own child, even though he was older than me.

We were still searching for help for Ken's mind. A new priest that we had in Purley suggested that we tried the Dympna centre. We had not heard of it, but it is run mostly for religious who have psychological or drink related problems. They felt Ken's problems were out of their area but they suggested a visit to Doctor Parienti in Harley Street, who they thought might be able to help. We made an appointment having received permission from our

Archbishop, who was always very supportive, and we found ourselves sitting in the luxurious waiting room with much
trepidation. Doctor Parienti wished to see Peter and myself with
Ken. The first surprise was that he was wearing a black yarmulke
(a skull cap) so we knew that he must be a Jew. Ken had always
shown racist tendencies and we were not quite sure how he would
respond. However, owing to his impaired powers of recognition
he initially did not notice. By the time he did know, all was well
because he viewed Doctor Parienti with some trust and obviously
liked his approach. He asked me in front of Ken to explain the
difficulties that we experienced with him, particularly his anger
and his abuse which still was very dominant if he did not get his
own way, and sometimes for no apparent reason. I found this very
difficult, because of my love for Ken I felt disloyal, yet felt that I
must tell the truth for Ken's own benefit. Ken firmly believed that
he was never angry, and if I challenged him he put the blame on
me for being unreasonable.

Doctor Parienti was very kind to Ken and could see that we cared
deeply. He was very hopeful that he could help him. He offered to
take him in to his private clinic for three weeks. He said he would
change the five different tablets that Ken was taking three times a
day and give him one tablet three times a day that would be better.
He also said he would arrange physiotherapy to help Ken's balance
and to teach him to go upstairs holding on to a rail. This pleased
Ken a great deal although he was loath to go away from home. The
Archbishop agreed for Ken to go under Doctor Parienti's care for
these three weeks. The nursing home was luxurious and Ken had
a very pleasant room. The only difficulty was that it was in North
London and I could only visit on alternate days. The journey by

car took an hour and thirty minutes each way. I phoned the local prayer group and found a lady who lived almost next door who was willing to go into Ken every day and see that he was all right. Father Luke, a German priest who we actually knew, ran the prayer group, and he took Ken communion, and prayed with him and had a chat each day. Ken was still very homesick. Although they did teach him to go upstairs, the greatest benefit was the changing of his tablets. Doctor Parienti supervised this personally. It was a difficult process as they had to risk stopping the ones he was taking and then wait for some hours and then establish the new ones. I am not sure whether there was any obvious physical improvement after this, but because the process was much simpler I was able to teach Ken to get his tablets ready himself. We devised a method with three egg cups. He would count them out in the morning and I would check them. This did a great deal for his confidence and sense of independence. He became quite skilled and was usually accurate. Because of his misshapen hands he had some difficulty in picking the tablets up, but with determination he was able to find a way.

As time went on and Ken's mind continued to heal he became more stable on his feet; I was able to teach him to make a cup of tea safely, and eventually he could get his own breakfast. I would leave a small jug of milk in the same place in the fridge, with some sliced bread in a plastic bag beside it. He could take a piece of bread and put it in the toaster, turn the toaster on, carry a plate and knife to the table and a cup and saucer, and then the jug of milk. We worked out a method of counting to pour the water on to the tea bag in the small teapot as he was unable to see when it was full, this worked most of the time. He was meticulously careful and repeated the process exactly every day, taking a great pride in the fact that he could do it all himself. If by any chance somebody moved the milk or the bread, he was flummoxed and had no idea where then to get it. I had to be very careful to remind everyone when they were all home not to move anything.

As Ken had become more adjusted we had been able to teach him more and more about saying Mass and gradually he was able to concelebrate. At first Peter and I had carried him up the steps of the sanctuary in the wheelchair and Peter had stood beside him and looked after him. Eventually with Peter beside him, holding him, and getting everything ready, he was able to say Mass on his own. There came a time when he graduated to saying a weekday Mass and two at the weekend. He always insisted on preaching a sermon and would not or could not grasp that many people found it difficult to understand him. This regime continued for several years, There then came a stage when it was thought Ken was ready to have a team of helpers to collect him and assist him on the sanctuary when he was saying Mass. A willing band of volunteers were gathered who were prepared to make this very big commitment. We created a rota and they looked after him with great love and care, and this was another great step forward. One of them would come to the house and collect Ken, and then get everything ready on the sanctuary. Ken always needed holding firmly to get up and down the sanctuary steps. He also needed closely watching so that he did not miss any prayers out of the Mass. There were many incidents and dramas. One day Ken turned over two pages without noticing and without his helper instantly being aware, he nearly missed out the consecration. We were not present, but it was an elderly lady who went quickly up to the altar and pointed it out. Another time one of the men, who was not as tall as Ken, was unable to keep his balance as they returned after communion and they both fell, scattering hosts everywhere. Evidently the whole congregation leapt out of their places to help. Ken's walking was always tottery and unsteady. Two ladies voluntarily sat at the front at 12 o'clock Mass on Sunday ready to go forward and help if necessary. Apart from not understanding his speech very well and seeing him stumble, most of his congregations at the Saturday and Sunday Masses knew little of the difficulties that Ken suffered and struggled with in his everyday life, particularly his bouts of anger and his tremendous depression. Occasionally they heard him shouting in the sacristy, but he was usually peaceful once he arrived on the sanctuary. Once he had a 'petit mal' just after the consecration and the Lord's Prayer. He felt quite ill and could not speak. I had taught him to always sit down if he felt this happening, so that he did not fall. He had a warning always because his mouth twitched very badly. Fortunately the ministers of the Eucharist were able to carry on and give communion. Ken sat for about 10 minutes and was able to give a blessing to finish the Mass and be helped to the sacristy. His speech became normal again after a while, but it was very frightening for everyone.

As Ken became more independent I started walking in the early morning on the days that he was at home. I found this time on my own a wonderful restorative for every thing that I needed. As soon as the spring came and the mornings were lighter I would wake about six o'clock or even earlier. I would dress quickly and gather my things together. I always took pen or pencil and note pad. Although eventually I had my favourite places to walk, I first explored the whole area within a certain radius. I took the car and always had to find somewhere to park it safely. I allowed myself 3 hours and by nine o'clock or soon after I would be home. I had to remember that wherever I walked I had to get back to the car, either by retracing my steps or taking a circuitous route. When Peter was at home I could be longer, and it was then that I explored the less known places. I walked the North Downs, starting from the fields on both sides of Ditches Lane, Happy Valley into Caterham, and the fields adjoining the motorways over the Merstham tunnel. I walked every inch of the country around Woldingham. I gradually expanded my radius as far as I dared go, I re-explored the whole area around Nutfield and Bletchingley which I had known so well as a child, now changed almost beyond recognition. The roads were always clear in the early morning, so travelling was easy. My favourite walk was from the millpond at Westerham by the lakes and then either way across the fields, one towards Limpsfield and the other back through Westerham, depending on the time. On this walk I had a favourite fallen tree trunk, which was very comfortable. I wrote many pages of my diary here but sadly over the years I watched the trunk's demise as it gradually rotted and fell to pieces. This time on my own was a time of prayer, if that is the right word. I just felt I walked with the Lord and chatted. He sorted out my ideas and put me right, and continued to bring me the peace which was essential for my task. I thanked God for my contentment and happiness. In my diary I could record the difficulties and the joys. Sometimes when I returned, I was very muddy, according to the weather. At this time Ken was a very sound sleeper and very regular in his habits. He rarely woke before nine o'clock or later unless roused by his alarm clock on the Thursday when he celebrated Mass, or the day he was looked after at the Convent. On Sunday his Mass was always at midday and Saturday at 6.30 pm. so there was lots of time to get him ready.

During this time I came to know the Sisters who had been part of the Sacred Heart Convent, now Woldingham School. They ran a Centre for Spirituality in a house on the beautiful school estate where they lived. They did offer to help Ken and I took him there for several afternoons but he made very little progress and did not enjoy any of their well thought out schemes for him and readily said so. He just wanted to sit quietly and be left alone to read his prayers, which he preferred to do at home. I benefitted greatly from the courses that they ran including the 30 days retreat of St. Ignatius' Exercises which we carried out weekly, and for some years one of the sisters was my spiritual director. I could leave Ken easily for a day after Peter retired and I could rest assured Ken was safe at home with him.

I had taught Ken to play a cassette on his own so that he could listen to music when I was not with him. It was now that I tried to teach him to run it back to the beginning and to turn it over to play the other side. He made good if slow progress but could never understand playing backwards or forwards. The best he could ever do was to turn the tape over and start again, which he never minded doing. He was always content to listen to his music even though it seemed to have a morose effect on him. As he became better, he would ask to see a psychiatrist, or a neurologist, or another physiotherapist. He always insisted that he was not difficult or argumentative. Appointments were made through our doctor, but on the whole the message given was that very little more could be done, it was just a matter of going quietly on. Each year we took Ken on holiday with us, sometimes he enjoyed it and sometimes he felt it was too difficult. Wherever we were he always had a long process of understanding anew what he had to do, and how he had to do it, and we could not leave him alone unless he was tucked up in bed. Each year he would also go into a nursing home, usually at Ramsgate, and later as his emotions became more reliable to Browside in Purley for two or three weeks so that Peter and I could have a time on our own. Ken hated this but put up with it. During the time he was at Browside, his team continued to collect him for Mass which was wonderful, and he looked forward to that.

The year he celebrated 25 years as a priest we had a party for him in the church hall and invited many people from his past life, and those who had helped him since his accident. We also went with him to the Holy Land. This was a journey he had always wanted to make. It was impossible to take him with a pilgrimage, so we made our own plans and hired a car. Peter and I had been previously so we knew our way about, and we could take our time. Although the two weeks was not without incident we thought Ken had enjoyed walking in the steps of Jesus, some of the time anyway.

Another year when Peter had to go away for a week I took Ken on my own to Lake Ochrid which is in the south of what was Yugoslavia and that was advertised in the local paper by two of their journalists who organised a different trip each year. One of them acted as a rep and accompanied a coach load of us from Croydon. This gave me a feeling of safety, as well as the fact that I knew the language a bit, much of it now forgotten. There were two hair-raising experiences in particular which I remember plainly. A trip on a boat was organised to sail south to the Albanian border where the saints Cyril and Methodius were buried. The scenery was beautiful and it seemed a good idea. Our hotel was on a cliff and to get to the lake we had to descend twenty two stone steps with no railing to hold on to. I took a firm hold of Ken's arm and we went one step at a time. There was not enough room for three people across the step, or someone would have supported him on the other side as well. I was horrified when we got close to the water to see that the lake was very rough. There was no protective harbour only a small stone jetty and the boat could only get in alongside in the usual manner. To board the boat, which was lurching about, we had to pull ourselves up, hold onto a bar and manoeuvre ourselves along a narrow ledge for about three metres and then get our legs over a barrier into the cabin, the boat heaving to and fro all the time. With others pulling and pushing we got Ken up onto the ledge, I held tightly onto the back of his trousers so that I had a good hold and he held onto the rail. With minute to minute instruction, "Now take a step to the left with your left foot, now move your right foot along..." we very slowly managed it. As Ken practically fell head first into the cabin many hands were there to catch him. I was really dreading the return journey home, and repeating the procedure in reverse, although on these occasions Ken was extremely trusting and obedient. The captain of our boat was obviously alarmed and afraid of losing one of his party overboard on the return. When we called in at the village before our stop, the captain came to get us explaining that he had ordered a limousine to be there waiting. Even though the lake was still rough it was a much easier landing stage, and we came back to the hotel in luxury. On that day two kind men had taken charge of Ken after lunch for the whole afternoon while we were at the Albanian border, walking with him one on each side assuring me that they would look after him. I think he enjoyed this, and it left me free to explore on my own and to have a chat with the other people.

The other disturbing event took place in the hotel dining room. One evening, as we were finishing dinner, a retired evangelical minister, who was in our party, came over to Ken and loudly and aggressively berated him for smoking. He shouted at him that as a minister of the church it was disgraceful for him to be smoking, saying that it was a bad example for the church. I was transfixed, wondering what was going to happen next. I felt protective of Ken, and put my arm round his shoulder. He said not a word; he just sat there looking at his plate silently. There was a pronounced hush in the dining room and the minister went out. His wife came back immediately to apologise for her husband, she was very embarrassed. I stood up and explained very quietly that Ken had had an accident and that his brain was damaged. I avoided contact for the rest of the time with this man. It was on the last day when we were assembled with our luggage that he came over to us and apologised to Ken for his very rude behaviour. He took his hand and shook it. I am to this day not sure whether Ken even remembered what had taken place earlier; he certainly didn't recognise this man as he had not looked at him. On occasions like this his policy of attack being the best kind of defence worked wonders. If he was attacking it was fine for him, if he was attacked, he just quietly ignored the person. One day someone shouted at him that he was drunk; he told me when he arrived home that he had taken no notice.

There are many stories to tell, but over the years Ken became more aware of the love that was being shown him by so many people and became slightly more able to control his own anger.

Chapter Fourteen

Peter

In 1991 the family were all going on well. Gerard and Celia were settled in Ottawa Canada, although Celia was still rather homesick for England. Their two boys Peter and Mark were growing up. We had spent a very enjoyable Christmas with all the family in their lovely house in Bankview Place, even though it was bitterly cold, with a wind chill temperature of -22°. Gerard was travelling an enormous amount for his job, and was sometimes away for three weeks at a time in Central and South America. He was then working for BA Banknotes. Ken was in Browside Nursing Home in Purley, until I returned from Canada.

After Christopher obtained his first degree in English and History and the usual celebrations were over, he eventually settled in a job in London with Sumitomo, setting himself up in a pleasant flat in Battersea which he decorated himself very tastefully. After a while he experienced some frustrations with the work he was doing and felt at that time he could do something more useful. He sold his flat and took a job in Nicaragua, originally through CIIR. This changed as he worked with others on his own projects, still in Nicaragua. He began to get involved with health and population research in the local community, investigating the reasons for the death of children in families who could not read or write, and who lived miles from medical help. He actually used this study for his PhD in 2001 in the Maternal and Child Epidemiology Unit at the London School of Hygiene and Tropical Medicine under the name 'Verbal Autopsy'. When he left Nicaragua he did a master's degree at Lancaster University in information systems, which has been endlessly helpful for Peter and myself. Christopher joined us from Nicaragua for Christmas 1991 and found Canada unbearably cold after the heat of Nicaragua. Clare by then had met Jonathan, who was to become her husband. She spent a long time on the phone to him. I think she wished that he could have come with her to Canada. She was working as a Probation Officer and was living in Windsor. Paul qualified in a four year teaching course, followed by a succession of jobs and had been working for nearly three years at Peper Harrow, a very exclusive school in Godalming for children with special needs of an extraordinary nature. The pupil and staff ratio was one to one and there were only twenty-one children. They occupied a beautiful house and estate, the grounds of which had been designed by Capability Brown. The year Paul should have taken up his position the main house, which was a heritage site, was badly damaged by fire started by one of the pupils. This was eventually restored and returned to its glorious original state. The pupils had all been referred to Peper Harrow by their local councils because no school could cope with their behaviour. Paul really enjoyed looking after and helping disadvantaged youngsters. He later did a degree in Social Work at Manchester University. Paul and Jane, who eventually married, were at this time planning a year-long trip to Africa.

I had arranged with Peter's support and the help of Archbishop